Praise for *Expert Secrets*

"Expert Secrets is the map that will allow you to turn your specialized knowledge, talents, and abilities into a business that will work for you! This is one of the shortcuts of the new rich."
— Robert Kiyosaki

EXPERT
SECRETS

ALSO BY
RUSSELL BRUNSON

DotCom Secrets

Traffic Secrets

All of the above are available at your local bookstore,
or may be ordered by visiting:

Hay House USA: www.hayhouse.com®
Hay House Australia: www.hayhouse.com.au
Hay House UK: www.hayhouse.co.uk
Hay House India: www.hayhouse.co.in

EXPERT
SECRETS

THE UNDERGROUND PLAYBOOK
FOR CONVERTING YOUR ONLINE VISITORS
INTO LIFELONG CUSTOMERS

RUSSELL BRUNSON

BUSINESS

HAY HOUSE, INC.
Carlsbad, California • New York City
London • Sydney • New Delhi

Published in the United States by: Hay House, Inc.: www.hayhouse.com®
• **Published in Australia by:** Hay House Australia Pty. Ltd.: www.hayhouse
.com.au • **Published in the United Kingdom by:** Hay House UK, Ltd.: www
.hayhouse.co.uk • **Published in India by:** Hay House Publishers India: www
.hayhouse.co.in

Cover design: Jake Leslie and Rob Secades
Interior design: Julie Davison
Interior photos/illustrations: Arturo Alcazar and Vlad Babich
Cover photography: Dan Usher and Erin Blackwell

A previous editon of this book was published under the same title (ISBN: 978-1-6835-0458-0).

Library of Congress has cataloged the earlier edition as follows:

Names: Brunson, Russell, author.
Title: Expert secrets : the underground playbook for coverting your online
   visitors into lifelong customers / Russell Brunson.
Description: 1st edition. | Carlsbad, California : Hay House, Inc., [2020]
Identifiers: LCCN 2020005093 | ISBN 9781401960476 (hardback) | ISBN
   9781401960612 (ebook)
Subjects: LCSH: Internet marketing. | Customer relations. | Electronic
   commerce. | Sales presentations.
Classification: LCC HF5415.1265 B778 2020 | DDC 658.8/72--dc23
LC record available at https://lccn.loc.gov/2020005093

Tradepaper ISBN: 978-1-4019-7060-4
E-book ISBN: 978-1-4019-6061-2
Audiobook ISBN: 978-1-4019-6082-7

11 10 9 8 7 6 5 4
1st Hay House edition, May 2020
2nd Hay House edition, August 2022

Printed in the United States of America

*To Daegan Smith, who reignited my passion
for marketing during a dark time in my journey,
when I almost threw in the towel. I'm so grateful that
your inspiration gave me a second chance.*

*To the experts I've met in my life who helped me
to become who I am today. Many of you have had
a huge impact on my life in wrestling, religion, business,
health, and my relationships. Thanks for being
willing to contribute so I could grow.*

*And to my amazing kids, Dallin, Bowen, Ellie, Aiden,
and Norah, who have given me a reason to try to
make this world a better place. Your future
is what drives me today.*

CONTENTS

FOREWORD

New Year's Eve 2007.

As the rest of the world went about celebrating the dawn of a new year heading into 2008, I lay in my bed, inside my large home that we had acquired not two years before.

My wife sat up next to me, and I can still remember the current of wind from the ceiling fan that I had become so addicted to, blowing down upon us.

We had these vast shutters over the left side of some giant windows that filled the master bedroom. I could see the moon reflecting through these giant shades off my wife's face.

She turned and looked at me, with tears pouring down her cheeks, and said, "I didn't sign up for this. How are you going to fix it?"

I lay down and put my hands back behind my head; closing my eyes, I felt every aspect of my being filled with rage.

My mind raced back to the summer, six months before, to me sharing the stage with Tony Robbins at the Mortgage Planner Summit in Las Vegas, Nevada.

My mortgage empire was expanding, and we were dominating, and yet, there I lay, heading into 2008, with everything crumbling around me.

The next four very dark years took me on a journey, trying to avoid divorce while I fought my way through the unknown of my Dark Soul. I discovered the practical science to unlocking measurable results in every area of my life every single day, a science I call the Warrior's Way.

My name is Garrett J. White.

I'm a married man.

I'm a family man.

I'm a businessman.

And most important:

I'm a Funnel Hacker.

I train married businessmen on the unique process of unlocking (nearly) unlimited power in marriage, business, and life without having to cheat on their wife, get a divorce, ignore their children, leave their church, or sedate themselves with drugs and alcohol through a gamified, metric-based system known as the Warrior's Way to Have It All.

I wasn't trying to become an expert.

I wasn't even sure what being an expert meant.

I wanted to set myself free after the banking crisis, and I had no idea that what would start with a decision to change my life would transform into a global movement thanks to the principles, frames, and support of this book you hold in your hands right now.

I launched Wake Up Warrior in 2012 with zero knowledge of online marketing, online sales, sales funnels, or automated systems.

I was a belly-to-belly businessman, and I had always sold products like mortgages, insurance, and real estate in person with prospects.

On top of that, I had never sold a product that was 100 percent created by me, and I had spent most of my career selling other products.

From 2012 to 2014, I struggled to get the message I felt in my heart and soul out to the world. Although we were having some success, I was paralyzed trying to figure out not only the psychology of being an expert online with my message, but also the science and technology of sales funnels.

Then in 2014, a powerful man in Boise, Idaho, I had never heard of launched a software weapon called ClickFunnels.

That same year late in the fall, while creating some sales copy on my MacBook, I got a private message from a client via Facebook chat asking me what I thought about ClickFunnels. (At the time, I had built a duct tape mess of a sales funnel with Kajabi, Infusionsoft, Leadpages, OptimizePress, WordPress, and Zapier. It was a ticking time bomb, but I had finally, after investing well over $200,000 in consultants, managed to get all the software to sort of work together as a junkyard dog of a sales funnel.)

I told my client, "No, I haven't heard of ClickFunnels, nor am I interested in adding yet another software to the huge mess I have already created!"

I was so frustrated in 2014 because it seemed like I had spent the previous three years investing 90 percent of my time into just managing online software systems. I wondered if I was ever actually going to focus on marketing my message or if I was doomed to struggle to get my message out because I wasn't a software coder or web designer.

A few days later, my client reached out to me again and said, "Garrett, seriously, you've got to check this ClickFunnels software out. It'll allow you to get rid of all your other software tools and just focus on marketing, selling, and fulfilling Wake Up Warrior programs!"

At first, I thought to myself, *No way!*

But his comment that I would be able to replace everything with one sales software tool caught my attention, so I agreed to check it out that afternoon.

Forty-eight hours later, I migrated my prospect lists, my client lists, and everything I had over to ClickFunnels.

I was blown away by how fast and how smooth and how quickly the software worked for a guy like me, who wasn't born in the matrix of online coding or knowledgeable about web design. Not to mention it radically accelerated my results in positioning, marketing, and sales.

In 2012, Wake Up Warrior did $50,000 in sales.

In 2013, Wake Up Warrior did $585,000 in sales.

In 2014, Wake Up Warrior did $1.4 million in sales (60 percent of it after the launch of our funnel).

My results on the ClickFunnels platform happened so quickly and had such an impact on the funnel-hacking community that I was invited to speak and share my Wake Up Warrior sales funnel at the first Funnel Hacking LIVE in Las Vegas in 2015.

Speaking at Funnel Hacking LIVE was an honor. As a speaker, I received a prerelease copy of what would become a runaway bestseller: *DotCom Secrets*. I read the entire book in one day while lying poolside with my wife in Cancún, Mexico.

In 2015, after being weaponized mentally with *DotCom Secret*'s master-level education, I took Wake Up Warrior to $3.6 million in sales.

I have come to be great friends with Russell over the years. He is my friend, mentor, teacher, and trainer on the at-times complicated combination of online sales psychology, married to the lethal software weapon of ClickFunnels. Many days, I feel almost like I have an unfair advantage to have access to books like the one you're holding in your hands.

In 2016, after speaking at the second Funnel Hacking LIVE, the *New York Post* came knocking to do an interview with me about Wake Up Warrior, and the press and brand of our funnels continued to skyrocket our success to the tune of $7.8 million in sales.

Then in 2017, Russell broke the game and launched what I consider to be the single most authoritative book on direct response marketing and online sales systems I have ever read in my entire 17-year business career.

Yes, I'm speaking about the book you're reading right now.

This book is not a weekend reading tool to overcome your boredom; it's an actual weapon and shows you step by step how to *win big* as an expert.

While prepping backstage to speak at the third Funnel Hacking LIVE with my family, Russell walked up to me and handed me one of 10 copies of the prerelease edition of *Expert Secrets*.

Even without reading it, I knew this book was the missing element I needed to truly position myself as an expert in the niche I was in and to establish my company and brand at the top as category king of the industry of masculinity for the next 30–40 years.

That night while my family slept, I stayed up and read the entire book cover to cover. I sent a text to Russell the next morning and said, "I can't believe you published all of this in one book; this book by itself should be $10,000 minimum!" I continued, "If a newbie or an established pro studied this book slowly and deliberately and then executed exactly what you have told them to do in these pages, there is no way they could fail!"

What Russell did for my life with ClickFunnels in 2014 he did again in 2017 with *Expert Secrets*.

I have studied this book from cover to cover more than 10 times.

You see, I'm not some celebrity businessperson who was paid to write this foreword. I'm a product of the product, and my results from following the principles and strategies that Russell teaches are inarguable.

I believe in this book so much that I purchased more than 1,000 copies of the first edition. I convinced Russell to speak to thousands of my clients in 2017 at Warrior Con 2 and again in 2018 at Warrior Con 3. I gave a copy of this book to every one of my event attendees.

Why?

Because the doctrine you will read in these pages is lethal and something I believe every businessman or businesswoman must consume and apply as an expert if they want to win.

In 2018, armed with the lethal yet straightforward marketing and sales frames Russell teaches you here in this book, I was able to take Wake Up Warrior companies to $15.4 million in sales.

In 2019, the Wake Up Warrior companies and my expert businesses have risen to $19.6 million in sales with a 40 percent profit margin and 17 full-time team members.

I don't share that with you to impress you. To some of you reading this, that is a ton of money, and to others, it's nothing. I share it with you to demonstrate what is possible when you learn, live, and leverage the wisdom of a master marketer like Russell Brunson.

This book plus ClickFunnels is the answer.

Myself and a tribe of 100,000-plus global Funnel Hackers are waiting for you to join us.

The man you're about to study with is one of the greatest men I have ever known, and my prayer is that you will give yourself, your family, and your future a chance to *win* just like I did.

So take a deep breath.

It's time for you to unlock the blueprint of a master and get to work.

Welcome to *Expert Secrets*.

—Garrett J. White
Founder, Wake Up Warrior
Author, *Be the Man* and *Warrior Book*

INTRODUCTION

HOW TO CHANGE THE LIVES OF THE CUSTOMERS YOU'VE BEEN CALLED TO SERVE

As I walked into my Inner Circle meeting that day, I saw two new faces who had just joined the group. They looked a little bit like deer in a headlight, not sure whether they were in the right room. There were 21 people in that mastermind meeting, including me, and we were sitting around three long tables that were laid out in a big horseshoe shape, with a spot for one person to present in front of the group.

As I started the meeting, I asked everyone to introduce themselves and tell us about their current businesses. When I got to Ryan Lee and Brad Gibb, I could hear the hesitation in their voices.

"We're successful financial planners, and about three weeks ago we saw this book online called *DotCom Secrets*. We bought a copy of it, as well as all the upsells. The next week we found out about the event Funnel Hacking LIVE. It was happening that weekend, so we quickly bought tickets, booked flights and hotels, and flew to the event. During Funnel Hacking LIVE, Russell talked about his Inner Circle program and we wanted to join, but we didn't feel like we were ready yet. We flew home, and that night couldn't sleep knowing that we needed to be in this group, so in the morning we applied to join through one of his funnels, wired him $50,000, and now we're here in Boise with all of you. We're not really sure how funnels work yet, but we're living proof that they do!"

Everyone started to laugh because the process of how all of them got into that room was very similar. "We want to be able to have our customers experience what just happened to us; we want to have our own funnels," they responded. "No one in our industry is doing anything like this, but we know it works."

After everyone finished introducing themselves, I told them that the meeting was going to be a little different than normal. You see, about a year earlier I had launched my first book, *DotCom Secrets*, which taught people how to grow their companies online with sales funnels. During that time, we saw more than 10,000 people join ClickFunnels and I watched as tens of thousands of new funnels went live online!

As exciting as it was for me to see so many funnels being built, I couldn't help but notice that most of the funnels that went live never generated any leads or made any actual money. There is a big difference between making a funnel and making a funnel that actually converts online visitors into lifelong customers.

"Over the next two days that you are here in Boise, we are going to talk less about your actual funnels, and more about how to get the people who come into your funnels to become raving fans. I'm going to teach you the fundamentals of persuasion, story selling, building a tribe, becoming a leader, and how to communicate with the people who enter into your funnels. If I do my job right, you are no longer going to look at your business as a product or a service, or even an offer, but *instead you'll look at it as a movement of people you've been called to serve.*" I then spent the next two days, for the first time ever, teaching the Expert Secrets frameworks that you are going to find in this book. These frameworks are the key to attracting your dream customers and breaking their false beliefs so you can serve them at your highest levels.

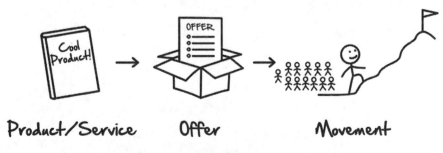

Figure 0.1:

As you become an expert, you'll find yourself moving away from just selling a product or service, to creating offers, and finally to leading a movement.

Little did I know how much of an impact those two days would have on so many people in our funnel-hacking community. Some of the people who were in the room that day shifted their businesses from product-based businesses to movements that have gone on to change millions of people's lives. I watched over the next few months as Brandon and Kaelin Poulin took their business, Tuell Time Trainer, and transformed it into the LadyBoss Movement that has helped transform the lives of more than a million women worldwide, selling supplements, coaching, and information products. Alex and Leila Hormozi went from gym owners to the leaders of the Gym Launch movement, which has helped thousands of gym owners attract members they can serve. Garrett J. White has built the Warrior movement, helping tens of thousands of men around the world to "have it all," while his wife, Danielle K. White, now leads a Big Money Stylist movement that helps stylists get paid what they're actually worth doing hair extensions.

Over the next year I shared these principles with thousands of other entrepreneurs and eventually wrote the first edition of this book, *Expert Secrets*. I've watched as entrepreneurs like you have been able to take these frameworks and weave them into their ads and funnels to get people to move through their value ladder.

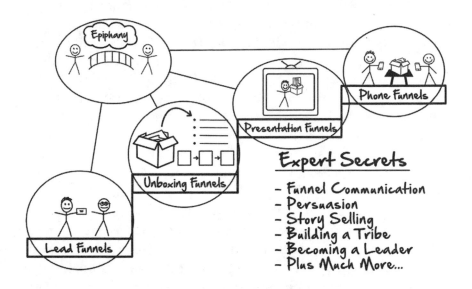

Figure 0.2:

Expert Secrets is the bridge that helps marketers master the art
of converting online visitors into lifelong customers.

I believe that your business is a calling. You've been called to serve a group of people with the products, services, and offers that you've created. People come into your funnels looking for a solution to their problems. By positioning yourself as an expert, and learning how to tell your story in a way that gets people to move, you are able to guide people through your value ladder, giving them the results they are looking for. This is how you change the lives of your customers, and this is how you grow a company.

The first edition of this book was very popular, selling more than 200,000 copies, and I've watched as the people who have taken these principles have been able to turn their online visitors into lifelong customers. I have a file with literally hundreds of stories that I could share with you in every market that you can dream of, but one of the ones I am most proud of is Brad and Ryan's story.

They came to that Inner Circle meeting as financial planners, in an industry that did not use funnels. There was no proven track record for the funnel concepts from *DotCom Secrets*, or for these new concepts of building a movement by building a tribe. Most people in this same situation would have said, "This works for other companies, but not a company like mine." Instead, they were humble enough to learn and then figure out how to apply the concepts to their business. As with any new framework, it takes time to figure out how to customize and apply it to what you do, but when they figured out how to apply it to their business, they created a movement. Within just months of setting their framework live, Brad and Ryan qualified for our "Two Comma Club" award (meaning they made more than $1 million inside one of their funnels); within a year they won a "Two Comma Club X" award (grossing more than $10 million inside of that same funnel)!

Inside this book, you're not only going to learn how to convert people inside of your funnels, but you're also going to learn how to become a leader. I believe that business and entrepreneurship is a calling we receive. My friend Ryan Moran once told me, "An entrepreneur is someone who takes personal responsibility for a problem that wasn't their own." While most of the world runs away from problems, especially the ones that are their own, we see a problem and feel called to step up and figure out a way to solve it. Every good business started this way, with someone feeling called to take on a problem that wasn't their own, and that calling is special.

Something you have experienced in your life started you on this path to create your business. It forced you to become more. You saw a problem, and then you had to read, study, and experiment with the things you learned in order to create the solutions you now offer your clients. By going through this refining process, you have become who you are today: an *expert*.

Most people then put their products up for sale, and don't understand that their expertise is the key to actually selling the product. Your story—why you created this offer and started your movement—is what gets people to convert initially, and continue to stay with you over time.

Your message has the ability to change someone's life. The impact that the right message can have on someone at the right time in their life is immeasurable. Your message could help save marriages, repair families, change someone's health, grow a company, or more . . .

But only if you know how to get it into the hands of the people whose lives you have been called to change.

> *Expert Secrets* will help you find your voice and give you the confidence to become a leader.

> *Expert Secrets* will show you how to build a movement of people whose lives you can change.

> *Expert Secrets* will teach you how to make this calling a career.

As Sir Winston Churchill once said:

> *To each there comes in their lifetime a special moment when they are figuratively tapped on the shoulder and offered the chance to do a very special thing, unique to them and fitted to their talents. What a tragedy if that moment finds them unprepared or unqualified for that which could have been their finest hour.*[1]

Your message matters, and this book is your figurative tap on the shoulder.

SECTION ONE

CREATING YOUR MOVEMENT

Figure 1.1:

To create a movement, you'll need an expert or guide,
a new opportunity, and a future-based cause.

I had been invited by David Frey to come to Salt Lake City to experience something that I had never seen before. It was a conference for a software company, and they had almost 3,000 distributors meeting to learn how to better sell the product. As I sat in the room, I was expecting to hear speakers teaching them how to sell and market the business better, but instead I watched for three days as they brought people onstage, gave them awards, and had them tell their stories about the product. Everything was a little different than I expected, but what shocked me most was how many people cried when they were telling their stories.

I leaned over to David on the third day and said, "I don't get it."

David knew that I had come from a direct response marketing background, and that this was going to be something new for me. He smiled and said, "Russell, they're not selling software; they created a movement, and that is what they are selling."

I sat back, and looking at this experience through this new lens changed everything for me. David hadn't invited me so I could learn how to sell software. He wanted me to see that the product was just a tool, but creating a movement is what actually changed people.

After I got home from that event, and for the next few years, I kept hearing David's words in my mind, "They're not selling software; they created a movement." After we came up with the idea for ClickFunnels and my business partner, Todd Dickerson, started to code the software, I knew that my role was to figure out this missing piece: How do we create a movement that will change people's lives?

Software, in and of itself, is boring. There were plenty of website builders out there, and although we had a better way of doing it (through a funnel), ClickFunnels was still just a website builder. I knew that if I wanted to create something like I had seen a few years earlier with David, I needed to create an actual movement.

So I started to study mass movements throughout time. I started initially by looking at great companies that had built movements around them, like Apple and Tesla. Then I started looking at religious movements like Christianity and Buddhism. And then, after looking at the light side of movements, I wanted to see the dark side as well. I studied many cults and negative political movements like Nazism.

As I dug deep, I started to notice a pattern showing up in every movement I studied, both positive and negative. The more examples I found, the more the pattern became clear. All the examples I found had three things in common that helped them build a mass movement:

- They each had a charismatic leader (or as we called it in *DotCom Secrets*, an Attractive Character). In this book we are going to take that role to the next level and call it an **expert/guide**.

- They each offered their audience a **new opportunity**.
- They then created a **future-based cause** that united the tribe of people they had attracted.

As with any pattern or framework, as soon as you are aware of it, you can actually use it. After I saw the pattern, I wrote down this statement:

The Expert Offers Someone a New Opportunity and Then Guides Them to a Result with a Future-Based Cause.

When I add in the value ladder and the value ladder mission statement from *DotCom Secrets*, it looks a little more like this:

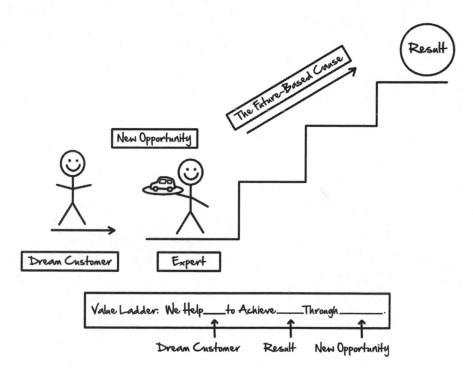

Figure 1.2:

As you introduce a new opportunity to your dream customers, you can guide them up your value ladder and build a movement by helping them embrace a future-based cause.

When you take these three elements that are essential in every mass movement and you weave them into the funnels and value ladder that you learned about in *DotCom Secrets*, you will not only create a business that can make money, you will also create a movement that can change the world.

As you learn these Expert Secrets, you'll learn how to position yourself differently in a way that will attract your dream customers to you. You'll learn how to find your voice and tell stories in a way that moves people so you can serve them at a higher level. You'll learn how to create and position your offers as new opportunities (instead of improvement offers), and you'll learn how to build a tribe and give members a future-based cause that will create the momentum they need to truly change their lives.

Becoming
the Expert

FINDING YOUR VOICE

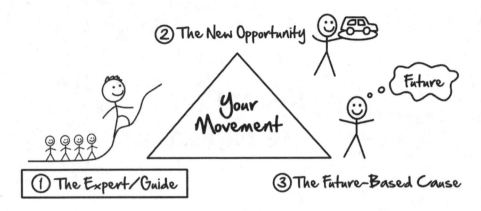

Figure 1.3:

The first stage of becoming the expert is to step into your role as
a leader to guide your dream customers to their destination.

I had heard my mom tell this story a dozen times before, but it was
my favorite story, so as she started to tell it to one of her friends,
again, I stopped everything I was doing so I wouldn't miss a word.

"He thought Russell was stupid," she said, talking about my
high school guidance counselor. "When we tried to get a letter
from him so Russell could apply to Brigham Young University, he
told us that Russell was a below-average student, and even if somehow he got accepted, he would never be able to pass the classes,
and that he should go to an easier school."

And that's when my dad jumped in to tell his favorite part. "So
we submitted the paperwork to BYU, and sure enough a few weeks
later we got a letter telling us that his grades were too low, and

that he wasn't accepted. The next month we went to Pittsburgh for the high school national wrestling tournament. You had to be a state champion to get invited to this tournament, and it's by far the toughest tournament in the country. Russell's weight class had more than 90 state champions in it (some states have multiple classes and could send more than one state champion per weight). He wrestled the best tournament of his life, beating multiple two- and three-time state champions."

Now this was the part of the story that was *my* favorite, and I had to jump in. "Dad, do you remember, after I pinned the two-time state champion in the semifinals and we were getting ready for the national finals match, one of the BYU coaches came over to us and asked me if I wanted to come on a recruiting trip to their school?!"

"Yes, and I told him that we had just gotten a letter saying that you weren't accepted, and he smiled at me and said, 'Don't worry, I'll take care of that.' Within a week of you becoming a high school all-American, we had your acceptance letter in the mail from BYU!"

Then my mom jumped back in. "But of course, as soon as the guidance counselor found out that you were going to BYU, he came back to me and warned me that you would never last the first semester."

Now, as cool as this story already was, my mom was waiting to give her update about what had happened almost 15 years later. When I launched *DotCom Secrets*, my mom had a job teaching home economics at the same school as the guidance counselor. She finished the story, "I took Russell's new book, marched right into the counselor's office, and asked if he remembered telling me that my son wasn't smart enough to go to BYU, and that he would probably fail after the first semester. He said yes, and so I *had* to tell him the good news. 'Well, that son is now a millionaire, and he just launched his first best-selling book, and I wanted to give you a copy!'" She then did the ultimate mic drop: She left the book on his desk and walked away.

I wanted to share that story with you for a few reasons. Besides the fact that the story makes me feel really good about myself and will probably build a deeper connection with some of my readers, I also wanted you to see that I really struggled in school. I was not someone who you would ever think would be an "expert" in anything. I graduated college with a stunning 2.3 cumulative GPA. I loved wrestling, and that is the one thing that kept me in school, knowing that if I didn't pass my classes, I didn't get to wrestle.

I don't remember liking to read or learn anything that the teachers gave me, and if I'm completely honest, I always thought I was dumb. It wasn't until the middle of my college career that I started to get exposed to different ideas that they didn't talk about in school. Google was in its infancy back then, and as I searched for and found things that sparked my interest, I discovered that reading became fun. Sleep became a burden as my mind raced with possibilities. Somewhere in this season of growth is when I first stumbled upon a small movement of people who were making a living selling things online. That initial spark started my journey to becoming an unlikely expert.

EVOLUTION FROM ATTRACTIVE CHARACTER TO EXPERT

One of my early mentors, Dan Kennedy, taught me that "we are all in a relationship business, not a product business." He explained to me that people may come into your value ladder because of a product, but they stay because of their relationship with you, the Attractive Character.

In *DotCom Secrets*, I first introduced the concept of the Attractive Character, and how you use your personality to attract people to you. In this book, I want to help take you and your relationship with your audience to the next level: Now that you've attracted someone to you, the next level is to lead them where they want to go. To become a leader or a guide, you have to grow into an expert.

Figure 1.4:

DotCom Secrets teaches you how to attract your dream customers.
Expert Secrets teaches you how to guide them to their desired result.

We use the Attractive Character at the front of our value ladder to bring people into our funnels, but then we, as the experts, are the ones who guide them through our funnels and ascend them up the value ladder. Jay Abraham once said, "People are silently begging to be led,"[2] and I believe that's very true. We are in the business of attracting our dream customers and then leading them to the results that we can get for them.

THE FIVE PHASES TO BECOME AN EXPERT

As you start on this journey, you will travel through five phases that will help you find your voice, build your tribe, and change the world. Each phase is important in your journey to help impact as many people as possible with your message.

Figure 1.5:

You have to go through five phases to become an expert: dreamer, reporter, framework creator, servant, and, finally, expert/guide.

Phase #1: The Dreamer (It Starts with a Spark)

Recently I read a post on Instagram from my friend Tom Bilyeu entitled "How to Develop Passion," but it could easily have been titled "How to Become an Expert." In this post he listed five things to develop your passion or expertise.[3]

1. Go experiment with a ton of stuff.
2. Identify things that spark your interest.
3. Engage deeply with those things.
4. As you engage, if it goes from interest to true fascination, go down the path of gaining mastery.
5. Fascination + Mastery = Passion

I didn't realize it at the time, but the path he laid out in that post is exactly what I followed to turn my spark and interest in marketing online into the movement that we've created today. I took my little spark, I engaged deeply, became fascinated with it, gained mastery, and it has become my true passion, my life's work.

Every great movement has a leader, and this spark is the beginning of your leadership. It's easy to assume that some people are just born leaders and others are not, but that's not true. Leadership and how to become an expert is something that you can learn. It's possible that your biggest fear when you first read the title *Expert Secrets* was that you aren't a born leader or don't feel like an expert.

When I started on this journey, I had the same feelings. Who was I to lead people when there were so many others who I felt were more qualified? I am by nature extremely introverted. I talk too fast. I barely graduated from school. But I put in the time to flame my spark, find my voice, and become the expert that my people needed to lead them.

For those of you who are nervous about having what it takes to be an expert, I want to spend a few minutes talking with you. My guess is that you are amazing. And I bet that the more amazing you are, the harder it is for you to believe it. Am I right?

I've had a really rare opportunity to coach thousands of experts around the world in almost every market you can dream of. What's interesting is when I look at all these amazing people changing the lives of tens of thousands (and in some cases millions) of others, most have felt an internal pull to want to serve and help people. It's almost like a voice inside them telling them they are destined for greatness. Yet at the same time, they have this other voice that consistently tells them they're inadequate, that they're not enough. Not smart enough, not focused enough, not thin enough, not experienced enough, not good enough . . .

The strange thing is that often the more they do and the more people they help, the louder the voice of inadequacy becomes. Whether you're just starting this journey or you've been at it for a while, know that the biggest hurdle you're likely to face is being okay with calling yourself an expert.

What's equally important to understand is that you're not alone. I really feel for people struggling with that negative inner voice because, in all honesty, that's the way I often feel. I feel like I have been blessed beyond what any human being should ever be blessed with on this Earth. And I feel that this gift I've been given from God is something I must share. In fact, if I don't share it, that would be an injustice to Him and the people I could serve.

Yet as I am out there in the trenches every single day building companies, working with entrepreneurs, trying to change the world in my own little way, I still wrestle with these feelings of inadequacy. As I talk to people, I realize that these same feelings keep most people from ever taking on the mantle of an expert. The voice keeps them from stepping up and stepping into that role.

And it's a tragedy for a couple of reasons. First, it deprives them of the experience and the opportunities they should have. And, more important, it deprives the people whose lives they could change. Those people you could serve by sharing your God-given talents and expert abilities—they might never be reached.

So I want to pause here and take a moment, not so much to convince you that you're an expert, but to give you whatever permission you might need to be able to move forward. You have the ability—and, I believe, the responsibility—to serve others with your gifts, whatever they are.

You've been blessed with talents, ideas, and unique abilities that have gotten you to where you are in life, and these gifts were given to you so you could share them with others. There are people today who need what you have. And they are just waiting for you to find your voice, so you can help them change their lives. What a tragedy for them if you don't develop your voice now.

Another problem that a lot of people suffer from is that our own unique abilities are things that come second nature to us, so they don't seem that amazing, and we dismiss them. My guess is that your superpower won't seem like that big of a deal to you. It will be something that comes naturally: something so simple that it couldn't possibly be that important. If you're an amazing cook, it's not that big of a deal for you. But to someone who can't cook, it's a *huge* deal.

Maybe you're good at playing piano, fixing motorcycles, building chicken coops, dancing, or something else. Look at what comes easily to you and what you love to geek out on, and chances are that's where your superpower is hiding, just waiting to be developed and shared with the world.

Phase #2: Taking on the Identity of the Reporter

Figure 1.6:

Your own knowledge isn't enough. You need to interview
other experts to gain different viewpoints.

I remember seeing an infomercial in the '90s with a guy named Howard Berg. He was in the *Guinness Book of World Records* as the world's fastest reader. On this infomercial, he would read an entire book in a few short minutes. After reading the book, he would have someone ask him questions to make sure he had actually read it, and he'd answer those questions with amazing accuracy. Years later I saw him on Fox News reading the entire health-care bill live on TV in under an hour, and then he had Neil Cavuto interview him afterward about what was in the bill. It was an amazing feat to watch.

Around the same time, I was speaking at an event in Dallas, and one of the event hosts told me after my presentation that Howard was in the audience and wanted to meet me! We quickly became friends and I even flew him to my office to train my staff on how to speed-read. During the launch of the first edition of

Expert Secrets, I had Howard read my entire book *live* on Facebook in just 4 minutes and 43 seconds! I then got to quiz him on what I wrote to make sure he remembered everything inside!

That night, Howard and I went out to dinner. I had a question that I had wanted to ask him for years. He had read more than 30,000 books on almost any topic imaginable, and I wanted to know his thoughts about God.

He smiled and taught me a lesson that I'll never forget. He told me that most people would read a book on a topic, then base their beliefs on what they learned. He told me that he likes to pick a topic, read a dozen or more books around the topic to see everyone's point of view, and create his own opinion based on seeing all sides of the argument. I spent the next few hours with him listening to his beliefs on God based on hundreds of books he had read. It was one of the most fascinating conversations of my life.

As kids growing up, we are all very teachable. We go to school and become sponges, learning everything that is placed in front of us. And then the worst possible thing happens: We get a degree. To the world, that degree means you know something, but to most people, it means you are done learning.

Your teachability index is how teachable you are at any given time. As a kid your index is high, but after you think you know something, if you're like most people your index drops to zero and you stop learning. This is the worst possible thing that can happen to an expert.

The next phase in your expert evolution is to start learning everything about your topic from multiple points of view. We need to keep your teachability index high so you are open to new ideas that you will need to create your own frameworks. The best way to do this is for your Attractive Character to take on the identity of the reporter and interview everyone you can get access to who is a few chapters ahead of where you are right now.

The fastest way to turn your spark into a fire is to get around others who are on fire already. I started to look for other people who were further down the path than I was, and I tried to get close to them to help my spark grow. There are a lot of ways that

I did that, but I'll share with you the three that had the biggest impact on my personal growth.

Going to live events: I found all the seminars and workshops that were happening in my industry, and I went to every one that I could. This gave me the chance to hear the other experts/speakers onstage, so I could quickly start to see what things were being taught and what things were resonating with people the most. I also loved the live events because they gave me the ability to network with other attendees. During these late-night networking sessions, I met some amazing experts who helped add to my abilities; I also learned what things people were struggling with and not finding answers to. This helped pave the ground for me as I started to design my own "category," as you will learn about in Secret #3.

Starting your own "show" or podcast: I go into depth about how and why to start your own show in *Traffic Secrets* because it's the fastest way to build a relationship from the other experts in your market and learn directly from them. Having your own show will open doors to experts you could never get access to otherwise. Interviewing a dozen or more experts who have different perspectives in your market is the equivalent of how Howard Berg would read a dozen books to see what the actual truth was. The more people you can interview the better. It will help you discover what gaps are in the market and what frameworks you can create for the new opportunity you will be offering your market.

Launching a summit funnel: In *DotCom Secrets*, we talk about the power of summit funnels. Not only can you use this funnel to build a large list of subscribers and followers, it is also an amazing way to interview the top experts in your field.

Taking on this role of reporter was for me one of, if not the most valuable parts of my education, as well as one of the most rewarding times in my life. I was able to take decades of someone's life work and get it compressed down to an hour interview with them. It's like having an author read you the CliffsNotes of their book while you get to ask your own personal questions along the way!

The first time I ever interviewed someone was after I read *The 12-Month Millionaire* by Vince James.[4] The book was about how a 28-year-old kid built a supplement company that generated more than $100,000,000 in just 23 months, all through direct mail, magazines, and online ads! I was so excited that I emailed Vince, asking him if I could interview him. Luckily for me he said yes, and he gave me six hours of his time, over two weekends, to ask any questions I had. I made a detailed outline of the questions his book raised in my mind as I read it. Then I asked him the questions and listened as the master told me the answers in his own words. It was amazing. I learned more about marketing during that interview than I would have if I had earned three MBAs! He allowed me to have the rights to our interview, and I later sold the recordings of that interview. They were part of the first offer I ever created that sold more than a million dollars, and it was the first time I ever qualified for the Two Comma Club.

I got so addicted by learning directly from the authors that I started to message every author of every book I loved, and most of them allowed me to interview them! This is how I met and built relationships with people like Dan Kennedy, Jay Abraham, Mark Joyner, and Joe Vitale. I loved their work, I asked them if I could interview them, and we built relationships while I had them explain to me the answers to my burning questions.

THE SHIFT FROM GROWTH TO CONTRIBUTION

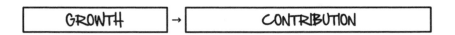

Figure 1.7:

After you've invested in your own growth, you're ready to move into contribution to start sharing your knowledge with others.

The first two phases are all about personal growth. That's how it typically starts. We get excited about a topic and we start geeking out on it. We learn, read books, study examples, listen to podcasts, and consume a lot of information. Next we put on our reporter hat and interview the people we have been learning from to get customized answers to our questions.

But then, at some point, we realize the only way to keep growing isn't to learn more, but instead to shift our focus from personal growth to contribution. It's only by shifting our focus to helping others that we continue to grow. As we help others and guide them through what we've learned, we start to grow again. Contribution is the key to continued growth.

The first time I truly understood that, I was in high school. I was a state champion and an all-American wrestler. I read and watched everything I could about wrestling. My dad and I would study videos and practice moves every day. We traveled to wrestling camps and got hands-on coaching from the wrestlers and coaches we looked up to. During this phase of my growth, I became a good wrestler.

The summer after my senior year of high school, one of my coaches asked me if I'd help coach at the wrestling camp. I'd never coached wrestling before, but I thought it would be fun. He had me work with some of the younger wrestlers on moves I was intuitively good at but that they couldn't figure out.

I would show the move, and then have them try it. Quickly I realized just showing the move didn't really help them understand how to do it. I brought the group of kids back together and I had to look at the move differently. Why did it work? Where were my hips? How did I position my elbows, and where did my feet have to go to make the move work? As I broke down the move into smaller pieces to teach to the kids, I started to look at the move differently. I saw the pattern and then taught it to them.

As I became aware of the details that made them work, I was able to better teach them, and the kids started to have success. But the big benefit that I wasn't expecting was that because I became more aware of why the move worked, I was able to do it at a level I hadn't ever been able to before. The insights I gained from coaching also made me a much better athlete. Contributing to other people's success helped me grow more than focusing on my own success.

This next phase of growth is the same. First, we become passionate about a particular topic. We study, we learn, and we implement, but eventually we can't grow anymore from study alone. We then shift our focus to helping others with what we've learned, and that contribution helps them, which in turn also helps us continue to grow.

Phase #3: Building Your Own Frameworks

Figure 1.8:

As you create your processes for achieving a certain result, you'll also test those frameworks on yourself.

As I am going through the process of growth, I'm looking for patterns of how to achieve a certain result. Each of these patterns is a process or a framework for success. As you get into creating content, telling stories, making offers, and taking on a lot of the other roles of an Attractive Character and an expert, having your own frameworks becomes essential.

As you've probably seen in my previous books, each chapter has a framework that I teach from. You'll notice that this chapter has a five-part framework for becoming an expert. Secret #2 is my framework for teaching frameworks. In Secret #3, I'll show you my framework for creating your blue ocean, and so on. Over the years as I've been studying each concept, interviewing others, and testing out the principles in my business and my life, I look for the patterns of what worked, then I create a process or framework to make it easier for others to replicate my success.

I will go deeper into how to build out and teach your frameworks in Secret #2, but for now I just wanted you to see that the end result from your growth phase is to identify patterns for success and then build your own frameworks to help facilitate that success for others.

For people who are authors, speakers, coaches, and consultants (traditional expert businesses), this concept of frameworks is pretty simple. Oftentimes service-based businesses or companies selling physical products or software struggle to understand how frameworks work for their types of companies. To understand how to use frameworks for other types of businesses, it's essential to remember that people buy products because they want certain results. My question for you would be: What is the framework that someone must follow to get that result? Your product is likely just a piece of that framework.

The result people are trying to get when they come to me is to grow their companies online. ClickFunnels is a piece of my framework, but it's not the framework. I teach the framework as a guide, and then my products or services become a step inside the framework of success I am giving.

If I were a dentist, the result people would want from me is straight, white teeth. Sure, my service may be part of that, but what is my framework for getting and keeping a beautiful smile? If I were a dentist, I would build out a framework which may include daily brushing, certain types of toothpastes, whitening strips, tongue scrapers for good breath, supplements to strengthen enamel, checkups twice a year, etc. Do you see how by switching from a product (teeth cleaning) to a framework, I position myself differently than every other dentist, I am giving people a replicable process for success, and I could then potentially sell a lot of other products that would help serve my clients at a higher level?

If I just sold ClickFunnels, I would have been like any of my competitors. Instead, I built dozens of frameworks that I am able to use to guide my dream customers toward the results they are looking for. In the process, they built a relationship with me because I was the one who gave them the frameworks and positioned myself as an expert. As a byproduct of that, people will often use the products and services I recommend (including my own) from within those frameworks to help get their desired results.

Step #1—Create your framework hypothesis: During your first two phases of growth as an expert, you will be spending time learning other people's frameworks for success. It could be by reading their books, listening to their podcasts, or watching them speak at live events. As you transition to your role as the reporter, you have a unique opportunity to dig deeper into their frameworks, ask them personalized questions, and gain a level of mastery in their process that very few people will ever have access to.

Your job now as the expert is to become a framework creator. You do this by taking the information you've learned from tons of different sources and other people's frameworks, looking at it, and organizing it into your own personal hypothesis for the perfect framework. During this step you are doing what Bruce Lee meant when he said, "Research your own experience, absorb what is useful, reject what is useless, and add what is essentially your own."[5] This process is similar to what my friend Howard Berg, the world's fastest reader, did when I asked him his opinion on God. He picks a topic, reads a dozen or more books around the topic to see everyone's point of view, and creates his own opinion based on seeing all sides of the argument. That is your job now: to build your own framework after seeing all the other ways and other opportunities people are using to try and achieve that result.

Christopher Vogler, author of *The Writer's Journey*, said in a lecture: "As you listen to . . . anyone's ideas . . . you'll find *Oh, there's a useful idea,* and *That's right, I agree with that,* and *That, oh, I never thought of that before.* But at some point. . . you make up your own [ideas] and you create your own lingo, your own shared language with the people that you work with. . . . Absorb it, take notes, and pull out a piece here and there that sounds right to your observation of the world. This is all about how you perceive things as an artist, so you've got to make it your own."[6]

Your framework hypothesis is the first draft you are going to create based on everything you're learning and the ideas and epiphanies that you've had during your journey of growth. The first thing to do is pretend that you are coaching your first client through this process. That client is you, when you first found your spark of interest in the topic. You are a few chapters ahead of where you were when you began. Sit down and write everything that you would want to teach yourself before you began this journey. Make a bullet list of as many topics as you can think of; the more the better. For example, when I wrote *DotCom Secrets*, my initial set of things I would have taught the younger version of me looked something like this:

- How to make a funnel that generates leads

- The concept of the value ladder

- How to use the Attractive Character in your communication with your list

- How to use a hook to get attention, a story to increase value, and an offer to close the sale

- How to create webinar funnels

- What happens if one of your funnels flops

- The secret of high-ticket funnels

- How to use book funnels

- The seven phases inside every funnel

- How to do a product launch funnel

- The "Who, What, Why, How" script

Keep doing bullet points like this until you have everything you would need to teach others to guarantee them the results you promised. After you make the list, you need to organize it into an outline in the order that you would teach the bullet points to yourself, similar to a table of contents in a book. In fact, if you look at the table of contents of *DotCom Secrets*, you'll see that I took these questions and then broke them down into sections and chapters. (I also did the same process for this book.)

- Section One: Sales Funnel Secrets

  - Secret #1: The Secret Formula

  - Secret #2: Hook, Story, Offer

  - Secret #3: The Value Ladder

  - Secret #4: The Attractive Character

  - Etc.

- Section Two: The Funnels in the Value Ladder

  - Secret #8: Lead "Squeeze" Funnels

  - Secret #9: Survey Funnels

  - Secret #10: Summit Funnels

  - Secret #11: Book Funnels

  - Etc.

If you flip to the table of contents of any nonfiction book, you'll see the author's framework for getting the result based on the topic their book is teaching about. For me, *DotCom Secrets* is my framework for using sales funnels to grow a company. *Expert Secrets* is my framework for converting online visitors into lifelong customers. And *Traffic Secrets* is my framework for filling websites and funnels with your dream customers.

Each section of the book is also a framework, as is each chapter. The Secret Formula in Chapter 1 is its own framework. Hook, Story, Offer in Chapter 2 is its own framework.

In fact, right now, this chapter you're reading is my framework for Finding Your Voice as an expert, and you're reading step three of five right now. Are you starting to see how this works? In the next chapter I will be giving you my framework on how to teach frameworks, and after that we'll move into my next framework, and so on.

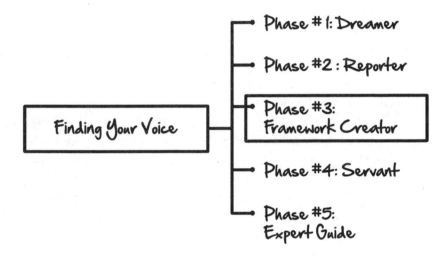

Figure 1.9:

Often, your larger frameworks will have smaller frameworks inside of them.

The better you are at creating and teaching frameworks, the more successful you will become. My hope is that by seeing me doing it over and over again (and making you aware of what I'm doing and how I'm doing it) you'll be better able to replicate it for your area of expertise.

Step #2—Test your framework hypothesis on yourself (human guinea pig): One of the writers I respect the most is Tim Ferriss, author of *The 4-Hour Workweek*, *The 4-Hour Body*, *The 4-Hour Chef*, and more. The reason I like Tim's writing is because he doesn't just learn something and republish it. He studies the best, interviews the top experts on the planet, and becomes a human guinea pig to test out their ideas and see if they work before he publishes them. In fact, *Newsweek* called him "the world's best guinea pig."[7]

To better understand how diet and supplementation affect his glucose levels, he had a glucometer implanted into his abdomen. He also took more than 1,000 blood tests, often taking them daily to see how different things affected his body.

The problem with most "experts" is they hear a good idea and then they go and regurgitate it as their own. This is not what you're doing when you create your own unique, proprietary frameworks. I told people after I wrote *DotCom Secrets* that I learned many of these concepts from others before me, but then I took every one of the ideas and tested them on my own businesses, refined the processes, found out what worked and what didn't, learned my own insights, formed my own hypotheses, and tested those hypotheses. From that process, I *earned* that book.

This is the step where you are going to start earning your framework. As I'll show you in the next chapter, you can stand on the shoulders of the giants you learned your fundamentals from, always giving them credit, but through this process, you will be creating something unique and proven by your own experience with it.

Often as you go through this process, you'll find that parts of your framework hypothesis don't work, or you figure out ways to do it better. There is nothing wrong with that; in fact, that is the goal: to find the holes and figure out better ways to get the outcomes your framework is designed to get. Even after years of teaching certain frameworks, things in the market will change, or I'll learn something new, or discover a better way to accomplish what I'm trying to teach others, and I update and change my frameworks when those things happen. Anyone looking at the first edition of either *DotCom Secrets* or this book will notice hundreds of pages of changes and updates to the frameworks I shared initially. This all came from years of testing the concepts with more and more people, and making adjustments as we found them.

Step #3—Give your framework a proprietary name: After you've created your framework, you need a name for your proprietary system. I like having an easy name for my framework so people can remember the process by the name itself, but also so it becomes a proprietary methodology that I own. For example, a few of the frameworks I've created that have become part of our industry jargon because we use them so much are: Hook, Story, Offer; the Perfect Webinar; The Value Ladder; and the Epiphany Bridge.

After I name the framework, I then want to have a description of what it is and what it will do if you follow the process. For example:

HOOK, STORY, OFFER:

My Three-Step System for Grabbing Your Dream Customer's Attention and Getting Them to Pay You What You're Worth!

So your framework description should fit into this sentence:

_____: *(your framework name)*

My _____-step framework (or system, process) for
_____*(insert result).*

At this point you should have the basic outline for your framework: Your framework's name, its description, and your outline of what you'll be teaching inside each step. You now have your framework hypothesis. In the next chapter, I'll be showing you how to teach this framework, but for now you're not ready; this is just a hypothesis, and you have to see if it actually works.

Phase #4: Work for Free
Serving Your Future Dream Clients

Figure 1.10:

After you've tried and tested your framework on yourself, you need to try
it on others to perfect it and ensure it produces the same (or better) results.

After (and only after) you have proven your framework works for
you—the human guinea pig—it's time to start testing the process
on other people. The next phase is one that most people mistak-
enly skip. This is where you prove the frameworks that you've
created don't just work for you, but will work for other people too.
It's also the phase where you have a chance to practice, refine your
message and your process, and perfect your frameworks. This is
important, because at first, chances are that you and your frameworks won't be very good, and that's okay. As my good friend
Garrett J. White once said:

> No matter what you do, in the beginning it's going to
> suck, because you suck. But you'll get better, and you'll
> suck less. And as you keep doing this, eventually you'll
> suck so little . . . you'll actually be good.

The next phase is all about testing your frameworks. Even if they have already worked for you, you need to test them and make sure that they work for other people too. Whenever I develop something new, the first thing I do is find a beta group of people I can test it with.

When I first launched my Inner Circle coaching program, I didn't have a track record as a coach for high-achieving entrepreneurs. Plus, I wanted to charge $50,000 a year for people to join. You could say I had a lot going against me. I could have done what most people do: put up a website and said, "Hey, my name's Russell Brunson. I'm the greatest coach in the world. You should hire me." But I didn't do that for a few reasons.

First, no one likes to hear you talk about yourself. It's not cool. Second, I knew that it didn't feel right. I wanted to serve some people first and prove that what I teach actually works.

One of the first things I teach people is to figure out who their dream customer is. I already had an idea about the types of entrepreneurs I wanted to work with. So I started looking around for those people, and soon I met a guy named Drew Canole, the owner of FitLife.tv. He was a super cool guy and had a successful business in a market I cared about. He was someone I thought I could help.

Eventually, a mutual friend introduced us. I went to Drew's house and talked with him for a bit. He mentioned some of the things he was struggling with. Then I asked him, "Would you mind if I came back and just worked a day for free to see if I could help?"

"Sure. But why would you do that for free?"

"If I am able to make a big impact on your business, then I'll probably charge a lot in the future. But for now, I just want to see if I can help you."

"What's the catch? What's in it for you?"

"There's no catch. I think what you do is awesome, and it'd be really fun to see if the stuff I do could help you at all."

Finally, Drew reluctantly agreed to let me come and serve his business for a day. I think he still thought there was some kind of ulterior motive.

About a month later, I flew out and met with his whole team. We found that their funnels were making money, but they weren't profitable. I helped them fix their current funnels, and we helped build a funnel for the upcoming launch of their new supplement, Organifi.

Overall, between the day I spent in FitLife.tv's office and the time going back and forth through email, I think I invested about a month coaching Drew's team through the whole funnel-building process for free. At the end of it, they launched their new Organifi funnel, which has gone on to make them tens of millions of dollars per year.

I didn't ask Drew for this, but in exchange for my help, he made a video for me talking about the transformation his business went through and the results I was able to get for them. After I saw that video, I knew I was ready to launch the Inner Circle, because I had proof that the frameworks I had created worked. I had real results for someone besides myself.

My team and I put the video into an online funnel and launched our new coaching program. People saw Drew talking about his transformation, and almost instantly the program started to grow. We set a cap of only 100 entrepreneurs in my Inner Circle at any given time and, despite the fact that we charge $50,000 per year to be a member, right now we have waiting lists of people fighting to get in.

The goal with this or any kind of business is not to lead with, "How can I sell my product?" Instead, you want to ask, "How can I serve people?"

Phase #5: Becoming an Expert

Figure 1.11:

The last step to becoming an expert or guide is to take on
that role and start leading others to their destination.

Once you've gone through the first four phases, you will be ready
to start using your frameworks and leading people as an expert.

"But Russell, I'm not certified. I can't help people yet."

This is one objection I hear *way* too often. "I'm not certified.
I don't have a degree. I haven't been to school for this. How can I
possibly claim to be an expert?" I always smile when I hear these
words come out of someone's mouth because I know where I
came from.

I ask them, "Well, I'm curious. You paid me $50,000 (or
$100,000) to teach you this stuff. What do you think my creden-
tials are?"

They think about it and usually say something like, "I don't
know. Do you have any marketing degrees?"

I say, "Nope. I barely graduated from college, and I got a C in
marketing." I didn't get good grades, and I don't have any certifications to my name. But guess what? I'm *really good* at getting
people results. My results are my certifications.

Tony Robbins told me that when he first started learning
neuro-linguistic programming (NLP), he signed up for a six-month
certification course, and after just a few days, he fell in love with

it. He gained the skill quickly and wanted to start helping people immediately. The trainers said, "You can't; you're not certified yet."

Tony said, "Certified? I know how to help people. Let's go help!" That night he left his hotel room, walked across the street to the nearest restaurant, and started helping people quit smoking and assisting them with lots of other amazing things. He ended up getting kicked out of the program because he was practicing without being certified. Yet he's gone on to transform tens of millions of people's lives using NLP—all without any certifications.

Your results are your certification.

I hereby give you permission to help people. You're ready now.

"But Russell, what if others know more about my topic than I do?"

There's a book (and a movie) called *Catch Me If You Can* that illustrates this point pretty well. It's the story of Frank Abagnale, a brilliant high school dropout and a famous con artist who masqueraded as an airline pilot, a pediatrician, and a district attorney, among other things. At one point, he starts teaching a sociology class at Brigham Young University. He teaches the whole semester, and no one ever figures out that he's not a real teacher. Later on when they finally do catch him, the authorities ask him how he could teach the class when he didn't know anything about advanced sociology.

Abagnale explained that all he had to do was be one chapter ahead of his students in order to teach the class.

That's the key. You don't have to be the most knowledgeable person in the world on your topic, you just have to be one chapter ahead of the people you're helping. There will always be people in the world who are more advanced than you are. That's fine. You can learn from them, but don't let it stop you from helping the ones who are a chapter or two behind you.

This first phase is all about finding what sparks your interest, geeking out on the topic, and giving yourself permission to help other people with the things that you've learned.

WHO DO YOU NEED TO BECOME AS A LEADER?

As I mentioned earlier, Jay Abraham once said, "People are silently begging to be led," and I believe that's true. So how do you become the type of leader they need? It starts with finding your voice. The secret to finding your voice is in sharing your message consistently for a long time.

On March 26, 2013, I launched the first episode of my *Marketing in Your Car* podcast, which later became the *Marketing Secrets Show*. It seemed as good a day as any to launch it, outside of the fact that in the prior few months I had fired about 100 employees, found out that I owed more than $250,000 to the IRS (which if I didn't pay soon would mean even more fines and possible jail time), almost bankrupted my company, and had almost no money left in the bank and tons of credit card debt piling up. Looking back now it seems like the worst possible time to launch a podcast teaching people my "secrets of marketing," yet that's exactly what I did.

I knew that if I was going to do my own show, I had to be consistent or it wouldn't work. Out of all the types of shows that I could publish (audio, video, or text), I knew that it had to be simple or I'd never stick to it. When I considered how to work it into my everyday routine, I realized that every day I had a 10-minute commute to my office. I figured that I could record each episode on my phone as I drove to work. In the episodes, I would share my thoughts about what I was doing to market my business and the lessons I was learning each day. That's how it got its original name: *Marketing in Your Car.*

The first episodes were not good. In fact, years later, my friend Steve J Larsen told me, "The first forty-five or forty-six episodes weren't very good, but then around that time is where it seemed like you found your voice, and they started getting better and better each episode after that." The good news for me (and also for you) is during your first episodes—the ones when you are the worst—no one is listening to you yet! If I hadn't done the first 45 episodes, I never would have gotten to episode 46, when I started to hit my stride. That's why it's so essential to start publishing your show now, even when you're not good at it. In the process of doing your show is when you will find your voice. I was lucky that I had no idea how to check the download stats to see if anyone was listening to me when I first got started. I am so grateful that I didn't know, because I'm sure that I would have been discouraged and stopped. Don't look at your stats, downloads, or numbers at first, because you're just trying to build the foundation for something great, and it will take time.

Interestingly, I learned how to check the download stats about three years into my podcast, and I discovered that I had tens of thousands of people listening to every episode! I also found out that the majority of the people who had joined my highest-level mastermind groups and coaching programs had been podcast listeners first! When I asked them about it, the pattern of how most of them came into our higher-end programs was shockingly similar. So many of them told me that they would listen to a few episodes, and then for some reason a particular episode would connect with them. It made them want more, so they would go back to episode #1 and binge listen to every episode over a week or two period of time. During the episodes, I documented my journey as I was building my company back up. I'd share stories of the people I had a chance to work with. Often even before they finished binging the episodes, listeners had applied to work with me!

Without selling ads in my podcast, promoting my own or other people's products (both things that you can and probably should do to make money from your show), I was just telling stories of my own and from my clients. I didn't promote anything, yet that podcast has converted more casual followers into raving fans than anything else I've ever done. But it didn't start that way; it took three-plus years of consistent publishing. Let me walk you through the steps that will make your show a success.

Step #1—Publish daily for at least a year: The first commitment you have to make is that you will be consistent. I knew when I started that if I didn't find a platform that was easy for me and easy to create the content, I wouldn't be consistent. What platform makes the most sense for you? If you're a writer, you will probably want to blog. If you like to make videos, you can start your own vlog. And if you like audio, your platform would be podcasting. First, figure out where you will publish, then decide how and when you are going to publish. Will you wake up each morning and write a 1,000-word blog post before lunch? Will you do a Facebook Live video before you go to bed each night, sharing the day's lessons? What works for you that will help you to be consistent? If you can publish every day for a year, you'll never have to worry about money problems again. During the process, you will find your voice and your audience will have time to find you.

One of my friends, Nathan Barry, wrote this post on his website recently, "Endure Long Enough to Get Noticed":[8]

How many great TV shows have you discovered in Season 3 or later? I started watching *Game of Thrones* after they had released five seasons. Pat Flynn had released at least 100 episodes of his podcast before I even knew he existed. I discovered *Hardcore History* years after Dan Carlin started producing it.

This is such a common experience. There is so much content being produced that we can't possibly discover it all. So instead, we wait for the best content to float to the surface after time. If step one in building an audience is to create great content, step two is to endure long enough to get noticed.

Seth Godin is very generous with his time and will appear on almost any relevant podcast—but you have to have recorded at least 100 episodes first. His filter is creators who have shown they are willing to show up consistently for a long time.

For those of you who have been around me for any amount of time, you know that this is a soapbox that I'm very firm on. You must be publishing or you will never become relevant, and you must continue publishing if you want to remain relevant. This part of the traffic flywheel does not go away.

Steve J Larsen knew when he bought his first tickets to Funnel Hacking LIVE that I was probably going to tell everyone this eternal truth, but as he packed his bags he told his wife, "I will do everything that Russell says at this event . . . except publishing my own show. I won't do that."

Before lunch on day one, I told everyone that the number one thing they could do from now until next year's event would be to pick a channel and publish on it daily. I told them that if they did that every day for a year, they would never need to worry about money again. And then I did something I hadn't before: I made everyone in the audience commit to me that they would start publishing that day.

Most of the people in the room raised their hand and were excited to take the challenge, but very few took what I said at face value. On the other hand, when Steve J Larsen made the commitment—the one that he went in saying he wasn't willing to make— he decided to go all in. He decided to start a podcast, and at that event he created his first episodes.

About a week later, he applied for a job at ClickFunnels and became my new head funnel builder. He sat next to me every day for the next two years. As I was working on my projects, he watched me share (i.e., publish) the lessons I was learning along the way. I was podcasting, posting on Facebook, doing Periscope shows, and more. He told me that he was shocked at how much I published, and so he modeled what I was doing.

For the next two years that he worked at ClickFunnels, he kept publishing his show; after a few months it started getting some traction. It kept growing over the years, and when he decided to make the jump from being an employee to becoming his own entrepreneur, he had a large following of people who were consuming everything he was publishing. That show and his following became the launchpad he needed to jumpstart his career. He had the fans and he had a following, so he simply introduced them to the new offers he created and became an "overnight success."

Step #2—Document the journey: The biggest question and the largest fear that most people have when I tell them to start their own show is they have no idea what they will talk about. One of the most powerful things I learned from Gary Vaynerchuk is a concept he calls "Document, Don't Create." I've reposted an article from his blog, which goes deeper into this concept:

> If you want people to start listening to you, you have to show up. What I mean by this is there are a lot of you out there who aren't producing enough articles or videos or pieces of content to build your influence. Too many "content creators" think that they only have one at bat—they have to make the one, most beautifully created video or image or rant on Facebook.
>
> But what they don't realize is that their hunger to make the perfect piece of content is what's actually crippling them.
>
> It's true that if you want to be seen or heard on social media, you have to put out valuable content on a regular basis. You should be doing a YouTube vlog or podcast or some sort of long-form audio/video series at least once a week. You should be posting on Instagram and/or Snapchat stories at least six to seven times a day.
>
> Now you're probably thinking: *Whoa, that's a lot. How do I create six to seven meaningful things a day?*
>
> I'll give you the biggest tip when it comes to content creation: Document. Don't create.
>
> In very simple terms, "documenting" versus "creating" is what *The Real World* and *Keeping up with the Kardashians* are to *Star Wars* and *Friends*. And don't get confused—just because you're "documenting" doesn't mean you're not creating content. It's just a version of creating that is predicated more on practicality instead of having to think of stories or fantasy—something that's very hard for most people (including myself).
>
> Think about it: You can ponder about the strategy behind every post and fabricate yourself into this "influential person" . . . or you can just be yourself.

Creating this influential persona might seem especially hard if you're just someone starting to climb the ladder. And I get it—for some of you there's a lot of pressure in that. You think that some 30- or 40- or 50-year-old is going to listen to your rant video with cynicism and think *What does this kid know?*

But, one of the biggest mistakes people make when creating content for their personal brand is trying to oversell themselves because they think that's what's going to get people's attention. Whether you're a business coach or motivational speaker or artist, I think it's much more fruitful to talk about your process than about the actual advice you "think" you should be giving them.

Documenting your journey versus creating an image of yourself is the difference between saying "You should . . ." versus "My intuition says . . ." Get it? It changes everything. I believe that the people who are willing to discuss their journeys instead of trying to front themselves as the "next big thing" are going to win.

So, when I say to put out those six to seven meaningful pieces of content a day, just pick up your smartphone, open Facebook Live, and just start talking about the things most important to you. Because in the end, the creative (or how "beautiful" someone thinks your content is) is going to be subjective. What's not subjective is the fact that you need to start putting yourself out there and keep swinging.

Starting is the most important part and the biggest hurdle that most people are facing. They're pondering and strategizing instead of making. They're debating what's going to happen when they haven't even looked at what's in front of them.

So do me a favor and start documenting.

"Okay, I started, Gary. Now what?" you ask? Keep doing it for another five years and then come back to me before you ask again.

People who are tuning in to your show are doing it typically because they're looking for some type of result. It's the same reason they buy your products, open your emails, and engage with your content. People listen to my podcasts, read my books, and watch my videos because they're trying to figure out more ways to market their business. I'm not publishing because I know everything about this topic, I'm publishing because I'm obsessed with this topic. I'm in a constant search for new and better ways to market my own company, and as I run across them, have ideas, read cool things, I'm sharing them with my people. As my friend Rich Schefren once told me, "We get paid a lot to think for other people."

So my first question for you as you start your show is this, What is the big result that you're obsessed with? What you are trying to learn for yourself anyway that you can document as you're discovering it in real time?

When you listen to the introduction to my podcast, I call out what the big question is that I'm answering on my show:

> "So, the big question is this: How are entrepreneurs like us, who didn't cheat and take on venture capital, who are spending money from our own pockets, how do we market in a way that lets us get our products and services and the things that we believe in out to the world, yet still remain profitable? That is the question, and this podcast will give you the answers. My name is Russell Brunson, and welcome to the *Marketing Secrets* podcast."

Inside that frame, I can talk about, share, and interview experts on anything related to helping people sell more of the things they believe in. As I mentioned earlier, I started this podcast on the back of a huge business failure. Most people would have thought it was the worst time ever to start a podcast, let alone one about marketing a business, but looking at it through the "Document, Don't Create" lens reveals that it was the perfect time to start the podcast. In fact, I wish I would have started it 10 years earlier when I first got online, because I would have had so many more interesting things to share as I was learning them for the first time. In any case, how cool is it now, six years later, that I have documented the entire journey from this business failure to growing ClickFunnels to a company generating more than $100 million per year? Even more important, hundreds of thousands of people have been able to follow us on that journey and learn the lessons as I was learning them!

Step #3—Testing your material: Recently, I was at a private mastermind retreat in Wyoming with a handful of influencers who collectively had made billions of dollars online and influenced hundreds of millions of people. One night as we were sitting around a campfire talking, Dean Graziosi shared an insight that has changed how I look at the material I'm publishing. His story, from the best of my memory, went something like this:

> You know how, when you watch an amazing comedian perform onstage on a late-night talk show, every joke he tells lands perfectly? You find yourself wondering, *How is this guy so funny?* But what you don't realize is that over the last 10 years of his journey to become a comedian, he would write out 10 jokes, go to the closest dive bar, stand up onstage, and deliver his jokes. He probably watched as one or two of the 10 jokes landed, and the rest bombed. He would then go back home, take the two jokes that landed, and write eight new ones. The next week he would find a new place to perform, deliver his 10 jokes, and find out that only one of his new jokes landed. He then has three jokes in total that landed. He goes back to his apartment and starts the process over again, doing this week after week, year after year, until he's found his 10 jokes. Now he's ready. That's when we get to see him, after he's perfected the material, when he stands up and lands every joke on the biggest stage in the world.

I look back at my journey and think about my first book. I was so scared when I finished writing *DotCom Secrets* that I didn't want to give it to people to read. But what most people didn't realize was that a full decade before I wrote that book, I *earned* that book. I was obsessed with marketing, and I read, watched, and listened to everything I could get my hands on. After that, I tested the concepts and ideas on the little businesses I was creating. I also tested the concepts on other people's businesses as a consultant. Some ideas worked, while others failed.

I started teaching at small seminars and workshops. I would explain concepts and watch to see which ideas made sense to people, and which ideas were confusing. At each event, I would teach the concepts again, over and over, tweaking and refining the ideas and stories every time. I did interviews, podcasts, videos, and articles, testing my materials over and over again. From this work came concepts like the value ladder, the Secret Formula, the three types of traffic, funnel hacking, the Attractive Character, and others. I was testing my material for more than a decade, and so while I was nervous for others to read that book, I was also confident knowing that it was ready.

The same thing happened with this book, *Expert Secrets*. I spent two years talking about the concepts on my own podcast and on other people's podcasts. I developed ideas on Periscope and Facebook Live. I ran events, workshops, and coaching programs, testing the ideas on others' businesses as well as mine, and the end product was the *Expert Secrets* book.

Publishing your show daily, as you're documenting your journey, will also give you a chance to start testing your material. You'll discover what messages connect with people, which episodes get shared and which ones don't. Which messages get people to show up and comment, and which messages don't connect. It's this very process of showing up consistently and publishing that will help you refine your message, find your voice, and attract your dream customers to you. It doesn't matter whether your end goal is a book, a webinar, a keynote presentation, a viral video, or something else, the more you publish and test your material, the clearer your message will become and the more people you will attract.

Step #4—Learn to be prolific: Your audience must be fascinated with you and what you teach. If you're boring, they're not going to connect with you. I've watched a lot of experts come and go over the past 10 years, and I have spent a lot of time trying to figure out why some of them last and others don't. The one thing I've noticed across the board with most experts who've had success and stayed relevant is that they are highly prolific.

When I say prolific, some people think I'm talking about producing a lot of content. While that is true, there is another definition for prolific: *someone who has abundant inventiveness.* They invent new, unique ideas and frameworks all the time. That's the type of prolific I'm talking about here. To make the biggest impact on the most people, and at the same time make the most money, it's vital that you fit your message into the sweet spot on what I call the Prolific Index.

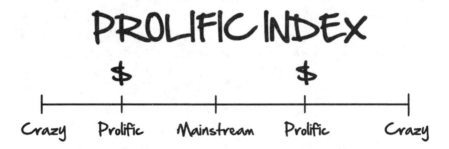

Figure 1.12:

**When you're constantly sharing new and innovative ideas,
you fall into what I call the Prolific Zone.**

In the middle of the Prolific Index is the mainstream. This area includes the ideas currently being taught to the masses via traditional mediums. For example, if you're a weight-loss expert, the mainstream advice hovers around the government recommendations like the four food groups or the food pyramid for nutrition. While some of these principles may be good, I'd argue that others are flat-out lies. Even if you believe those things are true, you aren't going to get anywhere teaching mainstream advice that people are currently getting elsewhere for free.

People can go to school and learn about all this stuff. It's common sense. It's not exciting. There's no money in the mainstream.

Now on both ends of this spectrum are what I call the "crazy zones." There are plenty of experts who live in the crazy zone. And while you can always recruit a few people into the crazy zone, it's difficult to get the masses to take action all the way to the left or the right.

One of my favorite examples of the crazy zone in the weight-loss world comes from a documentary I watched called *Eat the Sun*.[9] In this movie, they talked about how people can stop eating and just gaze at the sun. Yes, stop eating completely and just look at the sun. Kinda crazy? Well, the documentary did get me to spend a few minutes gazing at the sun, but I'm not crazy enough to give up food 100 percent. And I don't think anyone is going to make millions teaching that concept. (As a side note, I did actually love that movie.)

The sweet spot, the place where you will impact the most lives and make the most money, is right in the middle. Somewhere between the mainstream advice and the crazy zone is where you want to set yourself up. I call this place the Prolific Zone. When you're there, you're relaying ideas that are so unique, people will notice.

One of my favorite teachers in the weight-loss niche is Dave Asprey from Bulletproof.com. His origin story falls perfectly in the Prolific Zone. One day he was climbing Mount Kailash in Tibet and stopped at a guesthouse to shelter from minus-10-degree weather. He was given a creamy cup of yak butter tea that made him feel amazing. He tried to figure out why he felt so good. He soon discovered it was from the high fats in this tea, so he started adding butter and other fats to his coffee and teas.[10] This experience eventually helped him create a national phenomenon called Bulletproof Coffee. People put butter and coconut oil in their coffee to lose weight and feel amazing.

For those of you who are just hearing this for the first time, it may seem a little crazy—but not so crazy that you completely dismiss it. And it's definitely not something the government is going to recommend. Bulletproof Coffee falls directly in the Prolific Zone, and its message has made Dave a multimillionaire.

Did you notice how this message causes some polarity? The mainstream will probably hate it, yet there is something interesting there. When Dave tells the rest of his story and can back it up with science, it becomes a message that spreads quickly.

When your message causes polarity, it attracts attention, and people will pay for it. Neutrality is boring, and rarely is money made or change created when you stay neutral. Being polar is what will attract raving fans and people who will follow you and pay for your advice.

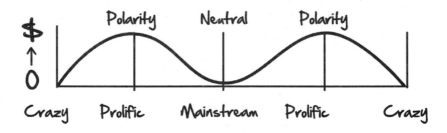

Figure 1.13:

**When you're in the Prolific Zone, you naturally create
polarity, which attracts raving fans.**

As you become more polar in your messaging, you will also notice that people on the other side of your message won't be happy about it. By creating true fans, you will always upset those on the other side. I wanted to warn you about this early, because often people (including me) really struggle when others get upset or disagree with their ideas.

For every 100 true fans who follow you, you'll likely get one person who doesn't like you. And for some reason, they always seem to be the loudest. If you search my name (or anyone's name who has tried to create change in others), you'll find tons of fans, as well as people who don't like us. It's just the nature of being a true leader. You've got to become okay with that, because without the polarity of your message, you can't get to your true fans and help create the change they need.

One tip I learned from Dan Kennedy that helps me cope with the small percentage of haters who disagree with my message is this: "If you haven't offended someone by noon each day, then you're not marketing hard enough."[11]

And Jay Abraham said, "If you truly believe that what you have is useful and valuable to your clients, then you have a moral obligation to try to serve them in every way possible."[12] And that is why I am so aggressive in my marketing. I honestly feel like I have a moral obligation to share my message, because it's changed my life and I know it can do the same for others.

I want you to start thinking about your niche. What do you teach, and where is it on the Prolific Index? Many times, people are either playing it safe with the mainstream, or they are way out in crazy land where there is no money. You need to find your sweet spot between the middle and crazy.

Step #5—Master persuasion: Throughout this book, you will learn how to persuade people. In fact, everything you learn in Sections Two and Three of this book is all about persuasion. But before we get too deep into that, I want you to understand the core foundation of persuasion.

One of my favorite books on this topic is *The One Sentence Persuasion Course* by Blair Warren.[13] Blair is a persuasion expert who spent more than a decade studying and using persuasion. During that journey, he broke down exactly how to persuade people into one simple sentence: "People will do anything for those who encourage their dreams, justify their failures, allay their fears, confirm their suspicions, and help them throw rocks at their enemies."

When I first read that, it made such a big impact that I wanted to remember it forever. So I made this graphic as a reminder.

Figure 1.14:

To turn your dream customers into true fans, you have to encourage their dreams, justify their failures, allay their fears, confirm their suspicions, and help them throw rocks at their enemies.

Here is a quick recap of why each of these actions is so important. I included Blair's explanations because he explains these concepts so masterfully.

Encourage their dreams: As the leader, it's vital that you first understand your audience's dreams, then encourage them inside the new opportunity you are creating for them. Parents often discourage their children's dreams "for their own good" and attempt to steer them toward more "reasonable" goals. And children often accept this as normal until others come along who believe in them and encourage their dreams.

When this happens, who do you think has more power? Parents or strangers?

Justify their failures: Most people who become followers and then fans will have tried to make a change before. You will not be the first person they have tried to learn from. For some reason, they didn't get their needs met from any prior encounters. It's important that you take the blame for past failures off their shoulders and place it back onto the old opportunities they attempted in the past. This way, they will be more open to trying your new opportunity.

While millions cheer Dr. Phil as he tells people to accept responsibility for their mistakes, millions more are looking for someone to take the responsibility *off* their shoulders. To tell them that they are not responsible for their lot in life. And while accepting responsibility is essential to gaining control of one's own life, assuring others they are *not responsible* is essential to gaining influence over theirs. One need look no further than politics to see this powerful game played at its best.

Allay their fears: To allay is to diminish or put to rest. If you can put people's fears to rest and give them hope, they will follow you to the ends of the Earth and back again.

When we are afraid, it is almost impossible to concentrate on anything else. And while everyone knows this, what do we do when someone else is afraid and we need to get their attention? That's right. We *tell* them not to be afraid and expect that to do the trick. Does it work? Hardly. And yet we don't seem to notice. We go on as if we've solved the problem and the person before us fades further away. But there are those who *do* realize this and pay special attention to our fears. They do not tell us not to be afraid. They work with us until our fear subsides. They present evidence. They offer support. They tell us stories. But they do not *tell* us how to feel and expect us to feel that way. When you are afraid, which type of person do you prefer to be with?

Confirm their suspicions: Your audience is already suspicious of you and others in your market. They want to believe change is possible, but they're skeptical about making the leap forward. When you can confirm in story format that you had similar suspicions and describe how you overcame them, it will bond people to you.

One of our favorite things to say is "I knew it." There is just nothing quite like having our suspicions confirmed. When another person confirms something that we suspect, we not only feel a surge of superiority, we feel attracted to the one who helped make that surge come about. Hitler "confirmed" the suspicions of many Germans about the cause of their troubles and drew them further into his power by doing so. Cults often confirm the suspicions of prospective members by telling them that their families are out to sabotage them. It is a simple thing to confirm the suspicions of those who are desperate to believe them.

Throw rocks at their enemies: One big key to growing your following is creating "Us vs. Them" within your community. Take a stand for what you believe, why you're different, and who you're collectively fighting against. Why is your movement better than the alternatives?

Nothing bonds people like having a common enemy. I realize how ugly this sounds and yet it is true just the same. Those who understand what I'm saying can utilize this. Those who don't understand it, or worse, understand but refuse to address it, are throwing away one of the most effective ways of connecting with others. No matter what you may think, rest assured that people have enemies. All people. It has been said that everyone you meet is engaged in a great struggle. The thing they are struggling with is their enemy. Whether it is another individual, a group, an illness, a setback, a rival philosophy or religion, or what have you, when people are engaged in a struggle, they are looking for others to join them. Those who do become more than friends. They become partners.

Step #6—Care . . . a *lot*: The next part of being an expert is showing people that you actually care about them. Theodore Roosevelt said, "Nobody cares how much you know until they know how much you care."[14] If your audience thinks you are just in this to make money, your vehicle for change will not last long. Your following will not grow. In fact, it will shrink very quickly. If you choose your ideal clients correctly, you'll have people you'd be willing to serve and teach and train for free because that's how much you care about them.

One struggle most of us have as we try to serve our audience is the guilt sometimes associated with getting them to pay us. There are two reasons it's essential to *their* success that they pay you.

First, those who pay, pay attention. Over the past decade, I've invited my friends and family members to sit in on events that others have paid $50,000 to attend. Not once in those 10 years has a single one of the people who sat in for free launched a successful company. Yet in the *same* room sat people who invested in themselves. They heard the exact same information and, because they invested money to be there, turned that same information into multimillion-dollar-a-year companies. Yes, those who pay, pay attention—and the more they pay, the closer attention they pay. You are doing your audience a huge disservice if you undervalue what you are selling.

Second, the more success you have, the less time you will have. I remember when I first started, how proud I was that I answered all my customer support emails and talked (often for hours) with everyone who asked me a question. I thought I was serving my audience, but because of how accessible I was to everyone, I wasn't able to serve many people at all. You will need to put up barriers to protect your time so you can serve more people. By charging for what you do, you are showing those who do invest how much you really care about their success.

Those are a few of the steps to finding your voice and building a tribe so you can change their world. Understand, though, that you don't become a leader overnight. Start sharing your message and become consistent with it so you can find your voice. Figure out where your message can polarize people into true fans. Share your backstory and flaws. Be transparent. And over time, you will naturally become the leader your tribe needs.

TEACHING YOUR FRAMEWORKS

I was sitting in a small room of very high achievers a few weeks after Dean Graziosi's new book launch for *Millionaire Success Habits*. This was an affiliate mastermind meeting for the people who had sold the most books during the launch. As I looked around, I could clearly see it included a who's who of the marketing and personal development industries.

During the meeting, Dean looked over at Brendon Burchard, who was also sitting in the room, and asked him if he'd be willing to share his "seven-day launch" framework with everyone. Brendon agreed, grabbed a marker, and spent about two minutes doodling out some squares and boxes and arrows without saying a word. When he was done, he turned around, pointed to what he had drawn, and said, "This is my seven-day launch framework."

Then he told a story about how he came up with it and walked us through a quick overview of the process. Then he pointed to the first part of his sketch and started teaching the tactics involved in executing that step.

He then moved to the next step, walked us through that step in the process, and so on. Everyone in the room was writing notes a mile a minute when someone asked Brendon a question. Brendon stopped, responded to the question, and looked back at his framework.

"Oh, I'm sorry, I didn't mean to throw you off," said the guy who had asked the question.

Brendon looked back at him and told him not to worry. He explained that because he was teaching from his framework, he just had to go back to where he left off and he was fine. And then he said something that has been burned in my mind since that day. He said, "Your framework is your savior."

You see, your framework is a map that helps you know where you're going. If you ever get stuck or forget what's next, your framework has all the answers you need to save you and put you back on track.

One of the other very powerful things about a framework is that you can take it and teach it as quickly or as methodically as you need to, depending on how much detail you put into each step of the framework. For instance, you could skim the surface in just two minutes on a YouTube video, go deeper in two hours on a webinar, or dive really deep over two days at a workshop. I can (and have) made quick videos teaching my Perfect Webinar framework, and I've also taught it in more detail at a live three-day event; it was the same framework in each case.

As you'll also see in Secret #5, when we start talking about how to quickly create information products, your frameworks are also the key there. Your framework can become a post on Instagram, a video on YouTube, an episode on your podcast, a lead magnet, a chapter of your book, a course, a membership site, a coaching program, a mastermind group, or something else. You will use your frameworks over and over again as the tool that guides your dream customers to the results they are looking for.

But in this chapter I'm not going to show you the different ways you can package your frameworks; I will save that for after we talk about new opportunities and creating offers. Here I want to focus on my framework for teaching frameworks (yes, I practice what I preach) as this is one of the primary skills that you will need to learn as an expert if you want to be able to guide your dream customers to their desired result.

HOW TO TEACH YOUR FRAMEWORKS

Figure 2.1:

To teach your framework, introduce it, tell a story about how you
learned or earned it, share the strategy (the *what* you do), teach the tactics
(the *how* you do it), and show how it has worked for others.

One of the worst feelings in the world is standing on a stage, or in
front of a group of people you've been called to serve, and trying to
explain to them a concept or framework that you know will change
their lives, but a few minutes into your explanation you see their
eyes glaze over. I can't tell you how many times I've been in that
situation and wanted to stop, grab their shoulders, shake them, and
yell, "Don't you understand what I'm trying to tell you?!" I knew
I had the key they were looking for, but I had no idea how to get
them interested enough that they would even believe me.

But I felt like I was called, and that my message was important,
so I kept trying. Most times I felt like I was shoving a round peg in
a square hole. I was a wrestler though, and I wasn't used to losing,
so I just kept trying, knowing that if I took enough shots, eventually I'd get a takedown.

As time went on, I tried different ways of teaching my frameworks, hoping to get a different result. Some things worked, and I remembered to keep doing those, and other things didn't, and I made notes not to try them again. I also spent a lot of time at events watching how other speakers delivered their presentations and I'd take notes on how certain things they did made me feel, and then I would try to add it to my presentations. Each time I stood in front of a small group, it was another audition to test my message and see if I could make it click. Over the years I got better and better, and eventually developed my "Framework for Teaching Frameworks" (that's what I call it). It's my four-step system to make sure that what I say is impactful so that the people I'm serving will listen and remember what they learned. Let me walk you through how it works.

Introduce the framework: Before I start teaching the framework, I must first introduce it. I do that by simply telling the audience the name of my framework:

"This is my Hook, Story, Offer framework" or
"Here is my Perfect Webinar framework."

Then I give them my framework description:

My ____(insert number)-step framework
(or system, process) for _____(insert result).

So when I was doing the Perfect Webinar framework, I'd say:

"This is the five-step framework for creating a webinar that
sells any product to a cold audience in less than 90 minutes."

Step #1—Share how you learned it or earned it: The big mistake that most people make as soon as they introduce their framework is they want to jump straight into teaching the strategy and tactics. I made this mistake for years because I would get so excited to teach the concept that I had spent years learning and mastering that I knew would change people's lives. I had spent so much of my time creating this framework that I wanted to share that it felt like the most special gift I could possibly give them.

When I finally had an opportunity to share it, I'd give people the concept that was so sacred to me, only to see most of them brush it off as unimportant.

Each time that happened, I would think of the scripture in the New Testament when Christ was teaching his Sermon on the Mount and said in Matthew 7:6, "neither cast ye your pearls before swine, lest they trample them under their feet." That's what I felt like. I had given them a pearl, and they gave it back to me and walked away.

I got so frustrated one day in front of a group, after I gave them the pearl and no one seemed to care, that I went off on a mini rant. "Do you not understand what I just gave you?" I asked the people at this small workshop. "Let me tell you what I had to go through to earn this concept so I could share it with you today." Then I spent about 15 minutes telling the story about all the pain I had to go through, the money spent, the time lost, the testing on myself as a human guinea pig, the tests I did with others to make sure the concept worked, and the iterations we had to go through to make this perfect.

After telling them this story, I then re-explained to them the same pearl I had shared just minutes earlier, and this time they got it. The first time I had given them the pearl, but they didn't respect it. The second time they were preframed to understand why it was so important. Handing them the pearl through this lens changed everything. Getting it now meant they saved themselves the pain and suffering I had to go through to get it for them; now they understood the value of what they were receiving.

The first thing I do after I introduce the framework is explain how I either learned it (your knowledge) or earned it (through your experiences). You've probably noticed in each chapter of this book (and all of my books)—and every presentation, podcast episode, blog post, or video I make—that I always start by telling the story of how I learned or earned it. This preframe creates the value of what I'm sharing. Without it, the strategy and tactics I share become worthless.

During this part of the process you should also acknowledge the giants that you learned any piece of your framework from. You've spent time learning and studying from others to build your framework. You've interviewed countless people. Whenever you share something that you learned from someone else, give them credit. Many people think that sharing the source of their knowledge somehow diminishes their status in the minds of the people listening, but the opposite is true. I try to always give credit to the person I learned anything from before I share it. Doing this has helped me keep great relationships with the people I learned from when I got started. It's helped me serve them back in a small way after they were so gracious with helping me on my journey. Your audience will respect you more because you don't steal ideas from others.

Step #2—Share the strategy (the *what* you do): The next thing I do is share the strategy of the framework. Many people get confused on the difference between strategy and tactics, but for this process it's really important that you understand the difference. The *Farnam Street* blog explained the difference between strategy and tactics like this:[15]

> Strategy is [an] overarching plan or set of goals. Changing strategies is like trying to turn around an aircraft carrier—it can be done but not quickly. Tactics are the specific actions or steps you undertake to accomplish your strategy. For example, in a war, a nation's strategy might be to win the hearts and minds of the opponent's civilian population. To achieve this they could use tactics such as radio broadcasts or building hospitals. A personal strategy might be to get into a particular career, whereas your tactics might include choosing your educational path, seeking out a helpful mentor, or distinguishing yourself from the competition.

During this part of my teaching I give them the outline of the framework, which is similar to sharing the table of contents of a book as it is the strategy of where we are and where we are going. For most people this is simply an outline, and that's okay. This is what my outline for my Perfect Webinar framework looks like:

The Perfect Webinar

- *Step #1—Grab Their Attention and Quickly Build Rapport*

- *Step #2—Tell Your Origin Story about How You Earned or Learned Your New Opportunity*

- *Step #3—Break and Rebuild Their False Belief Patterns with the Three Core Stories (Vehicle, Internal, and External)*

- *Step #4—Use the Stack to Position the Offer Correctly*

- *Step #5— Finish with Closing Techniques to Increase Close Rates*

If you're more of a visual person, you could doodle it out like I do in my books and when I teach most of my frameworks, but it's not essential. After I've presented the framework, I move into the five steps. You'll notice that in most of the chapters of this book, toward the beginning you see a doodle and some steps showing you the strategy, and then the content inside that outline is the tactical—or how-to—plan to execute each step in the strategy.

Step #3—Teach the tactics (the *how* you do it): This is where most of the content is taught. What are the principles and tools that you've learned and how can people use them in their lives? Walk them through the step-by-step process, just like you were teaching yourself back when you got started.

In our 30 Days Summit, we pose the question:

You suddenly lose all your money, along with your name and reputation, and only have your marketing know-how left. You have bills piled high and people harassing you for money over the phone. Plus, you have a guaranteed roof over your head, a phone line, an internet connection, and a ClickFunnels account for only one month. You no longer have your big guru name, your following, or JV partners. Other than your vast marketing experience, you're an unknown newbie. What would you do, from day 1 to day 30, to save yourself?

I love looking at my tactical teaching through the lens of a question like that. You should ask yourself these questions:

If I were to suddenly lose _____ (the results I've achieved that others are coming to learn from me), and I only had my framework left and I was starting over with no advantages, what would I do from day 1 to day 30 to get _____ (the big result) back?

This question will help you teach the principles of your framework in a simple process that will actually be possible for someone who is starting from ground zero to follow.

Depending on the length of time you have to teach, you may use parts of this same "framework to teach frameworks" inside each step of your framework. For example, when you teach the first step of the strategy, you can include Step 1, where you share how you learned or earned that step to create more value when you teach it, and then also include Step 4, where you show a case study of how it worked for someone else.

Oftentimes one of the steps of your framework will be another framework (just like this chapter of the book is a framework *within* the framework of the entire *Expert Secrets* book.) When that's the case, you may share Steps 1, 2, 3, and 4 multiple times within the one step of the framework.

I know that may sound overwhelming, but when you look at the table of contents of this book, you can see how Section One, "Creating Your Movement," is a framework. Here are the three steps (and strategy) of that framework:

- Step #1: Becoming the Expert
- Step #2: Creating the New Opportunity
- Step #3: Giving Your People a Future-Based Cause

But then inside of that framework, I have already shown you the framework for finding your voice. And now we're going through Teaching Your Frameworks. These are just embedded frameworks inside of my core framework that I can go into when time allows.

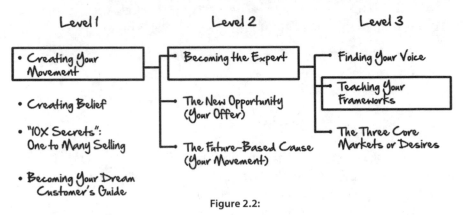

Figure 2.2:

You can go deeper into your frameworks depending on how much time you have. With each level, you can spend more and more time teaching that framework.

That's how we're able to take a simple framework and teach it in a two-minute YouTube video (Level 1), a two-hour webinar (Level 2) or a two-day live event (Level 3). You're still teaching the same framework, but you're able to go deeper into the embedded frameworks when you have more time.

Step #4—Show them how it works for others: In step #1, you tell them the story about how you learned or earned the framework, so they've seen how it worked for you. This last step is to show that it not only works for other people, but that you have the ability to transfer this framework to others.

This is a big reason why it's so important not to miss the step inside the Finding Your Voice framework of becoming the servant. The more time you can spend testing your frameworks out on other people the better. One reason is because it always takes some adjustments to get your process to work for others. You have life experiences and talents that others don't have that do give you an unfair advantage. By getting your process to work for others, you lose those unfair advantages and you have to adjust your process to make up for those shortcomings.

The other reason is that people are always skeptical of the expert. Even if they believe you, they will think it's because you have some type of special abilities that they don't have, so they will dismiss your ability to help them. Showing them that it didn't just work for you, but it also worked for people just like them, is the key to getting them to believe in your framework.

From the first minute you start applying your framework to others and every day after you start sharing these frameworks, you need to be gathering the stories, case studies, testimonials, examples, and proof that your framework can get results for the people you are serving.

Now that we've spent time focusing on developing *you* as an expert and the proprietary *frameworks* that you are going to be bringing to the market, I want to shift your focus to the *marketplace* and how to position yourself inside it so you can attract the dream customers you've been called to serve.

THE THREE CORE MARKETS OR DESIRES

Every so often, we run an event at the ClickFunnels headquarters called the "Funnel Hack-a-Thon" or FHAT Event for short. We usually pick a topic, teach a concept, and the rest of the day everyone works on that part of their funnel. These hack-a-thons typically go late into the night, oftentimes until 2 or 3 in the morning.

One night of the hack-a-thon was being run by one of my friends and lead trainers Steve J Larsen. He had just taught a session and everyone was working on their funnels when one of the attendees approached the left side of the stage.

"Hey, can I run my offer by you?" he asked.

"Sure!" Steve responded.

The guy then went on and explained all the things that he was going to include inside his offer. After he was done, he asked: "So . . . do you think that offer is sexy?"

Steve responded, "It depends. What market are you serving?"

He answered back, "Um, I don't know."

"Well then that's the *riskiest* idea I've ever heard in my life!"

"Wait, what?"

"Think about it, if you don't know *who* you're serving, anything you come up with is a guess, because you aren't the one buying it. You don't fill your own wallet. You need to figure out *who* you are going to serve first, and then you can create the offer(s) that they want."

THE THREE CORE MARKETS/DESIRES

There are three core markets or desires that every product is marketed through. The three desires (in no particular order) are health, wealth, and relationships. When people purchase a product or service, they're hoping to get a certain result in one of these three areas of their lives.

Figure 3.1:

Every product or service fits into one of these three core desires or markets.

So the first question you need to answer is this:

Which of these three desires are my future dream customers trying to receive when they buy my product or service?

For most people, this is a pretty simple question to answer, but sometimes people get stuck for one of two reasons.

Reason #1—My product fits into *more* than one of these desires: Many products can be marketed toward getting a result in more than one desire, but your marketing message can focus only on *one* of them. Any time you try to get your potential customer to believe in two things, your conversions will usually cut in half (most times by 90 percent or more). Focus only on one desire with each message you put into the market.

Reason #2—My product doesn't fit into any of these desires: This false belief was best resolved at one of our recent events, where someone told Steve J Larsen this exact same thing. Steve went on to tell the story of Gillette razors, and then he asked which desire a razor fulfilled.

At first everyone was quiet, and then a few people started guessing, "Health?" Another mumbled, "Or maybe . . . hmm . . ."

Steve then played one of Gillette's ads. In it, you see a story develop. First, a man is shown shaving. After the shave, a beautiful woman gets closer to him. Then the two go out for a night on the town. The ad ends with the two together back home.

After showing the ad, Steve asked the question again a little differently: "What desire was this marketing message created for?"

Instantly everyone responded, "RELATIONSHIPS!"

Most products could fit into multiple categories, and on the outside they may look as if they don't fit into any category, but remember that your marketing message must be focused on only one of the three core desires. As Steve often says, "If your product doesn't fit into one of the three core desires, then your sales message at least must!"

THE SUBMARKETS

When the markets first started, there were only three. The companies that started to sell their products inside each market had almost no competition. In their book *Blue Ocean Strategy*, W. Chan Kim and Renée Mauborgne call markets that have no competition "blue oceans."[16] But eventually other companies see the success they are having in this blue ocean, and they jump in and compete to serve the same market. Soon this blue ocean gets dozens of sharks coming and competing inside the same market, and the waters get bloody, which Kim and Mauborgne call a "red ocean."

After the three core markets became red oceans, companies started to look for ways to create their own submarkets (new blue oceans) within the three core markets. Inside each desire are multiple ways to fulfill that desire, and this is where the submarkets began.

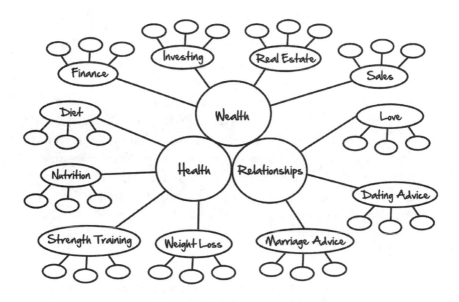

Figure 3.2:

Once markets get saturated, submarkets are created.

For example, inside health there are hundreds of ways to get that desire met. If you want to get healthy, you might want to do it by losing weight or gaining muscle. Similarly, if you want to be wealthy, you might want to do it through real estate or marketing online. If you want to improve your relationships, you might need marriage advice or dating advice. The list of submarkets is practically endless inside any of the three core markets.

So businesses started to create their own blue oceans, marketing directly to the new desires they identified in their customers. So here are the next set of questions for you to ask yourself:

What are the other submarkets inside my core desire that people are using to try to get that desire met?

What is the submarket that my product or service fits into?

As you are thinking about this submarket, I have three questions to consider to make sure you are picking the correct submarket.

Question #1: Would people in this submarket be excited about the new opportunity/frameworks you will be presenting them? I want you to start thinking about the new frameworks you are creating. Because you will be pulling people from this submarket into the new niche that you are creating, it's important to make sure they will be excited about what you want to share. Your new opportunity has to be something that will make people interested enough to take action.

Question #2: Are the people in this market irrationally passionate? Before we ask how passionate the market is, I need to ask you a personal question. Are *you* irrationally passionate about your topic? When you hang out with friends or family members, do you always bring it up, even if no one else seems to care? If so, that's a good sign. But are there others as irrationally passionate as you? Here are some of the things I look for to determine if my market is irrationally passionate.

Communities: Are there online forums, message boards, and social groups dedicated to this topic? How about Facebook groups and fan pages, YouTube channels, podcasts, or blogs with others geeking out on this topic you love so much?

Vocabulary: Does the market have its own special language? In the internet marketing world, you hear words like "autoresponder," "split testing," and "squeeze pages." In the health and biohacking market, they talk about "blood tests" and "ketones." An irrationally passionate market always has its own vocabulary. Does yours?

Events: Does this market have its own events? They might be online or offline conferences, seminars, summits, or masterminds. If events aren't happening in your market, you might have a hard time getting people to attend webinars and training. If they are already used to attending events, you'll have a much easier time.

Other Experts: Does this market have its own celebrities and gurus? There must be established experts already thriving and selling information products in your market. You don't want to be the first celebrity in a market. You want a topic or niche with its own subculture already established.

Question #3: Are these people *willing* and *able* to spend money on information? Sometimes people are *willing* to spend money, but they aren't *able*; they are broke. Other times people have all the money in the world; they are *able*, but *not willing* to part with a dime. Your submarket must be both willing and able to spend money.

For example, I had a friend who saw huge potential in the video game market. He spent a fortune trying to launch his product in this new niche. What he found was that even though there were plenty of kids playing video games, they didn't have credit cards. It's hard to sell your mom on why you need to buy a course that will help you play video games better. Even though the kids he was targeting may have been willing to buy, they weren't able to.

But the opposite is also true. One of my Inner Circle members, Joel Erway, started his expert business selling to engineers who had good jobs. What he found was that most of his dream clients did have money, but they were not willing to spend it on coaching. He spent almost a year trying different ways to sell his offers and had very few results. As soon as he started selling to a market that was willing and able to buy, he became an "overnight" success.

THE NICHES

As businesses started to carve out their own submarkets, in a very similar way to what happened with the core markets, other sharks saw the opportunities as well. Within time, many of these blue oceans became bloody with competition.

And that brings us to the market that we have inherited now. The core markets and the submarkets are red oceans, and now it's our time to go one level deeper to what I call the "niches." Each niche is contained within a submarket, and it's a specific way to fulfill the desire of the submarket, which in turn fulfills the core desire.

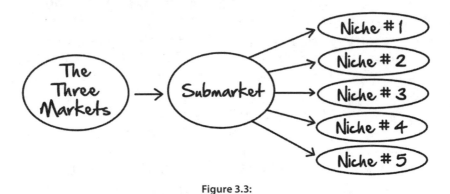

Figure 3.3:

Now that the core markets and submarkets have both become red oceans, you need to go one level deeper to find a niche where the water is still blue.

Inside each core market there are an unlimited number of niches. Here are a few examples of some niches inside popular submarkets.

Core market → submarket → niche

Health → nutrition → ketogenic diet

Health → nutrition → paleo diet

Health → nutrition → carnivore diet

Health → weight loss → weight loss for women

Health → weight loss → weight loss for college students

Health → weight loss → weight loss for couples

Wealth → real estate → short-selling houses

Wealth → real estate → flipping houses

Wealth → real estate → flipping houses on eBay

Wealth → online business → selling on Amazon

Wealth → online business → selling on Shopify

Wealth → online business → running Facebook ads

Relationships → parenting → dealing with toddlers

Relationships → parenting → dealing with teenagers

Relationships → parenting → dealing with marriage after kids leave

Relationships → dating → how to talk to a girl

Relationships → dating → how to recover after a breakup

Relationships → dating → how to know if you're in love

Do you see how each submarket can easily break into hundreds of niches or more? My next question is this:

What are all the niches inside the submarket you've chosen?

CREATING YOUR OWN CATEGORY (AND BECOMING THE CATEGORY KING)

The mistake most people make is looking at all the available niches and trying to decide which blue ocean to join. The problem is that jumping into an existing niche is swimming into someone else's blue ocean. And if you are the third, fourth, or fifth person in that niche, then the waters are already getting bloody.

In one of my favorite books of all time, *Play Bigger*, the authors define the leader of a niche or category a "category king."[17] This is the company that is the big player inside that market. The data shows that category kings usually eat up 70–80 percent of the category's profits and the market value. It's not necessarily the first, but the category king is the one who was the best marketer and sucked up the lion's share of the business. Historically it's almost impossible to dethrone a category king. The other sharks who come into their category often end up fighting over the 20–30 percent of the scraps that are left over. If you are trying to figure out which niche you want to join, best-case scenario is that you are going to be one of the sharks fighting over the scraps of an existing category, making the water bloody.

When we launched ClickFunnels, there were a lot of ways we could have positioned our company. We were a really good landing page builder, but there was already a category king in the niche of landing page software. We had really good marketing automation software, but there were existing category kings in that niche as well. The same was true with email marketing, split testing, and more. Each of these niches already had a category king. So we created our own new category called "sales funnels," which gave us the ability to quickly become the category king and suck up the majority of the market.

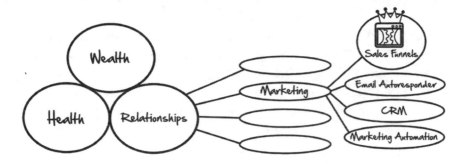

Figure 3.4:

Instead of joining someone else's blue ocean niche, create
your own category and become the category king!

We've seen our share of sharks come in and try to bloody the
water, but at this point they are just fighting over the scraps. My
last question is this:

What new category can you create
and become its category king?

The goal for you is to identify the niches in your submarket
and see what you can create that is truly new. In the next secret
we will spend more time going deep into how to create your new
opportunity.

MARKET SELECTION AND POSITIONING

After I published the first edition of this book, I started teaching
events, going deeper into these concepts with thousands of businesses around the world. Steve J Larsen, who I introduced you to
earlier in this chapter, taught most of these events with me. As
people got stuck understanding the markets, he started to develop
his own frameworks to better explain market selection and positioning, which he's going to share in this book. As he says, if you
have correct market positioning, even if you have C- or D-level
funnels and sales skills, it's almost impossible to fail.

MARKET SELECTION SECRETS BY STEVE J LARSEN

In 2014, when Russell Brunson, Todd Dickerson, and Dylan Jones created ClickFunnels, it was not the first time someone had tried to pull off what they were doing. Numerous attempts were made at developing a drag and drop editor for the sales funnel world. However, the three were a powerhouse of unique gifts, and once they created what many others had failed at, the next task was to learn how to sell the new software.

What most don't know is that ClickFunnels almost failed. Not because the software wasn't good, but because they didn't know how to sell their new product. Russell told me that he had tried to launch ClickFunnels six times before he learned *how* to sell it. The sixth attempt is when he got the correct market positioning, found the frustrated customers in the red oceans around him, and gave them a new opportunity.

Let me explain the details behind how this works, and then I'll come back to this story to show you how he used these principles to find his dream customers in the markets they were already in, and created one of the fastest-growing software companies of all time.

The market is a location, not a person: To illustrate this point, let's pretend that you are a fisherman and you live just outside a big village. You wake up, walk out of your hut, put on your sandals, and grab a basket of fish that you are going to sell for the day. As you look out over the village, you see a hillside filled with lots of other huts. Your family is counting on you to sell those fish, and with the distance to the village there's only enough time for you to set up and sell your fish in one spot today.

So where do you carry your basket of fish? I've asked this question on many stages now, and the majority of people respond, "You go wherever there's the most people!"

That's right! You'll walk to a location where many people are already in the habit of going, otherwise known as a marketplace or market. A market is a place for buyers and sellers to meet and exchange goods and services.

It's a mistake to think that the internet is any different from this example. While earning my marketing degree I was commonly asked, "Who is your target market?" However, as my village example now shows, a market is not a person; it's a location.

For example, my wife and I live in Boise, Idaho, about three miles south of ClickFunnels HQ. Several times, we've gotten up on a Saturday morning, put our three kids in the car, and driven to the Boise Farmers Market downtown.

Notice what I said? We *went* to the farmers market because I'm not the market. I'm a dream customer for those vendors. Your job is to first know who your dream customer is and then find out where they're already going to exchange money for products or services (online or offline). Clarity on who your dream customer is and where they already go to buy is a major milestone and shortcut to creating effective marketing for your business.

So the question is not "*Who* is your market?" Rather, the question is "*Where* is your market, and *who* is your dream customer who's already going there?" For example, ClickFunnels is my personal marketplace, and my dream customers are existing business owners who are already going to ClickFunnels. It's more lucrative for me and my business if I simply meet my dream customer at the same market, rather than walk around the village trying to hunt everyone down.

While your goal is to eventually create your own market, that does take time. So where is the market until you have your own? Go and sell to the frustrated customers in your submarket/red oceans that your dream customers are already in.

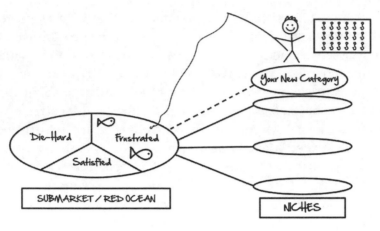

Figure 3.5:

**If you haven't created your own category yet, you can sell
to the frustrated customers in your submarkets.**

Fishing in the red oceans: Every red ocean is a marketplace full of people coming together looking for solutions to a certain problem. If you are offering a new way for people to get that result, doesn't it make sense to go fishing in these red oceans and pull these customers into your new category, your blue ocean? The first thing you need to understand is that not everyone in your red ocean is going to come to you, and that's okay. There are three core groups of people in each marketplace, and we are only going to target one of them.

The first group is "**the Diehard.**" The Diehard is such a believer in the current product they use that the logo may as well be tattooed on their foreheads. Trying to sell the Diehards is like sitting down to watch the Superbowl with two people trying to convince each other whose team is better as they cheer for opposing sides. No one wins and both people get mad.

After coaching thousands of businesses through their funnels and offers, I can tell you that one of the first errors I usually find is that the sales copy is written for a Diehard. I'm a ClickFunnels Diehard. You cannot convince me to change away from ClickFunnels. I'm so sold on the mission of ClickFunnels that you may as well put the logo on my coffin.

I absolutely love it when someone tries to tell me to use something else because of two reasons. First, I really don't know of any other viable option. And second, I love to fight the person who's trying to get me to switch.

Now see, that's the point. When you're choosing a market to serve, do not try to sell to the Diehards in that market. It's futile and expensive. They're so in love with the product they use that they may not know of many other options but they'd like to fight you anyway.

You know you're trying to sell a Diehard when you've entered a feature war with the person. Switching a Diehard to a new product requires a major identity shift.

The next group is "**the Satisfied.**" The Satisfied uses the product they bought but isn't in love with it like a Diehard. They've had enough success with the product to justify keeping it around, but the pain of switching to a new product can seem bigger than any discomfort they may be experiencing with their current product.

Typically, most people fit into this category. They're content but not fanatics. You know you're trying to sell the Satisfied when they're price shopping you, when they're looking up the value of everything in your offer, or guessing how long it would take to make the switch to your product. Switching the Satisfied to a new product requires a significant price or value benefit.

The last group, and the one we focus on the most, is "**the Frustrated.**" The Frustrated also use the product they bought, but they hate it. What was once an exciting purchase has now become so frustrating that they're eager for the next product. They're actively seeking a better product that can fit their desires. They have the shortest sales cycle and are often looking for reasons to give you money before you've even finished your sales script.

Often, they may not know what other products exist and can feel like they've exhausted all options they know about. This is my dream customer because after they buy, they move like they're hungry for my product and it makes fulfillment more enjoyable.

You know you're trying to sell the Frustrated when they've listed things they hate about their current product without you asking. Switching a Frustrated person to a new product requires finding them, gaining their trust, and giving them a small amount of education.

One of the things I realized in the first product I was selling was that my list was filled with a bunch of people who were either Diehard or Satisfied, which set me on an uphill battle during fulfillment from the start. If you decide ahead of time to sell only to the Frustrated in your market, you'll have a much more enjoyable business and customer experience.

Competitive or complementary: The offers you create will either compete with or complement the things that are already being offered in the marketplace.

Competitive: David Ogilvy was a famous advertiser who lived during the 1900s and has been called "the father of advertising."[18] In the 1950s, Dove approached David Ogilvy and hired him to sell its new soap.[19] Reluctant at first, David agreed to help Dove when he heard that Dove was going to sell its new soap with positioning that he didn't like.

After doing his own research and writing the ads, David helped Dove launch its new product with a tagline, "It's not soap; it's Dove!" Now wait a minute, but Dove *is* soap. So why does this work? With a single-sentence message, Dove stepped out of the competitive "soap" market and sold its product right back to those who were *in* the soap market. "It's not soap; it's Dove!" Dove was tossing rocks at the general soap market and telling everyone inside to leave that location for Dove.

The next thing David did was tell everyone Dove is a moisturizer first, but it also happens to clean like soap as a side benefit. So you still get the benefit of soap, but you're buying a moisturizer. Very clever.

Market positioning is how people *fit you* into what they already know. People already knew soap, so David simply anchored his message off of what people already knew and then threw rocks at it. This is called competitive market positioning.

Complementary: In the early 1900s, no one drank orange juice because orange juice wasn't a thing. Albert Lasker, coined as "the father of modern advertising," invented it. California Fruit Growers Exchange contacted Albert with a major problem.[20] For some reason that year, orange trees were overproducing and there were so many oranges that the company was cutting down its own trees. Albert's task was to dramatically increase orange consumption.

The first thing Albert did was change the company name to Sunkist. After figuring out that people could drink the juice from oranges and that a single glass took two to three oranges to fill, Albert set off to make drinking orange juice perceived as part of a healthy American breakfast.

So his firm invented the "orange juice extractor" (which is probably in your kitchen right now) and made an offer. For 10 cents you could buy the orange extractor plus receive a bundle of oranges for free! It worked. Inventory flew off the shelves and Sunkist was saved. The campaign, "Drink an Orange," is still used today.

Do you see how Albert used complementary market positioning to sell his new orange extractor? He created a product that complemented the existing products in the market, rather than throw rocks at the existing products in the market, like David Ogilvy did with soap.

I bring this up because many believe that the only way to create a new market is to throw rocks at the existing market, which is not true at all.

Can you see how these basic principles of market positioning can help? Understanding that the market is a location, and that you are fishing in red oceans for people who are frustrated in their current opportunity and presenting them a new opportunity is the big idea.

This was one of the big secrets to ClickFunnels' success on the sixth launch. Russell positioned ClickFunnels to be competitive with the website market. The sales script now called out frustrated website users to tell them there was a better way, capturing them in the middle of their frustration. A tagline of the new script warned frustrated website users of "the death of websites" and taught how ineffective websites are compared to a sales funnel.

Good market positioning taglines not only declare how you fit into what customers already know, they create a very natural sales message: "It's not soap; it's Dove." "It's not a website; it's a funnel" was said competitively to the website market, and the website market built the funnel market.

Indisputably, ClickFunnels has changed the world by handing the power of tech back to the entrepreneurs, but without the requirement of being "techies." Because of ClickFunnels, entrepreneurs get to be marketers again.

Products that don't make it are usually still great products. That's not the problem. The problem is that business owners often have no idea who they're selling to, where people are already buying from, and what kind of market positioning to use. Choosing a dream customer, selecting a market, and developing your market positioning will get you far more of a foundation than I ever understood during my first 34 product tries. It wasn't until I learned how to be a marketer with the lessons I've described that my wallet started gaining weight. As Joe Polish said, "There's no relationship between being good and getting paid. However, there's a huge relationship between being good at marketing and getting paid."[21]

DO YOUR HOMEWORK

I like sharing Steve's ideas about market selection and positioning because it takes the guesswork out of finding your future dream customers. Understanding this helps you to quickly identify them and know what to say to pull them into your new category.

A few years ago I had someone join my coaching program who was really successful at making money in real estate. He told me that he wanted to become a real estate expert and teach others what he knew. I was excited, because although I am not in that market, I am friends with two or three dozen people who are. I asked him about some of my friends, names everyone in that industry would know, and he had never heard of any of them. I told him that if I knew his market better than he did, that he was in trouble. My assignment to him was to find 20 or 30 other gurus who were already in his market, consume everything they had to offer, see what they were teaching, and figure out where he could carve his own unique spot in that ecosystem.

There are so many people who want to start a business, and they just start creating things without really understanding the history of the market, what the competitive landscape looks like, and where they're going to fit in that ecosystem. If you truly want to be successful, you need to do your homework and learn to understand the marketplace that you are entering into so you can create your own category. Once you do that, you'll be able to easily identify where your frustrated dream customers are currently congregating.

The New Opportunity (Your Offer)

THE NEW OPPORTUNITY

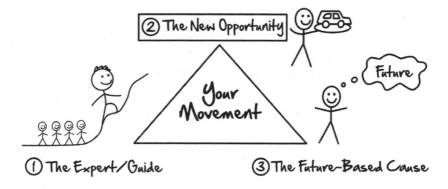

Figure 4.1:

The second stage of becoming the expert is to create your new opportunity.

On October 23, 2001, the Attractive Character of Apple, Steve Jobs, created and launched a new category of digital music players. He stood in front of the world and told everyone that he wanted to revolutionize the music industry (the submarket within which he was building his category). He talked about the other niches within that submarket: a CD would hold 10–15 songs, an MP3 player would hold about 150 songs, and a heavy hard drive would hold about 1,000 songs.[22]

And then Jobs did something that every leader of every movement throughout time has done. He did *not* present them with an "improvement offer" (something that is better, or faster, or almost any word that ends with an "er"). Instead, he created a new category and offered what we call a "new opportunity."

He said that his goal was to make it so that you could put your entire music collection in your pocket and listen to it wherever you go. He then reached into his back pocket and pulled out the first iPod and showed it to the world. This launched his new category, transformed the music industry forever, and made Apple the category king.

He followed this same pattern a few years later when he created another new category (smartphones) and revealed to the world Apple's *new* new opportunity: the iPhone. Later, he created another new opportunity with the iPad.

Jobs knew that consumers weren't looking for a faster CD or a better phone; they wanted something new, so that's what he created for them.

When you study any of the successful movements throughout time (both positive and negative), you'll notice that each of the leaders offered their followers a new opportunity.

Christ didn't give his followers a better way to follow the law of Moses; he offered them a new covenant where salvation didn't come from animal sacrifices and following the letter of the law, but instead came from a broken heart and a contrite spirit.

Hitler didn't offer the Germans a way to make Germany better or to pay off their war reparations faster. He told them that Germany wasn't responsible for the first world war, and that he wanted to tear up the Treaty of Versailles and launch his "New Order."

As you've seen Apple do this over and over again, it's also true with other companies like Tesla. Elon Musk, the Attractive Character, didn't make a better car; he made an electric car: a new category and a new opportunity. Facebook's Mark Zuckerberg and Google's Larry Page and Sergey Brin did the same in their submarkets. Snapchat's Evan Spiegel and Twitter's Jack Dorsey created a new category and offered a new opportunity. Tony Robbins did it with his personal development content, and I've done it with sales funnels. The pattern is repeated over and over again.

In *The True Believer*, which is one of the best books on how mass movements are created, author Eric Hoffer writes, "The practical organization offers opportunities for self-advancement. . . . [A] mass movement . . . appeals not to those intent on bolstering and advancing a cherished self, but to those who crave to be rid of an unwanted self."[23]

Our goal is not to fix what's not working. Our goal is to *replace* what's not working with something altogether different.

Most often, when people start thinking about the product or service they want to offer, they start by looking around at what is already out there and try to "build a better mousetrap." When you do that, you are not offering consumers a new opportunity; you are presenting them an improvement offer. When you do this, you are just one of the sharks swimming into someone else's blue ocean, and your best-case scenario is to fight over the scraps.

When you create your own category and offer your followers a new opportunity, this gives you a chance to become the category king and have the biggest impact on people's lives.

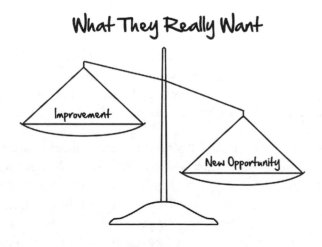

Figure 4.2:

Rather than trying to improve on someone else's product or service, create your own new opportunity to set yourself apart from the competition.

WHY PEOPLE DON'T WANT IMPROVEMENT OFFERS

Improvement offers are much harder to sell for a lot of reasons. Here are a few of the main reasons people tend to avoid improvement offers at all costs.

Improvement is hard: Most people have tried to improve in the past, and for some reason it didn't work. They've tried to lose weight. They've tried to make money. They've tried to make their relationships better. But if they're coming to you, then whatever they tried in the past didn't work for some reason. They know the difficulties they've had to go through, and there is pain associated with that.

   With a new opportunity, they don't know what the process will be, so they don't have to go through the known pain to get the result. Another amazing quote from *The True Believer*:

   "[Your customers] must be wholly ignorant of the difficulties involved in their vast undertaking. Experience is a handicap."

Desire vs. ambition: All people have desire, but very few have ambition. My guess is that less than 2 percent of the population is actually ambitious. Improvement offers are selling to overachieving, ambitious people. If you do sell an improvement offer, you are automatically excluding 98 percent of the world. You will be fighting an uphill battle. A new opportunity, on the other hand, plays on people's desires for the change they want in their lives.

Memories of poor past decisions: If your followers are in need of improvement, they must first admit failure. In order for them to say yes to your offer, they have to admit that the choices they made in the past were wrong. No one wants to admit when they're wrong, yet an improvement offer forces them to admit they've failed. Remember the *One Sentence Persuasion Course* from earlier in the book? We want to *justify* their past failures. A new opportunity does that.

Commodity pricing: When you are selling improvement, you are selling against dozens or hundreds of other improvement offers out there. You are stuck in the middle of a very red ocean, competing with everyone else who is selling similar options. This competition turns what you do into a commodity and pushes the pricing down. It quickly becomes a race to the bottom in terms of pricing.

Dan Kennedy once told me, "If you can't be the number one lowest-price leader in your market, there is no strategic advantage of being the second lowest price leader in town, but there is a huge strategic advantage of being the most expensive." In other words, if you can't be the cheapest, then you need to become the most expensive. And you can't do that when you are fighting inside this red ocean. When you present a new opportunity, you are creating a blue ocean, and all price resistance goes out the window.

But the *biggest* reason people don't want improvement offers is so important that I wanted to write a separate section about it. The number one reason people don't want improvement, and the reason they will or won't buy, is *status*.

STATUS: THE ONLY THING THAT CAUSES PEOPLE TO MOVE (OR NOT MOVE)

A few years ago, my friend Perry Belcher explained this concept to me. Once I understood it, I immediately changed how I interacted with everyone. He told me that status is the only thing that causes people to move toward you or not move at all. That's it. *Status* is the magic word in this business. When someone is presented with an opportunity, their subconscious mind is working on the answer to this question:

> *Is this thing I'm considering going to
> increase my status or decrease it?*

Figure 4.3:

If you want people to buy, you have to show them how your product or service will increase their status.

Status as I'm defining it here has nothing to do with how other people perceive you, but rather with how you perceive yourself.

Almost every choice in your life has revolved around status—whether you know it or not. For example, what school did you go to? You (or your parents) picked a school because you thought it would elevate your status. Who did you date? Who did you break up with? Who did you marry? You picked these people and made these choices based on who you thought would elevate your status. What school do your kids go to? What books do you read? What car do you drive? What car do you *not* drive?

All these things are tied into status. Almost *every* decision you've ever made was based on this one subconscious question:

> *Is this thing I'm considering going to increase my status or decrease it?*

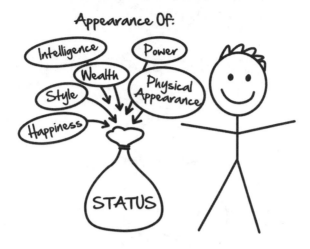

Figure 4.4:

While you should focus only on one core market or desire in your marketing, you *can* and should focus on as many status increases as you can that apply to your product or service.

When we're looking at any opportunity, we have to decide if it will make us appear smarter, happier, wealthier, more stylish, more powerful, or more attractive. All these things will increase status. If potential customers can say, "Yes, this will increase my status," they will move toward it.

What stops people from taking that new opportunity? Fear of decreased status. The sale-killing thought is: *What if I try this and it decreases my status? I will feel stupid.* There's this balancing act going on in our brains all the time. We're balancing hope of increased status against fear of decreased status. If you're selling a weight-loss solution and someone has tried and failed on 27 different diets, that fear is going to be pretty high. You're going to have to work pretty hard to get the sale.

If your brain thinks that taking an action will reverse your status, then you won't do it—*unless* it finds hope that by temporarily decreasing your status (spending money to try your new opportunity), you could increase it in the future. Your brain is always asking, "Will it be temporary and, if so, will the future gain in status eventually be higher?"

Figure 4.5:

Our brains are constantly trying to stay away from opportunities that might decrease our status.

When people first find you and your offers, it's probably not the first time they've tried to solve their problems. They've tried to lose weight. They've tried to make money. They've tried to do whatever your thing is. That's the big fear: *I know if I invest $1,000 or $10,000 or $100,000 with this expert and it doesn't work, I'm going to look stupid. I could lose money, or make a mistake, or damage or destroy a relationship, or embarrass myself in front of my friends or colleagues. My wife or my kids or my friends are going to see that, and they're going to think I'm an idiot.*

When someone invests in my $50,000 Inner Circle program, that money is leaving them, which causes an immediate decrease in status. But my members know that by taking that temporary decrease in status, the end result of being in the Inner Circle will be an increased status from what they learn and accomplish.

People are going to weigh the likelihood of success and elevated status against the risk of failure and the cost of that failure. Your job as the expert is to load up the elevated-status side of the scale and decrease the risk of failure. You can do that by creating an amazing offer and minimizing risk with things like money-back guarantees, risk reversals, and done-for-you options. The key to making a sale is 100 percent tied to this concept of status.

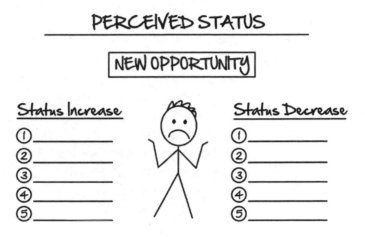

Figure 4.6:

Your goal is to load up the status-increase side and minimize the status-decrease side by including done-for-you tools and money-back guarantees in your offer.

When people look at your new opportunity, that is the only real question they are trying to figure out. I like to think through what their perceived status is, and then try to make sure I add as many things possible that would increase their status and take away as many things from my offer that would decrease their status. So you can probably see why that is the *biggest* reason we don't sell improvement offers. For someone to say yes to that, they have to admit to poor past decisions and create a huge decrease in status. Then you are forced to fight an uphill battle that few people ever win.

So which factors elevate status? Well, it's different for everyone, but here are a few that are pretty universal.

- Appearance of intelligence (anything that makes them look smarter)

- Appearance of wealth, power, or happiness

- Physical appearance (weight loss, makeup, supplements, etc.)

- Style (think Mac vs. PC)

Now you might be thinking, *I'm not affected by status considerations. I like to drive a reasonable car and live in a modest home.* If so, I'd like to pose a question. Why? Why do you like driving a car you feel is reasonably priced? Does it have anything to do with the fact that if you drove a Ferrari home one day, you're afraid that your friends, family, or neighbors would judge you? If they did judge you, how would that affect your status?

Status works on both ends of the spectrum. It's what makes some people fight for earthly possessions, and it's also what keeps others from desiring them at all. As much as we may hate to admit it, we are slaves to what we believe other people will think about us.

WHY PEOPLE CRAVE NEW OPPORTUNITIES

So now you know why improvement offers don't work. Here are a few reasons why new opportunities *do* work.

New discovery: When people discover your new opportunity for the first time, they're going to want to share it because sharing something new gives them an immediate increase in status. Just think about when videos on YouTube or Facebook go viral. What's happening behind the scenes? I've worked with teams who create viral videos for a living, and they've found that videos go viral when they are cool and new because others want to be the first to show them to their friends. Discovery immediately increases perceived status.

No pain of disconnect: Because they don't have to admit they made bad decisions in the past, there is no longer a huge pain of disconnect from what they are currently doing. They can just move on to something brand new. No pain of disconnect = no decrease in status. Improvement offers sell *through* the pain, whereas new opportunities sell *away* from the pain.

Dream replacement: One reason many people struggle to make the changes they want and need in their lives is the fear of failure. If they try to change and it doesn't work for them, then their dreams are dead. So they will give up potential success for fear of losing their dreams. In Proverbs 29:18, we learn that "where there is no vision, the people perish." When you make a new opportunity, you're giving people a new dream to move toward.

Greener pastures: We've all heard a million times that "the grass is always greener on the other side of the fence," right? Instead of trying to convince people that their grass is green or offering to fix their grass, allow them to follow you to the other side of the fence. That's where they want to be anyway. Stop trying to make existing things that aren't working better, and focus on fresh, exciting, *new* ideas that will inspire people to follow you.

HOW DO YOU CREATE A NEW OPPORTUNITY?

I hope by now you appreciate how important it is to create a new opportunity, but most people get stuck here. *How* do you actually create the new opportunity? And if you are already selling something else, how do you reposition it to become that new opportunity for your movement?

Step #1: What is the result your dream customers are trying to achieve?

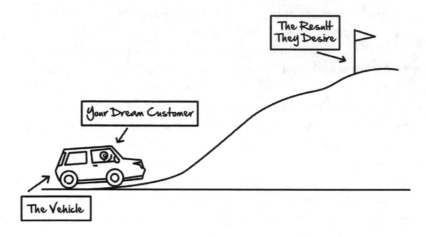

Figure 4.7:

Creating a new opportunity is as simple as creating a new way
for your dream customers to achieve their desired result.

The first step is to take your dream customers and look at the result they are trying to achieve. I first look at the three core markets or desires and ask myself: "Are they trying to get health, wealth, or relationships?" What is the result that they desire the most? Are they trying to lose weight, make money, build or save a relationship? If I had a chance to sit down with my dream customers and ask them one question, I would ask them this:

> *"If we were having this discussion three years from today, and you were looking back over those three years, what has to have happened in your life, both personally and professionally, for you to feel happy with your progress?"*

This came from the book *The Dan Sullivan Question*, and it quickly gets to the root of the result that someone really desires.[24] To be able to create your new opportunity, you have to understand at a very deep level what your dream customers really want.

EXERCISE

Talk to your dream customers to find out what result they desire the most.

Step #2: What is the "vehicle" they are currently using to try to get that result?

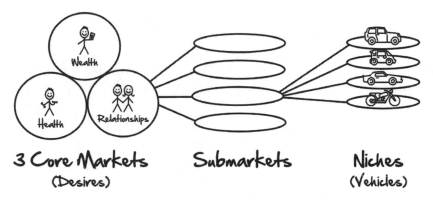

Figure 4.8:

Your dream customers have already been trying to get their desired result with other vehicles (niches) and those vehicles aren't working.

Now that you know what they want, you need to understand what "vehicle" your dream customers are currently using to try to get that result. The reality is that you are rarely going to be the first solution that someone tries when they are trying to get a certain result. They have been on this path before trying multiple different vehicles to solve their problem.

If they are trying to lose weight and they find you, it's likely you are not the first solution they've tried. The *LadyBoss* blog states that the average woman diets five times per year and still isn't able to lose the weight.[25]

If you're trying to make extra income, you may have tried selling things on eBay, Craigslist, Amazon, and Shopify with no success. Your desire hasn't changed, but the vehicle you've been using just isn't working for you.

The same is true in relationships and in every other market. Consumers know the result they want, and they've tried a dozen other vehicles to try to get that result. They aren't coming to you because they aren't trying; they're coming to you because the current vehicle isn't getting them to their destination.

EXERCISE

Write down all the other vehicles that your dream customers have been using (without success) to try to get what they desire most.

Step #3—The Opportunity Switch

Figure 4.9:

Rather than trying to improve the vehicles your dream customers have tried already (by creating an improvement offer), provide an entirely new vehicle for them to get to their desired result (by creating a new opportunity).

Now, the mistake comes when you look at those other vehicles and try to make them *better* or *faster* or any of the "er" words that create an improvement offer. If they are not having success with their current vehicle, they don't want a better version of it; they want something new.

When I built our new opportunity of sales funnels, I looked at all the other vehicles that people were using to grow their companies, and there were a lot. Here is a short list of some of the vehicles that our dream customers had tried with similar niches to ours:

- Website

- Email autoresponder

- Text message autoresponder

- Marketing automation

- CRM

- Landing page builder

I didn't offer people a better website; instead I told them that "websites are dead." I told people it was a broken concept, and I showed them the pain of how much money they had spent on those websites, and how little of a return they got on them. I threw rocks at the other vehicles and opportunities that they had tried to grow their company, and I told them it wasn't their fault, they had been lied to by others. Then I did an "opportunity switch," where I took them out of their old vehicle and switched them into my new opportunity by introducing them to funnels.

Opportunity switching takes consumers out of the pain they're currently in and gives them hope for a new future through a new vehicle.

Sometimes the opportunity switch happens when they are moving from one niche to the new niche (category) that you created in Secret #3.

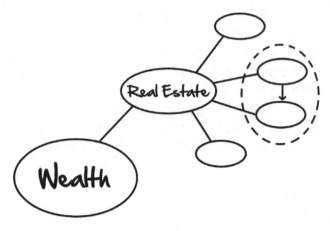

Figure 4.10:

You can create an opportunity switch by moving your
dream customers from one niche to another.

Other times it's actually switching them from one submarket
to another. For example, maybe they are moving from making
an income in real estate to making their living through internet
marketing.

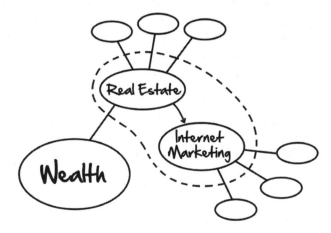

Figure 4.11:

You can create an opportunity switch by moving your
dream customers from one submarket to another.

If you look at everything I do on the front end of my business (the front of the value ladder), it's all tied to an opportunity switch: the books I write, the videos my team and I produce, the webinars I create, the podcasts I publish, and more. Every front-end offer I put into the market has a goal to switch someone from their current old vehicle into my new, sexy vehicle of funnels. This is my new opportunity.

Having lots of break-even front-end funnels allows us to "fish" in colder submarkets that wouldn't normally know about sales funnels, and this has been one of the key reasons our company has grown so fast. Our front-end offers specifically show how different business owners can use funnels to grow their business online. Here are a few examples:

- **BrickandMortarFunnels.com**—This funnel was designed to get local service-based businesses to have an epiphany about why they need a funnel.

- **ExpertSecrets.com**—This was created to get anyone who feels they have expertise to see why they need funnels.

- **ECommFunnelSecrets.com**—This funnel shows how people who are selling on Amazon, Shopify, or Etsy can use funnels.

- **NetworkMarketingSecrets.com**—This is to help network marketers and people in multilevel marketing see how funnels can help them generate leads.

- **FreelancerSecrets.com**—This is to show freelancers how they can make additional income by building funnels for their clients.

And we are continually adding more front-end offers to grab new segments of the market. If you want to grow your company, eventually you'll have to venture out of just serving your warm niche traffic, so creating front-end funnels that attract (and warm up) colder submarkets will help you expand your reach.

As you are creating your ads, lead magnets, and front-end funnels, do it through this lens of opportunity switching someone away from their old vehicle into your new opportunity, and it will change everything for you.

Step #4—The Opportunity Stack

Every business should have one and *only one* opportunity switch. The first few years I was in business I got really good at making new offers, and each offer I made was an opportunity switch. At first it worked great. I would launch an offer showing people this new opportunity, my team would sell a ton, and then a few months later I would launch a *new* new opportunity. People would get confused because just months earlier I had convinced them that my first new opportunity was the greatest thing since sliced bread, and later I was telling them about something new. Many people moved reluctantly to my second new opportunity, but they didn't know that behind the scenes I was secretly working on the third new opportunity that I would launch that year.

While the process worked and I made money, each new opportunity I launched after the first one lost the trust of my dream customers a little more. With each promotion, my lists would get less responsive, and eventually my business almost crashed.

Now, I'm guessing that some of you might be thinking that this is contradictory to what I taught about the value ladder. *I thought I was supposed to acquire a customer and then create new offers I can sell to them to provide more value.* My answer is yes, that is what you are supposed to do, and that is what I thought I was doing too.

It wasn't until I launched ClickFunnels that I saw what I was doing wrong. A few weeks after we launched ClickFunnels, my business partner Todd Dickerson told me that he was worried I was going to shift my focus in a few months and start selling something else after he had put so much work into the software. He asked me if I would commit to selling only funnels for at least 12 months. I was nervous because I had tons of ideas for other things

I knew people would buy, but I knew that I owed it to him and to our small team to stay focused, so I agreed.

For the next 12 months, the only thing I talked about was funnels. I did webinars on funnels showing people this new opportunity. I launched *DotCom Secrets* to introduce people to this new opportunity. Everything I did was focused on getting people to switch from whatever old vehicle they were using to get results to my vehicle/new opportunity of funnels.

At about this time we did our first-ever Funnel Hacking LIVE event in Las Vegas. We had about 600 attendees at the event, and while we were planning it, we knew we needed to make an offer to those in the room. Because it was our user conference, I knew that everyone who was there already had a ClickFunnels account and was drinking our Kool-Aid. I tried to think of a new opportunity that I could create for them, but no matter what idea I came up with, the team felt the offers would distract from our main focus: funnels.

One night a few weeks before the event, I realized that I didn't need to create a whole new opportunity for attendees. Doing that would cause confusion and break trust. Instead I needed to stack opportunities within the new opportunity they had already switched to! Since they believed that funnels were the greatest thing since sliced bread (and they are), what types of opportunities could I create and stack within that new opportunity?

As soon as I looked at it through the "opportunity stack" lens, I knew the answer. They already believed in funnels, so we should build a funnels-certification program and help them start a career building funnels for other people! It was not a new opportunity; it was the next level within that existing opportunity.

So we put together the certification program, and I presented it to my Funnel Hackers onstage at that first event. My goal was to get 50 people to sign up for the program, and when I announced the price, more than 150 people ran to the back of the room and got in line to join the program! In all my years of speaking from the stage up to that time, I had never seen a table rush like that.

That's when I realized the role of the other offers inside the value ladder. They weren't there to keep providing people new opportunities; they were there to take the new opportunity that dream customers already believed in, and package it in different ways to help serve them at a higher level.

Opportunity Switch to "The New Opportunity"

Opportunity Stacking
(Same Opportunity Packaged in a Different Way)

Figure 4.12:

You should offer only one opportunity switch (new opportunity), but you can offer as many ways as you like to package that same opportunity.

So inside the ClickFunnels value ladder, the ads, lead magnets, books, and webinars are all switching people into our new opportunity (funnels). After they come in, we figure out other ways to package funnels that will help them achieve their results. Some of the opportunity stacks that we offer inside our value ladder are:

- **ClickFunnels:** The software you need to actually build your funnels (ClickFunnels.com)

- **One Funnel Away Challenge:** A 30-day challenge to help you launch your first or next funnel (OneFunnelAway.com)

- **Funnel Scripts:** Software that writes the copy for the pages inside your funnel (FunnelScripts.com)

- **Funnel Hacking LIVE:** An event with live training and networking to help you have more success using funnels inside your business (FunnelHackingLive.com)

- **Funnel Agency Secrets:** A course showing you how to launch your own agency selling funnels to other business owners (FunnelAgencySecrets.com)

- **FunnelFlix:** A membership site with training content to help you become a master funnel builder (FunnelFlix.com)

- **Funnel University:** A monthly newsletter showing you behind the scenes of the best-selling funnels online (FunnelU.com)

- **ClickFunnels Collective:** A coaching program to help you grow and scale your funnels (ClickFunnelsCollective.com)

- *Traffic Secrets:* A book that teaches you how to get more people into your funnels (TrafficSecrets.com)

Do you see how none of these offers are new opportunities? Funnels are still the greatest thing since sliced bread, but now I'm helping you with different ways to implement them inside your company.

If I ran a health and fitness company, after I got someone to opportunity switch to whatever my new opportunity was, I would use opportunity stacking to sell supplements, coaching, meal plans, and more—all to better support someone inside the new opportunity.

The same is true with any business: Look at the result your dream customers desire and the new opportunity you have offered them, then package that opportunity in different ways to help them reach their desire.

MORE MONEY FOR THE SAME FRAMEWORK

Dang, I wish I would have brought some T-shirts. I look so stupid, I thought. It was the first business event I had ever gone to, and I wore a shirt and tie thinking that is what businesspeople do, but after walking in I realized I was the only one. All the other online entrepreneurs looked so comfortable in their own skin, wearing jeans and T-shirts. Instead I felt even more nervous because I was the introverted kid, wishing I had someone to talk to so I didn't feel so awkward, but I was too nervous to walk up to anyone and start that first conversation.

After we all found our chairs, the lights went down and I felt like a huge weight was being lifted off my shoulders, knowing that no one could see me anymore as we waited for the first speaker to step onstage. I don't remember much about what he said that day, but I did write down the name of a book that I had never heard of before that he kept talking about: *Think and Grow Rich.*

Throughout the event, I heard multiple speakers reference the book, so when I got back to the hotel room that night, the first thing I did was buy my own paperback copy on Amazon for $9.97. Within a week it showed up at my house. I ripped open the package, pulled out the book, and looked at it, knowing that the secrets to getting rich were inside!

Each night as I went to bed I would look at the book, and, being tired, I would make a resolution that "tomorrow" I would start reading it. One day turned into two, and then a month, and then six months. Each day I felt a little more guilty knowing that the answers to my problems were inside; I just needed to open the pages and start reading.

About six months later, I attended my second business conference. This time I wore jeans and a T-shirt and felt much more comfortable. I sat in the room, waiting to learn the secrets to getting rich, and sure enough, within an hour of the first speaker speaking, that book was brought up again. I started to feel a twinge of guilt rush over me, knowing that it had been sitting next to my bed for almost half a year, and I still hadn't opened it.

Why am I spending money traveling to events if I'm not even doing what I know I need to do to be successful? I asked myself. By that night I had heard the words *Think and Grow Rich* too many times to count, so when I got to my room I knew I needed to figure out a better way to get that book read. I jumped on my computer and searched for "Think and Grow Rich" again, but this time something else popped up. It was an ad for the audio CDs of *Think and Grow Rich*! (Yes, this was before audiobooks and Audible were a thing, so I was really excited.) I clicked on the ad and it took me to an eBay listing to buy the 10-CD set for $97. I was so excited, I bought it on the spot, and by the time I got home from the event the CDs were there! I started listening to them while I was in the car driving around town, and within a week of returning from that event, I had "read" the entire book!

I am sharing this story with you because it taught me a very important principle. People will spend more money for the exact same content (or framework) packaged in a different way. Think about it: What is the difference between the book, *Think and Grow Rich*, and the audiobook? The answer is: nothing. They are the same book, word for word, yet I paid 10 times more money ($9.97 for the physical book and $97 for the CDs) for the exact same content packaged in a different way. The audio CDs made the book simpler to read, so I happily paid more for a different user experience.

UNDERSTANDING HOW TO USE "INFORMATION PRODUCTS" TO GROW *ANY* COMPANY

During this chapter you'll learn how to create information products like books, courses, seminars, mastermind groups, and coaching programs. For those of you who aren't in a traditional "expert" business (usually authors, speakers, coaches, and consultants), don't worry, this process is still for you.

One of the big secrets to creating a new opportunity is understanding that while your product may not be a new opportunity, your framework has to be. ClickFunnels is a drag and drop website creation platform. In and of itself it's not a new opportunity; it's an improvement offer (a better way to make a website). When we introduced our funnel frameworks, *that* was the new opportunity, and the software became the tool that simplified the new opportunity.

Most of you reading this book do not yet have a true new opportunity. What you are selling, while it might be a better mouse trap, is just an improvement offer. That's why it's essential to create frameworks and wrap them around your core offers to make them a truly new opportunity. In this section I'm going to show you how you can turn your frameworks into information products. For some of you it will seem strange at first, but it will make your marketing and sales in the future so much easier. Here are a few amazing things that will happen when you start wrapping your products inside your unique frameworks.

- Complicated sales will become easy because the information products will indoctrinate potential customers about *why* they need your product or service.

- You will be positioned as an expert instead of a commodity, and people will pay you *more* for the same thing they could get somewhere else. The other options will become irrelevant, price resistance will disappear, and future sales will become easier.

- You will be able to acquire unlimited customers for free so every back-end sale you make will result in 100 percent profit.

- You'll be able to grow *much* faster.

Before we get too deep, I want to point out that there are two types of expert businesses. The tactics behind both are the same, but the strategies are a little different. Let me explain them so you can see which one best fits what you are trying to create.

Expert Business #1—Selling information products: The first type of expert business is the one that you're probably most familiar with. It involves taking the frameworks you've learned and packaging them into information products, coaching, and consulting. Being an expert and selling information products is (in my opinion) the greatest start-up in the world. You don't need venture or start-up capital, just a passion for what you're teaching and a willingness to learn how to tell stories in a way that will get others excited about it.

Figure 5.1:

You can sell information products without any start-up costs; you just need passion for what you're teaching and the ability to tell stories that move others.

Expert Business #2—Leveraging information products as fuel: If you have a company that is selling physical products or services, that's even better because you can use these information products as fuel to grow your company quickly. As you know, my company is a software company, yet we've used information products to grow quickly. I first focused on selling my frameworks, which created desire in people to use the core product we were trying to sell.

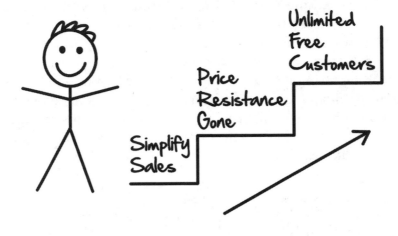

Figure 5.2:

You can use information products to create desire for the products and services you sell; by using information products to acquire customers for free, you can scale at will.

We use the information products we sell to get customers for free (through break-even funnels that you learned about in *DotCom Secrets*). We also bundle information products with our software to increase the perceived value of the service. During our first year we had more than 10,000 people pay us $1,000 for a course on how to use funnels, and bundled in that course they got a free trial to the software. In the next chapter we'll be going deeper into your Stack Slide and how you can create an offer, but understand that information products built from your frameworks is the secret to creating new opportunities and offers that are completely irresistible.

Figure 5.3:

Your frameworks can either be turned into information or tools.

Step #1: How to Increase the Value of Your Frameworks

Now that you understand the principle that by changing the experience and how you package your framework you can increase the value of that framework, I want to show you how you can repackage the same framework into each step of your value ladder.

The simplest way to increase the perceived value of your framework is to change the experience of how someone consumes it. That usually happens by moving things from one form to another:

- Written word → Audio

- Audio → Video

- Video → Live experiences

I see this happen every day in my business, where someone will buy one of my books, and then in the upsell of the funnel we will offer them the audiobook. Later, some of them will buy a video home-study course teaching the same frameworks from the books, but in much more detail, and then later they come to one of our workshops or seminars to get hands-on help implementing the frameworks. The frameworks are the same throughout the process, but the value of what we offer goes up at each stage.

The other way to increase the value of your frameworks is by changing how you fulfill on the framework. The three different ways that you can fulfill on a framework are:

1. Do It Yourself (Give them the framework and they implement it on their own)

2. Do It With You (Work with them to implement the framework)

3. Do It For You (You implement the framework for them)

Often times at the bottom of my value ladder, I will give or sell someone my frameworks, but they are responsible to learn and implement them themselves. As you move up the value ladder, I transition to working with them or doing it for them.

While there could be hundreds of ways to package your frameworks, I'll share the eight most popular ways that are used by experts in almost every industry.

Pre-funnel content (free): Your framework steps work really well as a hook for an ad that will pull people into your funnels. Usually you would just post one of your frameworks as a hook. One of my favorite couples who do this often on Instagram are Tom and Lisa Bilyeu. Here are examples of a few of the frameworks they've posted on their Instagram wall.

Figure 5.4:

You can create ads or social media posts using your frameworks as hooks.[26]

You can also teach your frameworks as pre-funnel content in YouTube videos, podcast episodes, blog posts, and more.

Lead magnet (free): You can also use your framework as a lead magnet. Oftentimes I'll record a 2- to 20-minute video of me teaching one of my frameworks and give that to people as the lead magnet they get when they give me their email address.

Figure 5.5:

You can teach one of your frameworks in a short video and use that
as a lead magnet in exchange for someone's email address.

Book (free + shipping): You can expound and go deeper with
your frameworks with a book. As you can see from this book, it's
one big framework with tons of embedded frameworks inside of
it. The negative thing with a book is that it's the hardest thing to
create and sell for the least amount of money, but its perceived
value and ability to position you in your market as an expert is one
of the highest ways you can package your frameworks.

Membership site ($10–$100 per month): Membership sites usually blend all the different learning modalities into one. Oftentimes there will be written content, audio, and video training,

along with an online community (live experience) for members to network together. The big advantage of membership sites over online courses is that because they are typically billed monthly, they give you the ability to drip out your frameworks to people over time as opposed to giving everything to them at once.

Online course ($100–$1,000): Courses are very similar to membership sites in terms of how the content is put together using all the different modalities. The biggest difference is in how you bill and deliver. Courses are finite, and even if you drip the content to members, it eventually ends, whereas with a membership site people are paying in perpetuity.

Seminar or workshop ($500–$5,000): This is where you start to take your frameworks offline. I define a workshop as an event where you are spending a few days teaching your frameworks; often these types of events are a little smaller and more intimate. My FHAT events are considered workshops because I spend three days teaching my webinar and selling frameworks for a group of about 100 people. At seminars there are usually a lot of different speakers teaching their own frameworks based around a topic. Our big Funnel Hacking LIVE event has about 5,000 people in attendance, and there are lots of different speakers teaching their own frameworks.

Mastermind ($10,000–$100,000): Mastermind groups are usually smaller events that aren't focused as much on teaching new frameworks, but instead on implementing existing frameworks that the group has already learned. My Inner Circle mastermind groups have about 30 people in them, and each person has a chance to get in front of the group, present their business, and get personalized help from everyone else in the group on the things they are struggling to implement from the original frameworks.

One-on-one ($10,000+): This is often the highest level of framework application, where people pay you to work one-on-one for them (services) or with them (coaching) implementing your processes. There is no leverage at this level as you are trading your time for money, which is why the pricing is so much higher.

Did you notice that even though the price changes for each way you package your frameworks, you're not necessarily teaching new frameworks at each level? You are changing the experience of how people consume and implement those frameworks, and the value goes up at each level of service. If you look at most people's value ladders, they're simply changing how the frameworks are delivered.

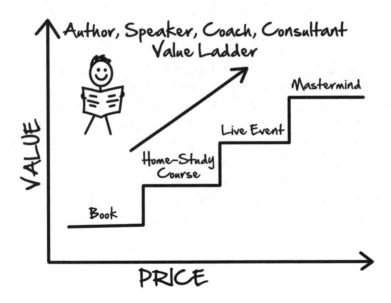

Figure 5.6:

While the frameworks usually stay the same, you can charge more when you deliver them in a different way.

Step #2: How to Create Even More Value by Turning Your Frameworks into Tools

During the gold rush in San Francisco in the mid-19th century, there was a local store owner named Sam Brannan who had a unique idea of how to capitalize on what was happening around him. He purchased all the picks, shovels, and pans he could find and ran around the streets yelling, "There's gold in the American River!" He had paid 20 cents for each pan, which he resold for $15 apiece.[27]

When everyone around him was searching for gold, Sam Brannan became San Francisco's first millionaire by selling the *tools* people used to get the gold they were looking for.

There are so many powerful lessons in this story. If you look at it through the lens that you are learning here inside *Expert Secrets*, you'll notice that his dream customers, those who had "gold fever," wanted a result: to find gold. Sam provided a framework for that.

Step #1: There is gold in the American River.

Step #2: You need three tools to extract the gold (picks, shovels, and pans).

Step #3: The only place to get the tools you need is at my store.

He made his fortune by giving them this framework and selling them the tools they would need to get their desired result.

My business is not much different. The end result I promise my customers is that they can grow their companies with sales funnels. I've compiled a bunch of frameworks that teach them how to get those results (some I give away for free, others I sell in my books, courses, and events). I then create software (or tools) that make the process I teach in the frameworks simpler.

Brandon and Kaelin Poulin at LadyBoss create and sell their frameworks for weight loss, but they also sell the tools (supplements, coaching, food, clothing) to create a shortcut to success for their dream customers.

How much money you are able to make as a business is in direct relationship to how simple you can make the process for your customers. The frameworks are a way to simplify the process, and you will get paid for that. Software or supplements, physical products, or services are ways to simplify the process inside your frameworks even more.

When you look at your frameworks, I want you to start looking at each part and asking how you could simplify that part of the process with some type of tool. Here are some ideas of things I look for when trying to create tools out of my framework.

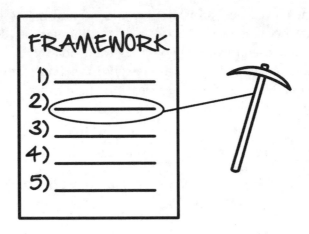

Figure 5.7:

Create a shortcut to success for your customers by providing done-for-you tools from your framework.

Software: The best tool you can create from your frameworks is software. The perceived value of software is huge, and (depending on complexity) can be pretty inexpensive to create. The first product I ever created, even before my potato gun DVD, was a software product called Zip Brander. I had the idea for the product, sketched out the idea on a pad of paper, hired a guy in Romania, and paid him $120 to build the software. He took my sketches, did whatever programmers do, and a few days later I had something I could sell.

ClickFunnels became the ultimate expression of my frameworks for building funnels and follow-up funnels. Funnel Scripts is software we created to make the sales scripts in *DotCom Secrets* and this book simple, where you can fill in the blanks and the software will pre-write your sales copy.

What parts of your framework could be automated for someone if you created your own software? Initially don't look for a ClickFunnels-size idea; look for smaller ones that you can get programmed for a few hundred dollars and start there.

Supplements: This will not be applicable to all businesses, but supplements are the ultimate "easy button" to get a result. If something inside your frameworks could be sped up through supplements, they are among the most powerful ways to increase the value of your framework.

Physical Products: Most people who have a physical product in our community start here, and then build a results-based framework around the product. For instance, if you were selling a survival flashlight, you could build an entire framework about how to survive during a disaster, and the flashlight then becomes a tool to help inside the framework.

The other way you can use this is to look at your existing frameworks and see if there is a physical product that you could create to help make the framework easier to implement. I've seen a lot of information-based companies create journals as a tool to make the implementation of their framework easier. If you purchased this book in the box set (found at SecretsTrilogy.com), you also got a free copy of the *Unlock the Secrets* workbook. This tool was created to help people implement the frameworks taught in my three books, and it increases the value of the box set.

By-products: As you have been using your own frameworks, what are the by-products that you've had to create that would be useful for your dream customers? As an example: When we started selling high-ticket products on the phone, we had to create scripts for the salespeople to use, training videos that would train our team, and we had lawyers make contracts for employees as well as for our customers. All these things were by-products that we had to create by using our frameworks. When we later sold our High Ticket Secrets coaching program, we sold our frameworks (training), but we were also able to bundle in all the by-products into the offer. With their purchase, our customers got access to the scripts, trainings for our own salespeople, and all the contracts we had paid for. These tools became some of the most valuable parts of the offer.

One of my Inner Circle members, Liz Benny, sells a masterclass for people who want to become social media managers. She gives away her contracts so her students don't have to hire expensive lawyers or come up with their own. While they certainly could draft their own, and she could teach them how to do that in the training, it's more valuable to just have them already done.

Basically, she's selling a by-product of her own business. She's already created the contracts for herself, so it's no extra work to offer them to others who are learning the same process. What by-products have you created that you could offer your customers?

People want tangible assets that make the core training easier to implement. Scripts, templates, cheat sheets, checklists, time lines, and schedules are all valuable tools you could create.

Information Products/Services: Every tool can be used to increase the value of any offer, but it can also help move people to the next level of your value ladder. Technically every type of information product we talked about earlier is a tool. A membership site can be a tool. Events and coaching are tools to help you better implement your frameworks. The top tiers of a value ladder have services helping people to implement the frameworks that you have given them earlier.

Remember, how much money your business makes is in direct relationship to how simple the process is for your dream customers to achieve their result. Creating done-for-you tools to give your customers a shortcut to success is one way to simplify that process. In the next chapter we'll bundle your product, frameworks, and tools into offers that your dream customers won't be able to resist.

Step #3: Turning Your Frameworks into an "Offer" with the Stack Slide

The next step is turning all these ideas into something that you can sell. In *DotCom Secrets*, one of the core frameworks I introduced you to is called Hook, Story, Offer. We talked about why it's so important to de-commoditize your business, not just selling a product like most companies, but to make it something unique by turning it into an actual offer.

The goal of an offer in its simplest form is to:

- Increase the *perceived value* of what is being sold.

- Make the thing being sold unique to you and available only within the special offer.

The simplest way to turn your product into an offer, increase the perceived value of that offer, and make it a true new opportunity is to wrap your product or service inside your frameworks. During this step we are going to make what we are creating and selling very tangible so you know exactly how you need to be packaging your frameworks and what tools you need to create for your offer.

We do that by using a tool I call the "Stack Slide." We will be using this Stack Slide in every story-selling script that you'll be learning in Sections Two, Three, and Four. It is the core foundation to everything else we will be doing in this book. The *first* thing I do when I am going to create a new offer is focus on the Stack Slide.

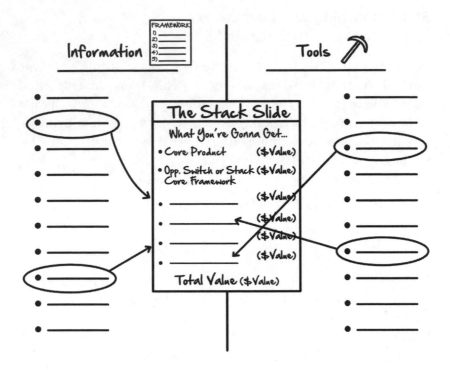

Figure 5.8:

**To increase the value of your offer, you'll include information frameworks
and tools that will give your customers a shortcut to success.**

In my Stack Slide, the first item is my core product, and the second item is the "opportunity switch" or "opportunity stack" core framework that I will be giving customers.

ClickFunnels example: In my presentations to sell ClickFunnels, my core product is access to the ClickFunnels software, and my opportunity switch core framework is my Funnel Builder Secrets online course. That's the way I decided to package my frameworks to help people learn them, but I can change the value of the offer based on how I deliver the frameworks:

- $9,997: two-day live event at my office
- $1,997: online course
- $97: smaller course or audio program

Physical product or service: If you are selling a physical product or a service, that would be your core product, so your core frameworks could be taught in whatever modality that matches how much you want to charge for the offer.

Information product or event: If the core product that you are selling is a course or event, the core product and the core framework will likely be the same thing.

Next, I need to figure out other things I can add to the Stack to increase the perceived value even more. Most times I will brainstorm with my team, and we'll sit in front of a whiteboard for hours talking about all the things we could potentially add to the offer. In the end, we'll decide which things the customers will actually get when they decide to buy, and those things end up on the Stack Slide.

I usually start on the left-hand side and brainstorm the different information products we could potentially create.

- Written word: Should we write a book or an e-book?

- Audio: Should we make an audio program?

- Video: Should we make a membership site? Would it be better to make an online course?

- Live experiences: Should we create a seminar or workshop, or would this work better as a mastermind group or one-on-one?

Then we talk about what each of those would look like if we did build them. What would be in the membership site? What modules do I need to record? Or if we decide to do an event, where would we host it? What other ways could we serve customers with our frameworks?

Traditionally I want only one or two information products inside the Stack. Having too much information can decrease the perceived value of an offer because it may seem like too much "work." Oftentimes the only information product I include in my

Stack is the actual opportunity switch or opportunity stack core framework.

Then we move to the right-hand side of the image and brainstorm tools we could create. Because tools often have a higher perceived value, I like to focus my Stack on as many of these as possible:

- Is there software we could create to make part of our framework easier?

- Could we bundle supplements into this offer?

- What physical products could we create to increase this offer's value?

- What are the by-products we've created during the implementation of these frameworks that have cost us time or money? Could any of them be passed on to our customers?

- Are there other information products or services we could bundle?

In Section Three, you will learn that there are three reasons why people don't buy from you. We'll go into much greater detail about them when we get to that section of the book, but I want to bring them up now because I try to make things inside my Stack that will help break those three core false beliefs.

False Belief #1—I don't believe this vehicle (your new opportunity) is the right vehicle for me: What false beliefs do your customers have about the vehicle/new opportunity you're presenting to them? What would keep them from believing that this vehicle is right for them? What tangible thing can you create to help them change their belief?

I love creating case studies or examples to include as a bonus. If I were creating a product about flipping houses on eBay, I'd go and find 20–30 examples of me doing this process or several case studies of my students having success with it. I'd put them together into a case study booklet or video training that people could watch or read as proof that the vehicle works and to provide better insight about how others are doing it. The more belief in the new opportunity I can create, the more likely others will be able to achieve the same results.

False Belief #2—I believe this is the right vehicle for some people, but I don't think that I could be successful with it: Once they believe in the vehicle, what beliefs do they have about *themselves* that make them think they can't succeed? For example, someone in your beta group might say, "That's cool, but I don't know how to_____." Or "I can't_____." They might believe in the new vehicle, but they don't believe in themselves. So you need to create something specific to help them overcome these false beliefs about themselves.

Maybe they think they're not technically inclined. What can you create to show them how to hire the right tech people? Maybe they believe they've never been able to stick to a diet. What tangible asset can you create that will help them overcome this internal struggle? Sometimes this element will be specific training that goes beyond what's in the masterclass. It could also be tangible tools or templates that will give them the confidence to realize they can truly do it.

One of my best-selling offers (Funnel Builder Secrets) taught people how to build funnels. While it was easy to get people to believe that funnels were the future, they often didn't believe that *they* could build a successful sales funnel on their own. I discovered that one of their biggest fears was writing the copy for the funnel pages. So for this element, I gave people my copywriting course along with my templates and swipe files so they could easily complete that part of the process.

False Belief #3—I believe that I could have success, but I have an external force holding me back from success: This is usually the last thing holding someone back from getting results. They believe that the vehicle is right, they believe they can do it, but there is still some outside force that might make it difficult for them to succeed. This outside force might be a bad economy, lack of time, or something else outside their direct control.

For my Funnel Hacks offer, getting traffic was the big external struggle everyone had. They believed in the vehicle, they believed in themselves, but they had fears that no one would ever click into their funnels. So we created a video course showing them how to drive traffic into their funnels.

For your opportunity, think about what outside things might possibly keep people from success, then create something to help eliminate or minimize that excuse.

Every item on the Stack Slide has a value attached to it. The goal is to show that you're giving 10 times as much value as you're asking for in price. So if you're selling a $97 product, you want the Stack Slide to add up to at least $997, preferably more. If you're selling a product for $997, then the value needs to be at least $9,997. If your value isn't 10 times higher than your price, then it's time to go back to the drawing board and figure out other ways you can package your frameworks or make new tools that will increase the value of what you're offering.

Learning how to create offers and build Stack Slides is one of the most important things you can learn to do in this business. This is not a one-time activity. Every time you have a new offer, you will go through this exercise again. Each step in the value ladder will have an offer and a Stack Slide.

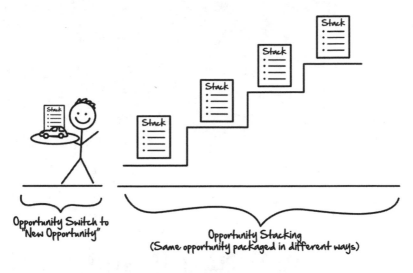

Figure 5.9:

Each step of your value ladder will have its own Stack Slide that shows that step's offer.

As a fellow Funnel Hacker, I would recommend watching people in as many markets as you can as they launch their offers. See what things they include in their offers, and you'll get ideas for different ways you can package your frameworks.

The Future-Based Cause

(Your Movement)

THE FUTURE-BASED CAUSE

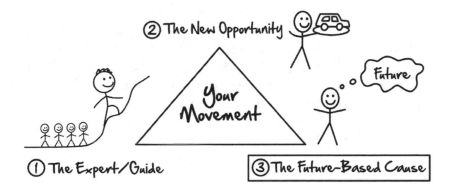

Figure 6.1:

The third stage of becoming the expert is to create a future-based cause.

For generations, people believed it was impossible to run the mile in under four minutes. They believed the human body wasn't capable of going that fast, and that it would collapse under the pressure. Some doctors and scientists said it wasn't just hard or dangerous but physically impossible. No one could run a mile in under four minutes.[28]

Then, on a cold, rainy day (May 6, 1954), six men entered a race held on the Iffley Road track in Oxford, England.[29] One of these men was Roger Bannister. As he crossed the finish line that day, he did something that was thought to be impossible. Over the loudspeakers the announcement came.

"Ladies and gentlemen, here is the result of event nine, the one mile . . . subject to ratification, will be a new . . . world record. The time was three . . ."

The announcement was drowned out by the crowd when they realized it was under four minutes! Bannister had finished the race in 3:59.4! He'd done what so many people believed was impossible; he broke the four-minute mile!

After the record was broken, it held up for only 46 days before it was broken by John Landy. Once people saw it was possible, it created belief in others that they could do it too. Since that time, more than 1,400 runners have broken the four-minute mile.

For me, there was a similar record shattered on August 17, 2004, that gave me the belief I needed to chase after my dreams. I had started my online business in 2002 while I was wrestling and going to school. My beautiful new bride was supporting her job-less student athlete, and I felt guilty because I wanted to help provide. But NCAA rules kept me from having a real job, so I turned to the internet with a goal of making an extra $1,000 per month. If my little business could do that, then I would feel like a success.

For about two years I was learning how this game was played, and had a few small successes, like my potato gun DVD, but nothing huge. At about that time, I heard about an online marketer named John Reese who was about to launch a new product he had created called Traffic Secrets. I heard rumors from friends that his goal was to make a million dollars selling that course. I didn't think too much about it at the time, but I was excited to buy a copy of his new course.

A few days before his launch, I went on a family trip to Bear Lake in southern Idaho. When I arrived, I realized there was no internet access anywhere on the lake, except in a small library that had a very slow dial-up modem. About halfway through our trip, I went into town and waited in line to get online so I could check my emails. When it was my turn, I opened my account and saw an email from John Reese with the subject line "We did it!"

I wasn't exactly sure what he was talking about, so I opened the email and read a story that changed my life. He said that earlier that day, August 17, 2004, his new course had launched, and in just 18 hours they had sold more than 1,000 copies, creating the first-ever "million-dollar day" for someone in my industry![30] As I read that email, I sat back in my chair and everything around me slowed down to a stop. He hadn't made a million dollars total selling his course, he had made a million dollars in less than a day! He had broken the four-minute mile for internet marketers.

As I thought more about that, my goal to make $1,000 a month seemed so small. I then realized that to earn a million dollars, John Reese had to sell 1,000 copies of a $1,000 course. And suddenly, it became so tangible and so real for me, and I realized that is what I wanted to do; I wanted to make a million dollars. It completely transformed what I thought was possible, and because of that, I started thinking and acting differently.

Within a year of reading that email, I didn't make a million dollars, but I got close. The second year I tried it and missed it again. But within three years, I had made a million dollars in a single year! Later I made a million dollars in a month, followed by multiple times when my company made a million dollars in a day! It was something I didn't think was possible. It didn't make logical sense; they didn't talk about things like this when I was in school, but because John did it, I knew I could do it.

In Proverbs 29:18 it says, "Where there is no vision, the people perish." Our job as an expert and guide for our audience is to help cast a vision for what is possible and bring our people to higher ground, to move them from where they are to where they want to be. The last step in creating your movement (after becoming the expert and creating a new opportunity) is creating a future-based cause. For every political, social, or religious movement throughout history, the charismatic leader paints a picture of the future they are trying to create and what life will be like when they get there.

In his book *The True Believer*, Eric Hoffer writes, "Fear of the future causes us to lean against and cling to the present, while *faith in the future* renders us perceptive to change." In circumstances where people fear the future, they typically stop moving forward. For you to have success in this business, you have to give your followers hope of something better so they will be perceptive to the change you are going to offer . You do that by painting a vision of the future that they want and showing them that it is possible.

Most people want to cast their faith and personal responsibility into something bigger than themselves. It happens in religion, it happens in political movements, it happens in the workplace, and it will be true for your movement. People want to plug in to something bigger than themselves, so it's your job to create that vision. Here are a few key principles that will help you create your future-based cause.

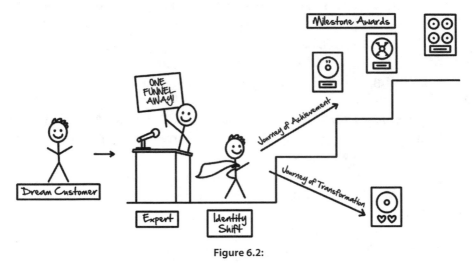

Figure 6.2:

Your job as the expert is to guide your dream customers on a journey of both achievement and transformation.

STEP #1: LAUNCH YOUR "PLATFORM" TO BE YOUR DREAM CUSTOMER'S GUIDE TO THE RESULT

Deciding that you want to create a movement is only half the job. The other half involves campaigning to your dream customers about why you are the expert or the guide to lead them. I realized as I was starting to build my tribe that there was a lot of noise in the market, a lot of other opportunities and other experts shouting from the rooftops trying to attract the same people I wanted to serve. I knew that if I wanted to get their attention, I needed to build a platform that I could "run" on as their expert or guide, just as I would if I were running for political office to try to be a state senator or the president of my country.

After having that thought—that I was running for president of my tribe, or "President of the Funnel Hackers"—it made me want to look closer at how successful political campaigns are run. I started a deep study of winning U.S. presidential candidates and what platforms they ran on.

I found a fascinating pattern that I believe most people completely overlook. Almost all the winning presidential candidates who were elected, from George Washington to today, won because of their ability to create a vision of the future that people want the most. Each of the winners interestingly enough also presented a new opportunity while the losers were offering improvement.

Year	Loser: Focus On Present (Improvement Offer)	Winner: Future-Based Cause (New Opportunity)
1980	Jimmy Carter: "A Tested and Trustworthy Team"	Ronald Reagan: "Let's Make America Great Again"
1984	Walter Mondale: "For New Leadership"	Ronald Reagan: "It's Morning Again in America"
1988	Bob Dole: "A Leader for America"	George H. W. Bush: "Read My Lips: No New Taxes"
1992	George H. W. Bush: "A Proud Tradition"	Bill Clinton: "It's Time to Change America"
1996	Bob Dole: "A Better Man for a Better America"	Bill Clinton: "Building a Bridge to the Twenty-First Century"
2000	Al Gore: "Leadership for the New Millennium"	George W. Bush: "Reformer with Results"
2004	John Kerry: "A Stronger America"	George W. Bush: "More Hopeful America"
2008	John McCain: "Country First"	Barack Obama: "Change We Can Believe In"
2012	Mitt Romney: "Believe in America"	Barack Obama: "Forward"
2016	Hillary Clinton: "Stronger Together" and "I'm with Her"	Donald Trump: "Make America Great Again"

Figure 6.3:

All winning presidential campaigns were won with a new opportunity or a future-based cause; the losing campaigns featured improvement slogans.

Isn't it interesting how the winners cast a compelling vision of the future, whereas the losers focused more on the present? Being a bett(er) leader or making America strong(er) or any of the "er"s make their entire campaign an improvement offer.

As I started to build my tribe within ClickFunnels, I wanted to create something that would unite our members and give them faith and hope in their future with us. If I'm honest, I didn't know I needed this at first, and actually stumbled upon it one day. But the minute I discovered it, it instantly cast a compelling vision of the future and united our members.

We were about to launch our third annual Funnel Hacking LIVE event, and I was trying to think of a headline for the sales page. I remember reading a story about the late Gary Halbert when I first started my business where he said, "You are only one sales letter away from striking it rich."[31] I know that for me, that statement created a vision that got me excited. I didn't know which sales letter or product it would be for me, but I had a perfect hope that if I would just keep trying, something would work. It created faith in my mind that what I was working toward was real, and even though I failed over and over again, that thought kept me moving forward through the ups and downs I experienced early in my career.

As I remembered what that statement did for me all those years ago, I started with that idea and tried to figure out how to create something similar for my members. After thinking about it for a while, I eventually wrote out a headline that said:

You're just one funnel away from being rich.

As I looked at it, for some reason I didn't feel it. I know that some people create sales funnels to get rich, but the majority of our members created companies and used sales funnels not just to get rich but, more important, to change the lives of their customers. So I went back to the drawing board. I wrote and rewrote that headline dozens of times.

You're just one funnel away from quitting your job.

You're just one funnel away from financial freedom.

You're just one funnel away from growing your business to the next level.

You're just one funnel away from sharing your message with more people.

The more I wrote, the more I realized that no matter what I wrote, it would reach only a percentage of my members. So I deleted the end of the sentence, hoping for some inspiration, and after sitting there for 10 or 15 minutes, I looked back up and saw something interesting. The headline read:

You're Just One Funnel Away . . .

That was it! Because having a funnel means something different to everyone, by not quantifying it I left it open for their interpretation. So each person could finish the sentence for themselves. If their compelling future was to quit their job, then *that* is the future I'm offering them. If their compelling future is to share their message with more people and try to change the world, then *that* is the future I'm offering that person.

At our last Funnel Hacking LIVE event, I told stories that showed how this vision was true for me. I talked about each major failure that I had during my career, and how each time I was saved by a funnel. Twice I've been on the brink of bankruptcy, and both times one funnel got me back to the top. Multiple times I've made poor decisions that could have (and probably should have) ruined me, but a funnel saved me. I shared story after story about how that was true for me, in hopes that it would give them hope of what's possible.

I now use that message in all my communication with my audience. I sign off in my videos by saying, "Remember, you're just one funnel away!" I've added it at the end of every email I send out. It's the theme of our events. It's a constant and consistent callout to our tribe, reminding them of the vision they have put their faith and hope into.

Since the first edition of this book when I first shared this concept, I've watched as my readers have created their own platform to win the votes of the members of their movements. Here are a few that I loved that should get the wheels spinning in your head as you are creating your campaign slogan or mantra.

The Expert(s)	The Movement	Slogan/ Mantra	Meaning
Ryan D. Lee, Brad Gibb, and Jimmy Vreeland (CashFlow Tactics)	We prove that anyone can be financially free in 10 years or less regardless of age, income, or experience. This has helped us form our message and draw a clear line in the sand. Simply making money is not good enough. Any strategy or opportunity that doesn't directly contribute to becoming financially free in 10 years or less doesn't work and should therefore be discarded.	Rise Up. Live Free.	We're not trying to help you make more money, pick the next great stock, or have more in your retirement account. We're helping you become FREE so you can live life on your terms. You can find your purpose and build a life you truly love.
Stacey and Paul Martino (Relationship Development®)	We have proven that it only takes ONE partner to transform a relationship...ANY relationship! Our mission is to empower people to get the Unshakable Love and Unleashed Passion they want in their relationship... without doing any couples work! We help you to transform your marriage, parenting, family, work and all relationships!	Changing the Way Relationship Is Done®	Together we are changing the way relationship is done! By doing this work with us, you are Breaking the Chains of Demand Relationship in your family's legacy. Your kids won't need us when they are 40 because they watched you live it. You become their example instead of their warning.
Jaime Cross (MIG Soap)	We deliver wildcrafted beauty experiences that transform the mind, body, and soul. We believe that beauty starts with purpose and radiance from the inside out, so we are activating human potential with products and tools that go far beyond the skin.	Seed to Skin. Skin to Soul.	We do more than help you attain softer skin. We are activating the human spirit to Rise, Run, and Become. Through our transformational True Beauty Experiences, and mentHERship platform, we are awakening you "unto life." You'll feel beautiful, capable, and ready to step fully in your journey of Becoming HER®.

Figure 6.4:

Our Funnel Hackers have created their own movements, complete with slogans that unite their tribe in a common vision.

Exercise

To create your platform, I want you to imagine that you're running for president of your movement. Think about what slogan would be great for your campaign. What do your people really want? Where do they want to go? How can you capture that in a simple calling you could put on a campaign sign?

STEP #2: GIVE THEM AN IDENTITY SHIFT

Figure 6.5:

When you give your customers a new identity, they will become your true fans.

After someone has joined your movement and taken you up on your new opportunity, the most important thing you can do is give them an identity shift. Their ability to have success with you is more tied to an identity shift than almost anything else you can do. You have to remember that your customers are real people and it's your duty to sell to them over and over again. If you don't, they will go back to their old ways and habits, or worse, chase the next new opportunity that someone else offers them. As my friend Myron Golden always says, "It's essential that you take them off the market."

If you don't, what are the repercussions of you not selling to them over and over again? Depending on what you sell, it could be a loss of health, a loss of money, or a loss of time. Remember what Jay Abraham said, "If you truly believe that what you have is useful and valuable to your clients, then you have a moral obligation to try to serve them in every way possible."

It's easy to sell someone something once, but to get them to buy from you over and over again (and be excited while doing it) you have to shift their identity. One of my favorite stories that illustrates how an identity shift will shift behavior is from James P. Friel. I've asked him to retell that story for you here.

MY IDENTITY SHIFT BY JAMES P. FRIEL

I had finished work early and was sitting in my office with the sliding door open, mesmerized by the crashing waves of the Atlantic less than 100 feet away. And, in what can only be described as a lightning strike of inspiration, I found myself online buying a set of drums after doing less than five minutes' worth of research.

My mind ran away with me—fast. I went from thinking it would be cool to play the drums to seeing myself as a rock star in about 40 seconds. I even felt cooler already.

Now, while I'm sure there are plenty of people who buy drums, I had exactly zero logical reasons to think this was a good idea. First, I have absolutely no rhythm. On top of that, the worst grade I ever got was from an ill-fated attempt to play the recorder in sixth grade music class. To this day, I can still hear the shrill squeaking of "Mary Had a Little Lamb." I'm convinced my teacher gave me that D out of pity, not because I earned it.

Yet, despite the scars of my laughing classmates, here I was looking at my purchase confirmation with a crazy new dream of jamming my heart out behind a drum kit. I already felt like a drummer. How hard could it be to bang on some drums? If Animal from the Muppets could be a drummer, then so could I.

I shut my laptop and immediately went into the other room to find my girlfriend, Yara, who had no idea she was about to become my first fan.

"You'll never guess what just happened," I exclaimed. "No. Really. I promise that you'll never guess."

She raised her eyebrow with equal parts concern and excitement.

"I'm a drummer now," I proudly told her.

"What does that even mean?!" she asked. "You've never even once mentioned anything about playing the drums."

"I know. I'm just as shocked as you," I replied, "but, my drums will be here on Thursday."

Now I really had her attention.

"Wait. You bought drums?!" A look of confusion washed over her face.

Playing the "air" drums to make my point, I nodded with a smile. Amazon Prime for the win.

She giggled in disbelief as I left the room. Meanwhile, all I could think about was playing the drum solo from "In the Air Tonight."

And so, for three long, tedious days, I could barely think about anything else than rocking out on my expectant drum kit like Animal. I wanted it so bad that when the package finally arrived, I could almost hear the sound of Phil Collins jamming inside the box.

As I opened it and saw what looked like 2,000 pieces, I felt my blood pressure rise, realizing for the very first time that I actually had no idea what I had gotten myself into. Admittedly, I had done absolutely no real preparation for this moment. Not one to be deterred, I tore everything open, and after about an hour and a half, the drum kit was fully assembled and ready to go. This was the moment I had been waiting for.

I sat down to play. Tap, tap, tap. Something was horribly wrong—there was no sound coming out of my drums. *You've got to be kidding me*, I thought. I quickly pulled up Google and discovered that in my haste to order my kit, I didn't order an amp. A not so minor detail that I had completely overlooked. With Google still open, I found a local music shop, ran out of the room, and jumped in my car to go buy one.

As I sped to the store, I started to feel myself become noticeably impatient. In the back of my mind, I feared that if the store didn't have what I needed, I might be forced to wait another few days to play.

So I shot into the music shop like a heat-seeking missile, going directly to the drum section, where I nearly accosted the guy at the counter. Thankfully, he was chill, showed me the right amp, and began to ring me up.

For the first time since my moment of inspiration, I had a startling realization. I had absolutely *no* idea how I was going to play the drums.

So I asked my new friend, "Hey, now that I've got everything I need, how do you suggest that I learn to play?"

"Actually, we've got an instructor who gives lessons right here." He pointed over my shoulder.

At that exact moment, my would-be instructor, Gregg, approached. He had wispy shoulder-length gray hair and wore a black Def Leppard T-shirt. I immediately knew this was my guy.

"My one o'clock lesson just canceled," Gregg said as he looked at me. "You can have your first lesson for free right now if you'd like."

My eyes widened in disbelief as I realized that luck was on my side.

"Yes. Let's do it!" I responded.

He showed me to his studio. There were two drum kits: one for me and one for him. My heart was racing as he handed me a pair of drumsticks. This was it. I was about to play.

Gregg demonstrated a basic rock beat for me. Bmmm, Tsss, Bmmm, Tsss.

"Now you do it," he said, looking at me.

As soon as I went to try what he showed me, I instantly discovered that somewhere between shaking Gregg's hand and sitting down at the drums, I had completely lost control of my hands and feet. It was kind of like rubbing your stomach and patting your head at the same time, but only 10 times more confusing.

My drumming was painfully slow, less coordinated than a three-year-old working a zipper on a jacket, and didn't sound like anything at all. Hardly the jam session I had been waiting for.

I instantly got a pit in my stomach and looked back at Gregg with a face red from embarrassment.

"It goes like this," Gregg said again. Bmmm, Tsss, Bmmm, Tsss.

With the patience of Mother Teresa, Gregg watched me attempt the beat again with my clumsy hands.

The sound of Phil Collins faded from my mind and was replaced by flashbacks from sixth grade music class and my horrible shrieking on the recorder. There was definitely no jamming and I was definitely not Animal.

With a bright red face, I said, "Dude, it's not like I can't hear how it goes. I just can't do it."

I hated the taste of those words coming out of my mouth.

Gregg smiled back at me. "It'll take practice, but you'll get it if you stick with it."

In an instant, my dreams came rushing back. I could see myself playing the drums again. I could feel the release of jamming on my kit. In that moment, I realized an important truth. I might be the absolute worst drummer on planet Earth, but I was still a drummer.

I took a deep breath. This was definitely going to take some serious work, but I was now a drummer. And, what do drummers do? Drummers practice.

So, practice I did. I religiously took lessons every week and practiced at home for hours on end. One painful note after the next. I practiced until my neighbors went from asking me to stop making noise to asking me to turn down the music. I practiced until I could jam. I practiced because I am a drummer.

BE A DRUMMER

I like sharing James's story because most people in that situation would have said, "I want to learn how to play drums." That is *not* an identity shift. When James decided to play drums, he knew that there was going to be a long, hard road to becoming good, and if he just wanted to "play the drums" he probably would never had made it to the finish line. But because he shifted his identity to "I am a drummer," he looked at it differently. It shifted him.

If you're a drummer, you have to figure out what drummers do. They have their own drums, they have their own sticks, they have a coach, and they practice a lot. Because being a drummer was now his identity, and not just something he wanted to do, it became easy in his new identity to do the things a drummer does.

When someone comes to me wanting to learn how to make more money or grow their company, it can be hard to get them to do the things that are necessary to have success. When they learn about the identity of a Funnel Hacker and they put on that mantle, it's no longer difficult because "that's what Funnel Hackers do."

Do you now see why creating that shift in someone is so important? Their likelihood of success will go up exponentially after they have that shift. As the leader, it's your role to design what that identity looks like so they can easily take it on.

Tribe identity: One of the mistakes many people make is trying to make their company and their movement about themselves. As long as your product or company name is your name, it will be hard for others to identify with the movement. My company's name is ClickFunnels, but our tribe is the Funnel Hackers. These are the people who believe in our new opportunity—funnels—and use the ClickFunnels tool.

I mentioned this earlier, but when Kaelin Poulin first launched her company, she used her maiden name and called the company Tuell Time Trainer. While she had some success selling to people once, it didn't create a movement. After I shared with her and her husband this concept of the tribe and getting people to self-identify with your movement, she realized that their current branding made it very hard for others to identify with it. They knew that to get to the next level in their business, they would need to make a change.

As they were flying home from the meeting, Kaelin had an idea. She thought: *LadyBoss Weight Loss. That's what it's going to be! Then they will say, "I am a LadyBoss."*

By the time they had landed, they had changed their messaging. They quickly launched their new movement, and within three months they saw their customer churn drop by 10 percent (which for them was equal to hundreds of thousands of dollars a year). On top of that, their *true* fans—the ones who purchase anything and everything they produce—now identify themselves as LadyBosses and their company continues to grow by hundreds of new people every day.

The first step to the identity shift is to create a name for your tribe that will make them want to belong. My tribe is the Funnel Hackers; Kaelin's is the LadyBosses. What's your tribe called?

Personal identity—The "I am" statement: For customers to be able to self-identify with your movement, they need to have an "I am" statement that quickly describes who they are. An "I am" statement is very similar to the tribe identity, but it's giving customers the ability to self-identify with the tribe. "I am a Funnel Hacker." My people can say that and it means something special to them. As you learned in the section above, after Kaelin named her movement, she imagined her tribe saying *"I am a LadyBoss."*

You can take this to the next level by creating T-shirts with your statements on them. Shortly after launching ClickFunnels and the Funnel Hacker movement, we made some T-shirts that simply had the word *#funnelhacker* on the front. We sent a free shirt to everyone who opened a ClickFunnels account. After giving away about 10,000 shirts, our accounting department asked me if we wanted to order more. They said they weren't able to see any benefit in doing it, as it was costing us almost $10 to print and ship out each shirt.

I almost told them to cancel it, until one day I got a message from someone who had joined ClickFunnels, received the T-shirt, and never logged back into his account. He told me that he never canceled his account because he loved his Funnel Hacker T-shirt. He felt like he was part of our tribe and didn't want to lose that part of himself. That was when I really realized the power of an identity shift. I told our accounting department that although these shirts were costing us a lot of money, the intangible benefits were worth more. Since then we have shipped out more than

250,000 #funnelhacker shirts to almost every country around the world. I've seen pictures from people across the globe wearing our brand and spreading our message.

Kaelin is also big on creating LadyBoss swag for her LadyBosses to wear. She told me that she looks at the T-shirts like capes that give her tribe members superpowers; when they put a LadyBoss shirt on, they become different, like Superwoman. It reminds them every day how empowered they are to do what they need to do, where they are in their journey, and to keep moving forward. Each time they put it on, they are proclaiming their new identity, and it will help them do the impossible.

To get people to identify with your movement, come up with something simple that you can put on a T-shirt your members could wear that would make them identify with your movement. Think *"I'm a _____"* or *"I _____."*

> *I'm a Funnel Hacker.*

> *I'm a LadyBoss.*

> *I build funnels.*

> *I see things differently.*

> *I'm a biohacker.*

What would your tribe wear proudly on their chests?

Create a "Title of Liberty" or manifesto: In the ancient Americas, Captain Moroni led an army into a war they couldn't win. Some of his troops lost faith in their mission, and some even left to join the enemy forces. The captain needed to do something quickly to save his army and his people. In Alma 46:12, the story goes that he took his coat, tore it into a makeshift flag, and wrote on it, "In memory of our God, our religion, and freedom, and our peace, our wives, and our children." Then he put that flag on the end of a pole and called it the Title of Liberty.

When people saw it, they rallied around their leader Moroni, and in a scene that I can only imagine was similar to Mel Gibson's famous freedom speech in the movie *Braveheart*, they renewed their faith in the cause and went on to win the war.[32]

Figure 6.6:

To inspire your tribe, create a Title of Liberty, or manifesto, that will rally them to your cause.

Your tribe needs a Title of Liberty that they can look to as motivation and a reminder about why they are trying to change. Something they can look at when they're feeling doubtful—a rallying call. Something that will help them know who *you* are, remind them who *they* are, and refocus them on where you are going together.

The first person I saw create and launch a manifesto for a tribe was Kaelin for her LadyBosses. She wanted to create something that would call out to the people she wanted in her tribe and repel those who were not a good fit. She wanted it to be something that would inspire her dream customers and be a reminder about who they are trying to become. One day she sat down with her husband, Brandon; he pulled out his phone and clicked the "record" button as she talked about what it meant to be a LadyBoss. They had the audio transcribed and turned into this image that her customers print out and hang on their walls and mirrors to remind them who they are trying to become.

THE MANIFESTO

A LADYBOSS IS THE COURAGEOUS WOMAN INSIDE OF US WHO TAKES RESPONSIBILITY FOR WHERE SHE'S AT. SHE ISN'T A VICTIM OF HER CIRCUMSTANCES. SHE DOESN'T MAKE EXCUSES OR COMPLAIN ABOUT WHAT SHE CAN'T CHANGE. SHE SPENDS MORE ENERGY DOING SOMETHING ABOUT IT INSTEAD OF TELLING EVERYBODY WHY SHE "CAN'T".

A LADYBOSS CAN HAVE IT ALL AND DO IT ALL WITHOUT HAVING TO COMPROMISE WHO SHE IS OR HER INTEGRITY. A LADYBOSS REALIZES THAT SHE SHINES THE MOST WHEN SHE IS AUTHENTIC AND TRUE TO HERSELF.

A LADYBOSS ISN'T ABOUT JUST TALK, BUT GETTING IT DONE. SHE RECOGNIZES THAT IF SHE WANTS RESULTS AND SUCCESS, SHE HAS TO PUT IN THE WORK. A LADYBOSS DOESN'T AIM TO PLEASE OTHERS EXPECTATIONS, BUT RATHER AIMS TO BE THE BEST VERSION OF HERSELF SHE CAN BE.

A LADYBOSS DOESN'T LISTEN TO ALL THE NEGATIVE HATERS AROUND HER WHO ARE AFRAID SHE WILL SUCCEED. A LADYBOSS FOCUSES ON WHAT SHE WANTS INSTEAD OF FOCUSING ON WHY SHE "CAN'T".

A LADYBOSS IS A NO BS, TAKE ACTION, GET IT DONE, NO COMPROMISE WOMAN WHO VALUES HER INTEGRITY, CONFIDENCE, SELF WORTH, AND DOESN'T CHANGE WHO SHE IS FOR ANYBODY.

A LADYBOSS IS IN CONTROL OF HER DESTINY, HER SITUATION, HER HEALTH, HER BODY, AND IN TURN, HER LIFE.
LADYBOSS IS A MENTALITY THAT YOU CHOOSE TO STEP INTO. IT'S YOUR CONFIDENT ALTER EGO. IT MEANS PUTTING ASIDE ALL YOUR DOUBTS, ALL YOUR FEARS, ALL OF YOUR EXCUSES, AND EVERY REASON YOU THINK YOU CAN'T DO IT.
BECAUSE YOU CAN DO IT...

YOU'RE A LADYBOSS NOW.

Figure 6.7:

Kaelin and Brandon Poulin created a manifesto to inspire
their customers and remind them who they are trying to become.

When I created our Funnel Hacker manifesto, I thought through a similar process. Who are my Funnel Hackers? What do we stand for? Who are we trying to become? After thinking through this for a while, I ended up creating this manifesto for our tribe:

A FUNNEL HACKER
Is A New Breed Of ENTREPRENEUR...
SMARTER, LEANER, FASTER, AND FREE!

A FUNNEL HACKER
Believes That Their Business Is A Calling...
Their Products, Services, And The Message They Share Have The Ability To Change The Lives Of The People They've Been Called To Serve.

A FUNNEL HACKER
Is In Control Of Their Destiny...
They Start Without A Safety Net, "Venture Capital" Is A Four Letter Word, And "Bootstrap" Is Their Middle Name.

#funnelhackers
Define Their Own Destiny.
Create Their Own Luck.
Build Their Own Empires.
Change The World.

I AM A FUNNEL HACKER
And I Am Just One Funnel Away!

Figure 6.8:

Funnel Hackers are entrepreneurs and business owners who are passionate about getting their messages, products, and services out to the world so they can change their dream customer's lives.

After Kaelin launched her manifesto, a short time later I saw her send all her customers a mini version of the manifesto that they could save as the background image on their phone. That way, every time they turned on their phone, they would be reminded of what it means to be a LadyBoss. I quickly created one for my Funnel Hackers as well. You can get your own Funnel Hacker phone background at ExpertSecrets.com/resources.

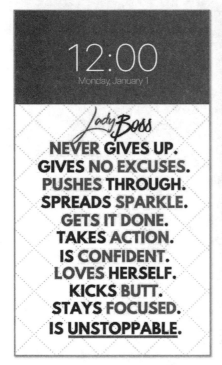 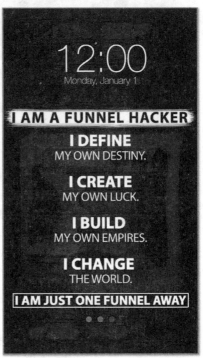

Figure 6.9:

By turning our manifestos into a background image for our tribe's phones, we're able to constantly remind our dream customers of the new identity they've taken on.

Creating an identity shift isn't limited to the ideas I shared here; they are just some of the things that we've used that have had the most success. The key is understanding that it's not just the name, or the T-shirts, or the words on their phone, it's how they feel about the movement and their role inside your community. They become a new person and they are connected to you as their guide.

STEP #3: CREATE MILESTONE AWARDS THAT PULL PEOPLE TOWARD THE RESULT (JOURNEY OF ACHIEVEMENT)

Figure 6.10:

We've created milestone awards that our Funnel Hackers earn when they hit the following sales in their funnel: Two Comma Club award ($1 million), Two Comma Club X award ($10 million), and Two Comma Club C award ($100 million).

Napoleon Bonaparte once said, "A soldier will fight long and hard for a bit of colored ribbon."[33] I know that as soon as I started wrestling, I found out that the "colored ribbon" for wrestlers in high school was to be a state champion. As soon as I knew that was the prize, it was the only thing I wanted. I would cut 20–30 pounds every single week to make weight for weigh-ins, and within hours after I was allowed to eat or drink again, I'd gain it all back. I missed meals, parties, and hanging out with friends. I also climbed rope every night, lifted weights, and ran every day on top of doing two to three hours a day of wrestling practice. I literally gave blood, sweat, and tears, all for the hope that I could someday win that title. By junior year I won my state title, and immediately I wanted to know the next colored ribbon I could go for.

I found out that after the state tournament there was a national tournament, and if you placed in the top eight, you would be an all-American! That's all I needed to know. I put on my plastics to lose weight and started running again. Within 12 months of learning what it would take to be an all-American, I took second place in the nation and got my colored ribbon.

Within minutes of my finals match, I started looking for the next match, the next level, and within a month I had signed on to Brigham Young University's wrestling team to start chasing the next ribbon.

Often in business, someone will join our movement because they are looking for a result. Unfortunately for most people, the result itself often isn't a strong enough pull to keep them in momentum long enough to achieve it. Other times the goals they set for themselves aren't very tangible, like, "I want to grow my company" or "I want to feel more successful." The result that most people are seeking is simply growth, so it can be hard to define a finish line. Because of that, we decided to create milestone awards that people can achieve while they are growing their companies inside of our new opportunity (funnels).

The first award we created is called the Two Comma Club award (because there are two commas in $1,000,000), and at our third Funnel Hacking LIVE event, we gave this award to everyone who had made at least $1 million inside a funnel! That first year we gave away 73 awards onstage, and I watched as the rest of the audience was transformed. They saw people around them break a four-minute mile that they may have dreamed of but didn't believe was possible. That award was the colored ribbon to chase after.

Over the next few years since we launched that award, we have had hundreds of entrepreneurs each year come onstage and receive that award! It helps to keep them tied to our movement, and it gives them the feeling of progress and accomplishment on their journey of achievement.

As soon as we awarded that first group of entrepreneurs their Two Comma Club awards, they immediately started asking, "What's next?!" What's the next colored ribbon they could chase? We then created a Two Comma Club X award signifying they made more than $10 million inside a funnel, and at the next Funnel Hacking LIVE event we had 17 people who won that award! Since then, we've also created a Two Comma Club C award (C is the Roman numeral for 100) for those who have made more than $100 million. We also have plans as our students keep growing to give one of the first-ever Three Comma Club awards! You can see the names of the people who have achieved these awards at TwoCommaClub.com.

What is the four-minute mile for your movement that you could create an award around for your people? Initially, the four-minute mile will need to be something that you've already accomplished, so you can show them it's possible and give them hope and belief that they can do it too. As you shift your focus to helping others accomplish the same results and breaking their four-minute mile, you'll notice something strange will happen inside your community. Their focus will be taken off of you, the expert, and shifted outward toward their tribe. This is important because people usually come into a community for the expert, but they stay for the community. As more of your members break the four-minute mile, more people will be attracted to your movement and it will start to grow faster than you ever thought possible.

STEP #4: UNITE WITH A SOCIAL MISSION (JOURNEY OF TRANSFORMATION)

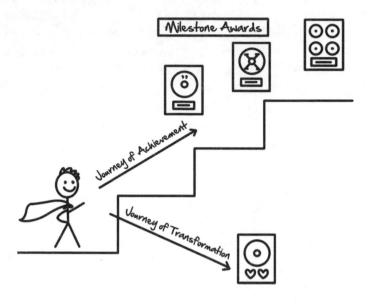

Figure 6.11:

We've also created a milestone award that our Funnel Hackers earn when they donate more than a million dollars to charity: the Two Heart Club award.

When you get to the story-selling section of this book in Section Two where we talk about the Hero's Two Journeys, you'll learn that in every story there are two journeys the hero goes on. You will soon master this story structure as you learn to tell your own stories, but it is also a real journey that you are taking your tribe on within your movement. I'll explain it to you quickly now, but you'll understand it in much more detail soon.

The first is the journey of achievement. We just talked about how you as the expert help guide tribe members through that journey to their end goal. The second journey that every hero unknowingly takes is called the journey of transformation. This transformation is who the hero becomes while on the journey of achievement.

If the only thing you do with your tribe is help them achieve a result, eventually they will leave you. There is no long-term fulfillment in achievement alone. Even if they do achieve the results you promise them, they will then start looking for other places to get their other needs met.

When we first launched ClickFunnels, we knew that we wanted to weave into the DNA of the company and also the culture that we were givers. A lot of people say that they'll give when they're successful, but I'd suggest that for most of us, we became successful because we gave. When we launched ClickFunnels, we set it up so that every time a funnel went live, we would donate $1 to a charity I love called Village Impact that builds schools for kids in Kenya. Each year at our Funnel Hacking LIVE event, we present a check for how many funnels our community has built to my friends Stu and Amy McLaren, founders of the charity. We've also had the chance to take a group of Funnel Hackers to Kenya to experience how their giving is changing the lives of so many people there.

A few months before our fourth Funnel Hacking LIVE event, I had a chance to meet Tim Ballard, who runs an organization called Operation Underground Railroad that helps save children from sex slavery. I didn't realize it at the time, but it's estimated that there are more than 2 million children right now who are being used for sex and organ harvesting. When we learned about this cause, we knew we needed to help. We decided to help fund the documentary *Operation Toussaint* that we premiered at Funnel Hacking LIVE. After screening the movie, we were able to raise more than $1 million for the cause, enough to save 400 children.

Tony Robbins, who happens to be O.U.R.'s biggest donor, was also our keynote speaker that year. After the event was over, I was backstage with him and showed him how much money we had raised. He told me something that changed me. He said, "What I love that you're doing now is you're teaching them to be givers, and helping them to see the value in that, and getting them hooked on that. . . . To me, that's the most important thing of all."

I realized in that moment, while I had always assumed that my mission was to help my tribe achieve something, that was just a distraction from the real goal, which is to help them transform into something more.

When we got home from that event, we rallied our community around this cause and created a funnel to help promote the documentary. (You can watch it at OURFilm.org.) At the time of this writing, that funnel has helped raise more than $2.5 million and that number is growing every day.

When I was in Kenya on our last donor trip, I started thinking a lot about these two charities that mean so much to me. While they are very different, they both have the same spirit. As I contemplated how to weave them deeper into our movement, two words came to my mind: *Liberate* and *Educate.*

As soon as I heard that, I saw how these two charities tied together, but also why they meant so much to us as a community. Operation Underground Railroad helps liberate children from slavery, and Village Impact helps educate children by building schools for them.

ClickFunnels' mission has also been to liberate entrepreneurs from the technical hurdles that have held them back from having success, and educate them through the books and coaching programs we have created.

Liberate and Educate: This is what we do for entrepreneurs during their journey of achievement, and during their journey of transformation we give them opportunities to help the children who can't help themselves. We've also recently created a new award to encourage giving even more called the Two Heart award for those who donate more than $1 million to charity. I'm excited to see how this new colored ribbon will help move people to give even more. (You can learn more about our mission, Liberate and Educate, at LiberateAndEducate.com.)

CREATING BELIEF

I was onstage in front of 4,500 of my fellow Funnel Hackers doing my opening keynote at Funnel Hacking LIVE. The energy in the room was intense. Everyone was wearing some type of ClickFunnels swag, many made their own custom ClickFunnels suits, others dyed their hair, and one guy in the front row had real ClickFunnels tattoos on both of his arms.

These weren't just users of ClickFunnels; these were our die-hards. We had almost 100,000 members using our platform, but these were the 4,500 fans who were the most obsessed and left their families and businesses for a week to be with their fellow Funnel Hackers.

As I stood onstage, I wanted to share the most important thing possible that would have the biggest impact on them over the next year. I wanted to make this first presentation so valuable that if they only got that, it would have been worth the time and money they spent to be there. What would be the most powerful thing I could share?

In the weeks leading up to the event I had identified a new framework that I had been unconsciously using for the past decade; it was so simple, yet I would say it was the most important discovery in my 15-plus-year career. The framework I shared with them that morning was: Hook, Story, Offer.

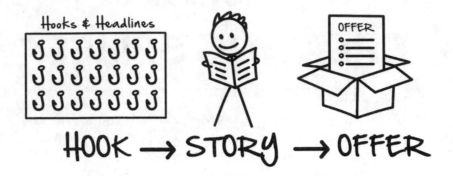

Figure 7.1:

Though I had been using the principles in the Hook, Story, Offer
framework for 15 years, I had never taught it before as a complete
framework; once I did, I realized it was crucial to business success.

I'm not going to go into great detail here, because *DotCom Secrets* is based on this framework and you can geek out and learn how to master this principle there. But I did want to introduce it to those of you who haven't read that book yet, because you'll see how what you're learning and where we're going in this book fits into that framework.

I told everyone at the event that day that if something wasn't working in your funnel, it was always the hook, the story, or the offer. The hook is how you grab your dream customer's attention, the story is how you build up the perceived value of what you sell, and the offer is what you are selling. I then showed how each page in your funnel has a hook, a story, and an offer: your ads, emails, social media posts, blog posts, podcast episodes, landing pages, sales pages, upsell pages, and more. Everything you put into the world has these three elements, and if something is not working, it's always either your hook, your story, or your offer.

I share that here because the first section of this book has gone deep into the third part of this framework: how to create powerful offers. The higher the perceived value of your offer is, the easier it will be to sell it. If your potential customers see your offer and feel it's worth $1,000, and you are only selling it for $100, they will buy it every time. But if they think it's worth $50, and you are selling it for $100, you will never make the sale. The secret is to get the perceived value to be more than the actual cost. When you can do this, people always say yes. Here are a few things we have done to increase the perceived value of our offer so far:

- We changed what we sell from an improvement offer to a new opportunity.

- We developed proprietary frameworks that are unique to us.

- We created our own category inside the marketplace where we can become the category king.

- We packaged our frameworks in different ways to increase the value.

- We gave our people a future-based cause they believe in.

- We brought them into our tribe.

- We helped them have an identity shift that will allow them to feel part of our community.

All the tools you've learned so far were designed to increase the value of your offer. This next section of the book is also going to be increasing the perceived value of your offer, but it does it through a different process. Here we use story as a preframe that will increase the perceived value of the actual offer.

Figure 7.2:

Your stories preframe your offer to increase its perceived value.

Just as you share a story about how you learned or earned your framework before sharing it with someone so your story increases the perceived value of your framework, you'll also share a story about how you learned or earned what you've created inside your offer to increase its perceived value. If I tell you a story about the offer, and I do it in a way that drives the value of the offer way past how much money I am asking for it, then it becomes really easy to get you to buy. Learning how to tell stories the right way will do more to increase the perceived value of what you have to offer than anything else you can do. In this section you will master story selling.

THE EPIPHANY BRIDGE

Have you ever made a critical decision while in a sugar coma? I was at Kneaders in Boise, Idaho, having their all-you-can-eat chunky cinnamon French toast, which is not like normal French toast. It's two inches thick and drowned with their homemade caramel syrup, strawberries, and whipped cream. I'm pretty sure the founder of this new start-up lured me there and got me sugar drunk before pitching me on his new idea, but either way, the idea sounded great and I agreed to be a partner.

The next week he sent me the sales script he had written for their front-end sales video. As I read through it, I felt a little dirty. It was a very traditional video pitching people on why they should join the new opportunity. It had all the copywriting tricks and sales tools weaved in, yet it didn't make me want to sign up. I knew instantly what was wrong. The problem was that he was trying to sell me on why I should sign up. Your goal isn't to try to sell anyone anything. Your goal is to guide them to their own decision.

Knowing the problem, I quickly sent this email:

> Hey - I'm really excited to be part of this project, but the sales video is all wrong. The mistake is that you are trying to sell them on why they should be joining. That is the wrong approach.
>
> What I've found is that if you are directly trying to sell something in your video, it's not as strong, and it doesn't create the emotion you need to really cause action. If you want people to adopt a new concept and want to get their buy-in, you have to lead them to the answer, but you can't *give* it to them. They have to come up with the idea themselves. You plant the idea in their minds with a story, and

if *they* come up with the answer, they will have sold themselves. The buying decision becomes theirs, not yours.
When that happens, you don't have to sell them anything.

He wrote back, a little confused, and asked me if I'd be willing
to take a shot at writing the script for our new start-up. I spent the
next few hours writing what I call an "Epiphany Bridge" script,
which we used on launch day. Within six weeks of that video
launching, we had acquired 1.5 million users with $0 in adver-
tising spend! That is the power of a story when you use it the
right way.

So what is an Epiphany Bridge? It's simply a story that takes
people through the emotional experience that got *you* excited
about the new opportunity you're presenting. For this exercise, I
want you to think about yourself before you got started on your
path. Back in your expert journey when you were in the growth
phase and it was just a spark and you were first learning what you
teach now, can you remember what life was like back then? It's
important to get back into that state, because that is the state that
your future dream customers are in now.

Now try to remember, what was the experience that caused you
to have the big aha moment (your epiphany)? Something happened
where you realized that everything had changed forever. These big
epiphanies always come from a guide. Sometimes the guide is a
person who gave you the answer you needed, and other times the
guide is God, and he gave you the inspiration or idea you needed.

For my journey to learn about my new opportunity—
funnels—my aha moment came after Google raised its prices and
I had to stop selling my potato gun DVD online. Then a guide
(in this instance it was Mike Filsaime) called and told me that he
had started to create upsells (he called them "one-time offers,"
or OTOs) for all his products, and one out of three people who
bought his first product also bought his upsell.

Boom! That was it! That was the epiphany I needed. I ended
up adding OTOs to my potato gun funnel and was able to make
enough money to cover my ad costs from Google. I was back in
business.

Figure 7.3:

Your epiphany is the aha moment when you learned about your new opportunity.

So the first question is for the story you are telling: What was the epiphany that your guide gave to you?

After you have that big epiphany, you are *emotionally* bought into the concept. That usually starts you on your journey of growth. This is what drove you to become an expert on the topic.

Figure 7.4:

Your epiphany sets you on a journey to learn everything you can about the new opportunity.

You started geeking out and going deep into the subject, learning the terminology, and understanding the science and technical aspects behind why it worked, and then you became *logically* sold on the new opportunity.

This is where most people mess it up. Because they are now backed with the logical proof of their argument and armed with the data, they go out to make their first sale, and the first thing they do is spew these facts on their unsuspecting prospect. It's confusing to most people when they find that the people they try to sell logically never get as excited as they do, and are usually very resistant to the new ideas. Has this ever happened to you?

The problem is that you started to speak a language we call "technobabble." One of my friends, Kim Klaver, identifies technobabble as the number one sales killer in her book *If My Product's So Great, How Come I Can't Sell It?*

Figure 7.5:

In your journey, you gain so much knowledge that usually when you try to talk to others about your new opportunity, you speak in technobabble and they get confused.

We all love our ideas so much. We want people to understand why they should follow us and use our products and services. But for some reason, as soon as we try to explain our beliefs to someone, we automatically spew the technobabble we've learned in order to logically convince people to buy. We talk about why this concept is the best and potentially mention the science behind what we do. We talk about how we're "leading the industry" with "groundbreaking" products. We share industry numbers and jargon.

But the logical stuff that strengthened our own beliefs in the new opportunity will not help people buy unless they've *already had the same initial emotional epiphany that you had.* All the logic, features, and benefits you give people before the epiphany will just annoy them. It's frustrating and often completely offensive. There's a time and a place for logic, but you have to convince them emotionally first before they'll be excited by your logic.

Figure 7.6:

You have to step away from the technobabble, meet your dream customers where they are, and help them feel the emotion you felt when you had your epiphany so they can move *with* you.

Think about it. *You* didn't buy into the new opportunity because of the logical technobabble. You bought in because of some emotional experience that happened *before* you geeked out. You had an epiphany *first*, and that caused you to move forward. People don't buy logically, they buy based on emotion. Then they use logic to justify the purchase decision they've already made.

For example, let's say I purchased a Ferrari. I am emotionally invested in the feeling I want to have when I'm driving it. That's why I bought the Ferrari (or a big house, expensive clothes, watches, etc.). But then I have to logically justify to myself, my friends, or my spouse why it was worth spending that money. I have to explain how it gets better gas mileage, it was on sale, or it came with a great warranty. Logic is justification for the emotional attachment I've already made.

If you think about it, there's a status consideration on *both* sides of this equation. I'm emotionally attached to the status that the new Ferrari will give me, but I need to justify it logically to my friends and family so I don't lose status with them. But good luck selling me logically if I don't already have the emotional connection with that car—it's pretty much impossible.

Logic doesn't sell. Emotions sell.

To create those emotions, you have to go back and remember what it was that gave *you* the epiphany that caused you to believe in the new opportunity. That story—your Epiphany Bridge story—provides the emotional connection and bridges the gap from the emotional to the logical side.

If you can tell a story about how you got your big aha, and if you structure the story right, potential customers will have the same epiphany and will sell themselves on your product or service. Then they'll look for ways to logically justify the purchase and learn the technobabble on their own. Your job is to learn how to tell these stories in a way that will lead people to the epiphany, and they will do the rest. This time you are the guide who is going to help them have the same epiphany that your guide gave to you. That is the key.

So my first question for you is "What was the core Epiphany Bridge story that made you believe in the new opportunity that you are sharing with others?" We'll worry about how to structure that story over the next two secrets, but for now I want you to think back to the original experience that gave you your first epiphany and brought you on this journey.

Do you remember what happened? What was happening around you? How did you feel? It's important to remember those details, because they are key to telling a good story.

EFFECTIVE STORYTELLING

Have you ever noticed that two people can tell the same story with completely different outcomes? In one, you're emotionally captivated and engaged. Then someone else tells you a story about the exact same experience and you fall asleep. What's the difference? What makes some people better storytellers than others?

Oversimplification: The first key to telling captivating stories is oversimplification. When you're telling stories, you need to speak at about a third-grade level. Many of you will struggle with this because you like to use big words and show off your vocabulary to sound sophisticated and smart. There may be a time and place for that, but it's not when you're telling stories. People are used to digesting information at about a third-grade level. When you go above that, you start losing people quickly. There is a reason the news stations speak to their audiences at this level.

During the 2016 U.S. presidential primary elections, a study looked at the speeches of the Republican candidates and ran them through the Flesch-Kincaid test that shows the grade level of their speech.[34] Donald Trump averaged speaking at a third- to fourth-grade level during each of his speeches, whereas other candidates, like Ted Cruz, spoke at a ninth-grade level; both Ben Carson and Mike Huckabee spoke at an eighth-grade level. Using big words may make you feel smarter, but it will not influence others.

"Kinda like" bridge: Sometimes you have to talk about complex ideas. So how do you take a complicated idea and simplify it quickly? You do it using a tool I created called a "kinda like" bridge. Every time I run into a word or a concept that is past a third-grade level, I stop and think about how I can relate that concept to something customers already know and understand—the same way I would try to explain complex ideas to my kids.

Figure 7.7:

If you need to teach a concept that's past a third-grade level, say
It's kinda like . . ." and relate it to something customers already know.

For example, in one of my sales scripts, I was trying to teach a process called ketosis, which is kinda like a way to lose weight by eating fat. (That sentence right there was a mini "kinda like" bridge! Did you notice that?) In the sales script, I mentioned the word *ketones* and I watched as the audience zoned out. I discovered that if they don't know what a word means, they stop paying attention to everything you say afterward. So I started using a "kinda like" bridge like this:

> *The goal is to get ketones into your body. Now what are ketones? Well, they are kinda like millions of little motivational speakers running through your body that give you energy and make you feel awesome.*

I take this new concept or word that people may not understand and add the phrase "it's kinda like . . ." to the sentence. I'm connecting the new word or concept to something they already understand, something that makes total sense to them, so they get it. My audience knows what a motivational speaker is. And they can imagine what it might feel like to have millions of little ones running around in their bodies.

In that same script, I was trying to explain what it feels like to be in ketosis, and that's a hard thing to understand. It feels good. It feels awesome! So I had to take this concept and say:

> When you're in ketosis, it's kinda like the old video game Pac-Man. Remember? You spend the whole game running away from the ghosts. But every once in a while, you get a power pellet and suddenly you get tons of energy, and then you're actually chasing the ghosts, and you feel ON. That's what it feels like to be in ketosis.

Again, I'm taking this concept that's vague and hard to understand and bridging it with something audiences understand, using the phrase "kinda like."

Any time you're speaking (or writing) and you hit a friction point where some people may not understand what you're trying to convey, just say "It's kinda like . . ." and relate it to something easy to understand. This keeps your stories simple, entertaining, and effective. Oversimplification is the key.

Making them feel: The next way to improve your storytelling is to add feelings and emotions. In film, it's often a lot easier to get people to feel something. One of my favorite examples is from *X-Men: First Class*. In this movie, we are taken back into the X-Men's past and given a glimpse of what it was like for them growing up and discovering their powers.[35]

In one scene, young Magneto is taken to a Nazi concentration camp. As they pull him and his family into the gates, they notice the metal fences around their compound move as he starts to resist them. They want to see what his powers are, so they bring him into a very small room with a Nazi leader who wants a demonstration of his powers. They also bring Magneto's mother into the room so they can use her as leverage to get him to do what they want.

The leader points a gun at Magneto's mother and asks Magneto to try to move a metal coin on the desk with his mind. He nervously tries to move the coin but isn't able, so the leader pulls the trigger and kills his mother. Then you see a scene so powerful that—without a single word being said—you feel the pain that Magneto is going through.

You watch as his eyes shift from sadness to anger. He then uses his powers to crush a bell on the Nazi leader's desk. From there, he starts yelling, and everything metal moves inside the room. He crushes the guards' helmets, killing them instantly, then he completely destroys everything around them. And that's when he finds his power.

When you're watching the film, you are able to see all of this happen without any words, because you see his face, you experience the room, you hear the music, and you actually feel, in some way, Magneto's pain and suffering. That is the power of film.

Now most of us aren't producing films to sell our stuff, but we have to learn how to tell stories in a way that helps others feel as if they're watching a powerful movie.

Imagine if Magneto just came in and said something like, "Yeah, so when I was a kid, I was in a Nazi concentration camp and they wanted me to move a metal coin with my mind. I wasn't able to do it, so they killed my mom. I was really mad, so I blew the whole place up."

Did you feel anything there? No, you wouldn't have had the same emotional experience that you needed to connect with that character. Yet that's how most people tell their stories.

If you study the work of a good fiction author, you'll notice that they'll have the character come into a room, then they'll spend several pages describing the room. They'll talk about the lights, how things looked and felt, and everything they need to set up the scene. Then they go deep into how the character is feeling. And that is the key. You have to explain how you feel, and when you do that people will start to feel what you were feeling.

For example, what if I tell a story like this:

I was sitting at home, in a little office next to the kitchen. I had a small desk that was covered with Post-it Notes and pads of paper with dozens of half-baked ideas scribbled on them. In the other room I could hear my kids playing, not realizing what had just happened. Then I heard my wife tell the kids to wash up, meaning it was time for dinner. As I heard them running to the sink, fighting over the soap and whose turn it was first, I knew I needed to get out of my chair and join them.

But as I slowly stood up, I felt a shooting pain in my stomach. It felt like a heart attack, but it was lower in my gut. On top of that, I felt a pressure coming down on my shoulders; I felt like someone was sitting on my neck. It got so heavy that I couldn't lift my head. The only thing I could see were the palms of my hands, and they were sweating, yet I was freezing cold.

What would my wife say when she found out that I didn't have any money for Christmas? What would the kids' faces look like tomorrow morning when they found out that Santa hadn't come this year?

As you read this story, you probably actually felt the things I described. How many of you felt a pain in your gut, a weight on your back, or sweaty palms? As I explain how I felt, you almost instantly will feel something similar. If I'm telling you my Epiphany Bridge story, I need you to be in the *same* state that I was in when I received my aha moment. If you are, chances are you will have the same epiphany that I had. If you aren't, you will likely miss the whole point of my story.

Have you ever had the experience where you told someone a story about a situation that was really funny or exciting, and after you told it to them, they didn't quite get it? They understood, but they didn't "get" what you were trying to share with them. So you try to tell the story again another way, and then again another way, and after a few attempts, you throw up your hands in defeat and say something like, "Well, I guess you had to be there." That's what happens when you don't get people into the same state that you were in when you had that epiphany originally.

Now that you understand the basics of an Epiphany Bridge, how to simplify your stories, and how to get people to feel things when you tell your stories, I want to transition into story structure. When you learn the right structure for telling your stories and apply the concepts you learn here, you will become a master at storytelling and story selling.

THE HERO'S TWO JOURNEYS

It was 1984, about a year after George Lucas had launched the third film in the *Star Wars* series, *Return of the Jedi*. He decided to attend an event in San Francisco about the inner reaches of outer space; he attended because his guide, his "Yoda," was teaching the class.[36]

His name was Joseph Campbell, and while he and Lucas had never met before, the work that Campbell had done decades earlier was what had helped to create the storylines for *Star Wars*. Campbell had spent his life studying the universal themes and archetypes (and what I would call frameworks) that are present in storytelling across history and across the world. In his studies, he found that the framework was present in mythical stories regardless of the time in history or the culture in which it was set. Almost all successful stories throughout time followed a 17-stage framework.

In 1949, Campbell wrote a book detailing his findings called *The Hero with a Thousand Faces*.[37] In it, he laid out his 17-stage story framework, which he called the "The Hero's Adventure":

1. **The Call to Adventure:** Hero receives calling to the unknown

2. **Refusal of the Call:** Obligations or fear prevent hero from starting the journey

3. **Supernatural Aid:** Magical helper appears or becomes known

4. **Crossing the First Threshold:** Hero leaves their known world and ventures into the unknown

5. **Belly of the Whale:** Final stage of separation from the known world

6. **The Road of Trials:** Hero must pass a series of tests to begin transformation

7. **Meeting with the Goddess/Love:** Hero experiences unconditional love

8. **Temptation:** Hero faces temptation that will distract from their ultimate quest

9. **Atonement with the Hero's Father:** Hero must confront the person who holds ultimate power in their life

10. **Peace and Fulfillment before the Hero's Return:** Hero moves to a state of divine knowledge (usually through some form of death)

11. **The Ultimate Boon:** Achievement of goal

12. **Refusal of the Return:** Having found bliss and enlightenment in the other world, hero may be reluctant to return

13. **Magic Flight:** Sometimes the hero has to escape with the boon

14. **Rescue from Without:** Sometimes the hero needs a rescuer

15. **Return:** Hero retains wisdom gained on their quest and integrates it into human society by sharing their wisdom with the world

16. **Master of Two Worlds:** Hero achieves balance between the material and spiritual (inner and outer world)

17. **Freedom to Live:** Free from fear of death, hero lives in the moment without concern for the future or regrets of the past

Lucas was introduced to Campbell's frameworks as he started to write *Star Wars*. In an interview, he said that after he had Campbell's framework he was "able to take ideas that go through all societies, through all the ages, and bring them down and put them into a razzle-dazzle . . . action-adventure film."[38]

Over the next few years they became great friends, even though, shockingly, Campbell had yet to see any of the *Star Wars* films. Lucas invited him to come and watch the shows with him. This was decades before people ever binge-watched movies, and Lucas said "it was actually the first time anybody had ever seen all three of [the movies] together at one time." They watched the whole trilogy in a day. When the last film ended, they sat quietly in the dark, and then Campbell said, "You know, I thought real art had stopped with Picasso, Joyce, and Mann. Now I know it hasn't."

THE HERO'S JOURNEY

Most of Campbell's work focused on myths and legends and folklore, and while his frameworks are amazing, it was difficult for me to figure out how to pull that story framework into something I could easily use on a Facebook Live, or in a webinar, or onstage at an event. So I started digging deeper to find ways to simplify that framework into something I could use.

During my journey trying to figure out how to use stories better in my marketing, I came across the Christopher Vogler book *The Writer's Journey*. While he was working as an executive at Disney, he took Campbell's framework and figured out how to simplify it to fit into film. Vogler popularized calling the process "The Hero's Journey," and his simplified story framework has just 12 stages:[39]

1. The Ordinary World

2. The Call to Adventure

3. Refusal of the Call

4. Meeting the Mentor

5. Crossing the First Threshold

6. Tests, Allies, Enemies

7. Approach the Innermost Cave

8. The Ordeal

9. The Reward

10. The Road Block

11. The Resurrection

12. Return with the Elixir

If you look at most popular movies, you will see this framework used over and over again.

Harry Potter and the Sorcerer's Stone	
The Ordinary World	Harry Potter lives in the cupboard under the stairs
The Call to Adventure	He receives a letter to attend Hogwarts
Refusal of the Call	He doesn't believe he's a real wizard
Meeting the Mentor	Hagrid takes him to Diagon Alley
Crossing the First Threshold	He learns about his parents' death at the hands of Lord Voldemort
Test, Allies, Enemies	He adjusts to life at Hogwarts
Approach the Innermost Cave	Harry, Ron, and Hermione plan to get the Sorcerer's Stone before Snape
The Ordeal	They overcome the obstacles set up to protect the stone
The Reward	Harry enters the room where the stone is hidden
The Road Block	He faces Professor Quirrell, who has been hosting Voldemort in his body
The Resurrection	Harry wakes up in the hospital; Dumbledore explains that he was protected by his mother's love
Return With the Elixir	Harry returns home for the summer, happy to belong at Hogwarts

Figure 8.1:

Vogler's 12-stage "Hero's Journey" framework is found in *Harry Potter and the Sorcerer's Stone*.

The Lion King	
The Ordinary World	Simba is heir to the throne in the Pride Lands
The Call to Adventure	Scar kills Mufasa and tells Simba to leave
Refusal of the Call	Simba, scared and alone, retreats to the desert
Meeting the Mentor	Timon and Pumbaa introduce Simba to life in the jungle
Crossing the First Threshold	Simba embraces the "hakuna matata" life
Test, Allies, Enemies	Nala finds Simba and the two fall in love
Approach the Innermost Cave	Nala asks Simba to return to the Pride Lands and take the throne from Scar
The Ordeal	Simba must choose to save his kingdom or to keep living his new life
The Reward	Mufasa's ghost tells Simba he must return to the Pride Lands
The Road Block	Simba returns and faces Scar
The Resurrection	Simba learns that Scar killed his father; Simba throws Scar off Pride Rock
Return With the Elixir	Simba ascends Pride Rock and reclaims the throne

Figure 8.2:

Vogler's 12-stage "Hero's Journey" framework is also found in *The Lion King*.

THE HERO'S TWO JOURNEYS

As I studied Vogler's new frameworks, I found an audio course he had created with Michael Hauge called "The Hero's 2 Journeys."[40] As you can probably guess, I was already geeking out on the Hero's Journey, and to open a loop like this—that there were potentially *two* journeys—well, needless to say I didn't sleep that night. I bought the course, listened to it a few times, and then called Michael Hauge and got to know him personally.

Hauge has been one of Hollywood's top script consultants and story experts for more than 30 years. He's the guy the top screenwriters and directors call to make sure their movies are following correct story structure for maximum emotional impact. He specializes in understanding the inner life of the characters and heroes in film as well as their character arcs and their invisible qualities.

While Campbell and Vogler talked about the hero's journey of achievement, Hauge brought to light the fact that inside every great story is an even more important second journey: the journey of transformation.

Think about it. Harry Potter may have beaten Voldemort, but who did Harry become on that journey? Simba may have killed Scar and reclaimed his throne, but what were the internal transformations Simba had during this journey? Most times the second journey is what gives the audience the biggest payoff.

In the movie *Cars*, Lightning McQueen doesn't get his journey of achievement; he loses the race. Just seconds before he crosses the finish line to get the thing he desires the most (the Piston Cup), he slams on his brakes and watches as Chick Hicks beats him. Lightning backs up, goes to find the King, who was in a huge wreck, and pushes him through the finish line. Through his entire journey, he has been doing everything possible to achieve his greatest desires, and then at the last minute, he gives them up to become something more. We see the death and rebirth of his identity. We see the new beliefs he has created. We see his transformation. That is the key to a great story.

THE HERO'S TWO JOURNEYS FRAMEWORK

After geeking out on stories for years, I tried to take all the things I learned from Campbell, Vogler, and Hauge, plus what I learned from mentors like Daegan Smith, and I built a story framework that simplified the core story concepts so you can become a great storyteller.

THE PLOT: CHARACTER, DESIRE, CONFLICT

Good stories are really simple. There can be layers of complexity, but at the core they are all very simple. Depending on the complexities I share, I can tell the same story in 60 seconds or 60 minutes—all with the same desired effect. Michael Hauge taught me that every good story is built on three foundational elements: character, desire, and conflict, also known as the plot.

Figure 8.3:

The plot of every good story has three simple elements: character, desire, and conflict.

For example:

> *Once upon a time, there was a girl named Little Red Riding Hood. She wanted to take a basket of cookies to her grandma, who lived in the woods. What she didn't know was that the Big Bad Wolf was waiting to gobble her up.*

- **Character:** Little Red Riding Hood
- **Desire:** Take a basket of cookies to her grandma
- **Conflict:** Big Bad Wolf

These are the basic elements of every movie, book, play, TV show, opera—really, any type of story. After showing me this, Hauge explained, "Every good story is about a captivating character who is pursuing some compelling desire and who faces seemingly insurmountable obstacles to achieving it. That's it. If you've got those three things, then you've got a good story."

Phase #1: Separation from Ordinary World

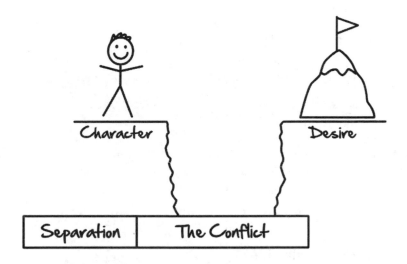

Figure 8.4:

In order for the character to go on a journey to achieve his desire, he has to separate from his ordinary world.

The story always starts with our hero in their own ordinary world. The first 25 percent of most stories involves the hero separating from something. During this separation it's essential that the storyteller gets the audience to care about the hero, so we have a vested interest in their journey. We do this through two things.

- Build rapport with the hero
- Introduce the desire

Build rapport with the hero: If we don't build rapport with the hero in the story, then no one cares what else happens to them on their journey. If you do a good job of building that rapport up front, the audience will be engaged throughout the story. You want people to build rapport with the hero quickly. We do that by giving our hero at least *two* of the following things:

- Make the character a **victim** of some outside force, so we want to root for them.

- Put the character in **jeopardy**, so we worry about them.

- Make the character **likable**, so we want to be with them.

- Make the character **funny**, so we connect with them.

- Make the character **powerful**, so we want to be like them.

Introduce the desire: Every story is about a journey either toward pleasure or away from pain. There are four core desires that drive most heroes: to win, to retrieve, to escape, or to stop. Two desires move the hero toward pleasure, and two desires move the hero away from pain.

Toward pleasure

- *To win:* The hero may be trying to win the heart of someone they love, or they may want to win fame, money, a competition, or prestige. But as you now know, they are really looking for an increase in status.

- *To retrieve:* The hero wants to obtain something and bring it back.

Away from pain

- *To escape:* The hero desires to get away from something that's upsetting or causing pain.

- *To stop:* The hero wants to stop some bad things from happening.

Phase #2: The Journey, the Conflict, and the Villain

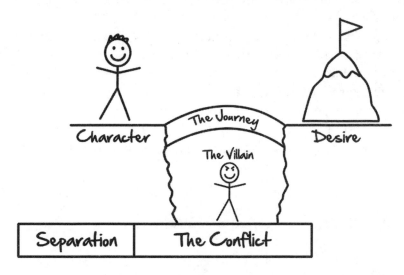

Figure 8.5:

The villain's role in the story helps us root for the hero to achieve his desire.

During this next phase, our hero has left the ordinary world to pursue their desire. This is the first journey, the one that everyone listening to the story is aware of. There's a visible goal with a finish line that the audience can see. It's the reason the hero sets out on the journey in the first place. We are all rooting for the hero to accomplish this journey. While this journey is what drives the story forward, it's the second journey that matters the most. In fact, in many stories the hero never actually achieves their end desire. Or if they do, they give it up for the real transformational journey that they've been on throughout the story.

During this journey there will be different points of conflict they encountered along the way. The conflict is what makes the story interesting. The number one tool we have to create conflict is to introduce a villain. The worse the villain is, the stronger the bond the audience will have with the hero.

Batman has Joker, Luke Skywalker has Darth Vader, and your hero will need a villain to fight against too. The villain can be a person, or it could also be a false belief system. Our job is to vilify the belief system and defeat it so we can give our audience the truth.

Campbell, Vogler, and Hauge have many different frameworks showing the different turning points of conflict, as well as the types of characters that are in most stories to help or hurt a hero along their journey. If I had room, I would add another 200 pages in this book going deep into conflict, but it's outside the scope of what most of you will be using your story for inside your funnels. Just know that conflict in your story is the key to the emotional connection with your audience.

Phase #3: The Mentor/Expert/Guide

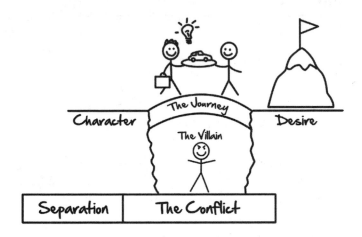

Figure 8.6:

The hero can't achieve desire without the help of a guide.

During the journey, the hero meets a mentor or guide to help them along the way. Think about almost any movie—our hero always finds a guide. Luke Skywalker has Yoda, Rocky has Mickey, Frodo has Gandalf, and Moana has Maui. I could go on and on, but hopefully you're thinking about your favorite movies and identifying the hero, the villain, and now the guide.

For our purposes with storytelling, the guide is the person who gives us the epiphany and the frameworks. Sometimes the guide is an actual person who gives you your big aha; other times the guide could be God, giving you inspiration, ideas, and thoughts (epiphanies) that form your frameworks for the new opportunity.

The journey then becomes the hero using the plans/framework they receive from the guide to defeat the villain and achieve their desire.

Phase #4: The Achievement

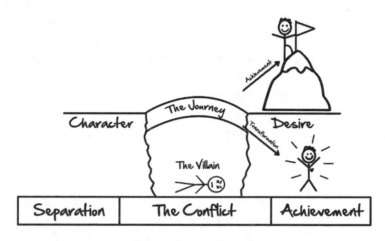

Figure 8.7:

As the hero finally ends their journey, they're transformed into a new person.

This last phase is where the hero finishes their journey. Sometimes heroes get what they have been trying to achieve throughout the story, and oftentimes they don't. Rocky Balboa didn't beat Apollo Creed, and Lightning McQueen didn't win the Piston Cup, but during their journey both heroes were transformed. This is the hero's second journey. Who have they become and how have they evolved? This journey is the death of their old identity, and their rebirth as a new person. This invisible journey is the real journey that our hero has been on the whole time.

I created this simplified framework of the Hero's Two Journeys to help me see the most important aspects of good story framework. As I was studying, I found a lecture where Christopher Vogler said, "As you listen . . . to anyone's ideas . . . you'll find *Oh, there's a useful idea,* and *That's right, I agree with that,* and *That, oh, I never thought of that before.* But at some point . . . you make up your own [ideas] and you create your own lingo, your own shared language with the people that you work with. . . . Absorb it, take notes, and pull out a piece here and there that sounds right to your observation of the world. This is all about how you perceive things as an artist, so you've got to make it your own."

After hearing that, I realized that while Vogler took Campbell's 17-step framework for myths, legends, and folklore and built a framework that was very specific for film, I needed to take both concepts and my experience of more than 15 years of using stories to sell products online and make a framework that would be simple: first for me to use, and later, after I had perfected it, to introduce to my people. In the next secret I will be sharing my framework that is built off the Hero's Two Journeys, but modified and simplified for use inside your funnels.

THE EPIPHANY BRIDGE SCRIPT

It's the question I had been asked almost daily since we launched ClickFunnels, and although I love funnels more than any other human on this Earth and had spent countless hours trying to figure out a quick way to answer the question, I didn't have one.

"So . . . what is a funnel?" a woman asked me.

I smiled for a second, knowing that the only way I could get her to understand was to tell her a story. "Do you mind if I tell you a quick story about how I found out about funnels? I think that'll be the best way for you to understand what they are." She agreed, and I started my Epiphany Bridge story about how I discovered funnels (my new opportunity).

THE BACKSTORY

Backstory/Desire? When I was in college, I met my wife, Collette, and fell in love. I asked her to marry me, and though she said yes, I know she was nervous because I didn't have a job or any prospect of a job.

(External) I was a student athlete wrestler, and NCAA regulations wouldn't let me get a full-time job, so she was working two jobs to support us. I wanted to make money to help support my wife and myself on our new journey together.

(Internal) But what I really wanted was to figure out a way my wife could retire from her job and we could start our family. She wanted to be a stay-at-home mom more than anything else in this world, and I wanted to give that gift to her soon.

Old vehicle? I tried a lot of different things to make money online that didn't work. I tried selling things on eBay, and I set up websites to sell computer parts with no success. Everything I tried ended up costing me more money than I made. Each new experiment I tried got us deeper and deeper in debt.

THE JOURNEY/CONFLICT

The call? At about that time I saw some people who were selling "how to" information products online and it seemed like they were doing really well. So I decided to create my first "how to" product; the problem was that I didn't have any unique skills that I thought people would pay for. The only thing I could think of that might work was that a few weeks earlier I had made a potato gun with a friend. I talked that friend into letting me film us making a potato gun, and I turned it into a DVD that I eventually started to sell online.

Villain? The way I ended up selling the DVDs was by setting up a simple website and buying Google ads that promoted the DVD. I spent about $10 a day on ads, and sold on average one DVD per day priced at $37. I was finally having success with my own business. But then Google decided to change the rules. They increased advertising costs dramatically, and soon I was spending more than $50 per day to sell a $37 DVD.

What if? Almost overnight my business stopped working. That meant that I either needed to quit wrestling and get a job, or my wife would have to continue working two jobs to support us. Both options seemed horrible, and I felt completely hopeless.

NEW OPPORTUNITY

Guide? I ended up turning off my Google ads because we were losing so much money every day. About a week later I got a call from someone I had met online who was doing a similar business to mine, selling "how to" information online. His name was Mike Filsaime and I had assumed that because my business was now dead, that his was too.

Epiphany? I asked Mike how he was doing, and he told me that business was better than ever before. Confused, I asked him how, and then he gave me the big aha. He told me that he had added one step to his website that changed everything. He said that it was similar to how McDonald's works. After you order a Big Mac, they ask if you would also like fries and a Coke. After someone bought one of his products, he added an upsell page asking them if they wanted to buy one of his other products at a discount. He said that one out of three people who bought his first product ended up buying his upsell as well! Because of that he was making more money from each customer and he could now afford to keep paying Google for traffic.

I got so excited. I quickly tried to find something that I could add as an upsell after people bought my potato gun DVD. I found a company that sold potato gun kits, and I worked out a deal where I could sell the kits and they would ship them to the customer. I added that upsell, created my very first funnel, and just like Mike said, one out of three people who bought my DVD ended up buying the potato gun kit! I made enough money to pay for the Google ads and keep a hefty profit!

New opportunity? I realized from that experience that the secret to success online wasn't what I was selling, but how I was selling it. This simple funnel was the secret to me selling a lot more potato gun products.

THE FRAMEWORK

Strategy? I got so excited by the secret I had discovered that I wanted to see if it would also work for other products. Soon I launched funnels selling weight-loss products, dating advice, couponing classes, network marketing, iPhone apps, supplements for people with diabetic neuropathy, and more. I found that some of the funnels I created worked better for online businesses and others worked better for service-based businesses. I tested hundreds of different variations and started building different funnel frameworks for each type of business. I found frameworks that worked for generating leads, others for selling physical products, and others for services.

Your results? Each market my company went into, if we created the funnel the right way, it would explode overnight. We created one funnel that generated more than 1.5 million leads in just six weeks! We've created funnels that have taken a brand-new start-up to eight figures in sales in less than a year! We've also used some of our funnel frameworks to generate more than $2 million in sales for a charity that we believe in.

Others' results? As exciting as that is, I've also shared these frameworks with thousands of other entrepreneurs. I've watched as Brandon and Kaelin Poulin have taken their LadyBoss start-up from an idea to a business with funnels that help more than a million women with their weight-loss journeys. I've seen Dr. Anissa Holmes fill her dental practice with hundreds of new clients each month and help countless other dentists do the same thing!

ACHIEVEMENT AND TRANSFORMATION

Achievement? After I learned about funnels, my wife was able to quit her job. The funnels my company has created generate more than a thousand new leads per day and generate millions of dollars in sales each month.

Transformation? But what was even cooler than that was my wife was able to retire from her job. She was able to become a stay-at-home mom, and we now have five amazing kids! On top of that, we've watched as hundreds of other entrepreneurs have been able to free themselves and better serve their audiences because of the funnels they've used to launch their companies.

"Wow, I run a _____ company, do you think a funnel would work for what I do?" is usually the response I get from most people after sharing my Epiphany Bridge story. Depending on who I am telling it to, I determine which sub-stories I'll then share. If I were speaking to a dentist, I wouldn't share Kaelin Poulin's results, but I would tell Anissa Holmes's story. If I had two minutes to tell that story, I could, but if you gave me two hours, I could tell a lot more of the details, I could share more emotion, and I could help you have stronger feelings about it. Regardless of how I tell the story, though, it always fits into that five-step framework.

THE EPIPHANY BRIDGE FIVE-STEP FRAMEWORK

The Epiphany Bridge script is an adaptation of the Hero's Two Journeys that I have been developing over the past five years. I use this for podcasts, Facebook Lives, ads, emails, sales videos, webinars, speaking engagements, and pretty much anytime I tell a story (which is a few dozen times a day). After perfecting this script, I gave it to my Inner Circle members and have watched as they've used it to make hundreds of millions of dollars in sales. It is just 5 phases and answers 14 questions that, depending on time, I can use to tell a story in 2 minutes or 2 hours. I can expand on each detail to fit the time allotted.

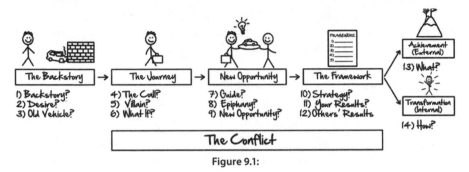

Figure 9.1:

The Epiphany Bridge script is the framework for telling stories in videos, podcasts, webinars, and more.

I keep a picture of the framework for the Epiphany Bridge script on my desk, and I use it all the time when I'm telling my stories. You'll be telling a lot of stories too, so mastering this script will become one of the most important things you will do as an expert. All you have to do is answer these 14 questions to tell your full story. I will go into more detail for each question later, but for now, let me show you how quickly it can work just answering these questions.

Phase #1: The Backstory

1. What is your BACKSTORY that gives us a vested interest in your journey?

2. What is the DESIRE or result that you want to achieve?

   External: What are your external desires?

   Internal: What are your internal desires?

3. What are the OLD VEHICLES that you tried in the past to get this same result that didn't work for you?

Phase #2: The Journey

4. What was THE CALL or the reason that made you start on this journey?

5. Who or what is THE VILLAIN that is keeping you from having success?

6. WHAT will happen if you don't have success on this journey?

Phase #3: New Opportunity

7. Who was the GUIDE who gave you the epiphany?

8. What was the EPIPHANY you experienced?

9. What is the NEW OPPORTUNITY you created from this epiphany?

Phase #4: The Framework

10. What is the STRATEGY or frameworks you developed to get you to the desire you wanted to achieve?

11. What were THE RESULTS you got by following the frameworks?

12. What were OTHERS' RESULTS from following your frameworks?

Phase #5: Achievement and Transformation

13. WHAT end result did you accomplish or achieve? (External Desires)

14. HOW did you transform during your journey? (Internal Desires)

For many of you, this outline and these questions will be enough to give you the framework to tell any story. But I want to dig a little deeper into each question so you have a clear understanding of how to answer those questions.

THE EPIPHANY BRIDGE SCRIPT

The Backstory

Figure 9.2:

Your backstory will share your external and internal desires as well as all the old vehicles you tried in the past to achieve your desires.

Backstory? What is the backstory that gives us a vested interest in your journey? Most good stories start with the backstory. For an Epiphany Bridge, that means remembering where you were before you had your big aha. Go back to that time and place and remember the circumstances that caused you to start on your hero's journey. Usually this backstory starts at about the same point where your listener is in their life right now.

They desire the same result that you have already achieved. But when they see you as the expert and see what you've accomplished, it can be hard for them to relate to you and trust you. That's why you must come down from your positioning as an expert and return to the beginning, when you were struggling with the same things they are. When they see that you were once where they are now, they will have faith that you can take them where they want to go.

Desire? Here is where you talk about what it is that you desire the most. As you learned earlier, your desire is usually to win, retrieve, escape, or stop.

(External) The external struggle is what drives the journey of accomplishment—the hero's first journey. People are usually willing to share their external struggles, "I'm trying to lose weight" or "I want to start my own company and make some money."

(Internal) The internal struggle is the journey of transformation from fear to courage—the hero's second journey. Sometimes it's hard to share or even know what the actual internal struggles are. But if you're willing and able to get vulnerable and share your internal struggles, this will build rapport faster than anything else you can do. Why? Because your audience also shares these same internal struggles. Most people never talk about them, but when the audience hears you get vulnerable and expose what you are really struggling with, they will form an almost instant connection with you.

When you get to the end of the story, typically you've solved the external struggles and accomplished what the hero has set out to do. But for your story to be truly impactful, the hero needs to have done more than just accomplish their goal. They need to have become someone different in the process.

Old vehicle? The backstory builds rapport with the character, then takes the listener to the moment of frustration that causes your hero to start on their journey. Chances are this wasn't the first time that you have tried to achieve this desire or result. Tell them about the other vehicles you tried that didn't work for you. This wall is the frustration you felt because of the current opportunity you have been using to try to accomplish your desires. This old opportunity is not working and it's the reason you (as well as your listeners) are willing to go on a journey to try something new.

The Journey/Conflict

Figure 9.3:

As you share the beginning of your journey, we're introduced to the villain in your story, which creates conflict.

The first 25 percent of any story is spent with the hero in the "ordinary world." During that time we get to know and care about them, find out what their desires are, and learn what things they have tried in the past to get the result they desire.

This next phase in the story is where they change their desire from something they *should* do into something they *must* do. Usually something happens that causes the hero to do something drastically different and leave where they are comfortable to start a journey into the unknown.

The call? In your story, this is where something happens that causes you to go on the journey. It may have been a feeling or impression you got, something you learned, or an event you went to. Something happened that made you decide to try again to reach your desire, despite the failures you had in the past.

Villain? As you start this journey, who or what are the things that are fighting against you? For your story, the villains are often false beliefs that are holding you back or belief systems that are hurting the market you are in. This is the person or ideas that you will be throwing stones at.

What if? If you don't know what's at stake, it's hard to get excited about the outcome. If you don't have success this time, what does that mean? What is the worst-case scenario if you don't achieve what you are searching for?

New Opportunity

7) Who Is the Guide?
8) What Was the Epiphany?
9) What Is the New Opportunity?

Figure 9.4:

To explain your new opportunity, share who (or what) led you to your new idea.

In this third phase of the story, the hero discovers the new opportunity. Your goal in this phase is to help your listeners feel how you felt when you experienced the epiphany for the first time.

Guide? The guide can be a person or it can be an inspiration from God. Sometimes for me the epiphany comes directly from something someone said to me, and other times it's an idea that comes while I'm moving forward on my journey. Who is the guide who gave you this epiphany?

Epiphany? What is the big aha moment that gave you the missing piece? The goal is to get your listeners to have the same aha that you had as you tell the story.

New opportunity? From this epiphany, what was the tangible thing that you were given or that you decided to create? This is where the opportunity switch takes place that you change from the old vehicles you used in the past to try to get your desired result to this new vehicle.

The Framework

Figure 9.5:

As you share your frameworks, explain the strategy behind them and share the results you and others got by using them.

186

Now that you've discovered the new opportunity, this is where you build and test your frameworks to see if the new opportunity is the one that is going to get you to your desired result.

Strategy? What is the plan that you put together to try and apply this new opportunity? What are the frameworks you've built based on what you've learned from your guide?

Your results? What are the results that you got from applying these frameworks? You are the human guinea pig; share this part of the story so we can understand how these frameworks could work for us as well.

Others' results? After you got results for yourself, did these frameworks work for others? If so, please tell us the case studies and results that others have also had with this new opportunity.

Achievement and Transformation

Figure 9.6:

Give closure by sharing not only what you accomplished
but also how you transformed on your journey.

This is the last phase of the story. It's the payoff for the listener who has now gone on this journey with you.

Achievement? When you started on this journey, you set out to achieve a desired result. Share the aftermath of what happened so people can see the results that you got from the new opportunity.

Transformation? Here you talk about who you became through this process. This is the resolution of your internal struggles—the death of the hero's identity and the rebirth of your new belief systems.

As you will see in the next secret, the goal of good stories is to break old belief patterns and rebuild them with new ones. When you create your stories this way, you are helping people break free from their old belief systems and create a new future.

That's the script for writing an Epiphany Bridge story. We've covered a lot here, so you could understand the power behind each section of the Epiphany Bridge story. But remember that stories are simple by nature. You can make stories more complex by going deeper into the settings, emotions, other characters, etc. But at their core, they follow a very simple progression.

THE 30-SECOND EPIPHANY BRIDGE SCRIPT

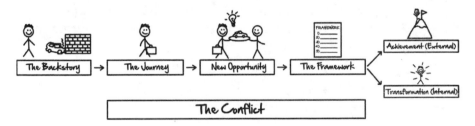

Figure 9.7:

To share a shorter Epiphany Bridge story, simply skim the surface of the five core steps.

There are many times when you won't have the convenience of spending 10 or 20 minutes telling a full Epiphany Bridge story. Other times, like in the Perfect Webinar framework, you will be telling one big Epiphany Bridge story, followed by a lot of smaller stories to quickly break any other false beliefs that weren't covered by the main story. When I do these faster versions of my story, I don't answer all 14 questions, but I do make sure to cover each of the five phases. For example, here is how I could tell my potato gun story if I had only 30 seconds:

Backstory: I wanted to make money to support my wife.

Journey: I started selling potato gun DVDs but later got shut down by Google.

New Opportunity: Mike Filsaime told me about an upsell, and I discovered funnels.

Framework: I built funnel frameworks to grow my companies.

Achievement: I made a ton of money, and my wife retired so she could have kids and be a stay-at-home mom.

The majority of the time your stories will cover only these five phases. When time permits you can go into more detail answering each of the questions under each phase.

Now that you understand story structure and you've created your first Epiphany Bridge story, in the next section we are going to dig deeper into the false beliefs people have about your new opportunity, and then look at the stories we need to create to break these false belief patterns.

THE FOUR CORE STORIES

My wife and I had been invited to come to a private mastermind meeting in Puerto Rico with some of the top personal development and marketing gurus in the world. Sitting around that small table was more than a billion dollars a year in sales among the companies that were represented. One of the guys who I looked up to the most in that group is Craig Clemens. I consider him one of the best living copywriters on the planet today.

When I first became aware of Craig, I found a few of the video sales letters he had written, and they were so good, I used to watch them over and over again on my big-screen TV the same way I would a new blockbuster movie. What's crazy to me, though, is the fact that while the goal of most Hollywood films is to gross a billion dollars in sales while they are in the theaters, Craig's sales videos have been so powerful that they've grossed his company more than a billion dollars in sales online in just the past few years.

As we sat around the table that day, on a small porch overlooking the ocean, Craig made a comment that I'm pretty sure most people missed. It was so simple, yet so powerful, I'll never forget it. He said: "My goal in my marketing is to rewrite the story that's inside of people's heads."

Tony Robbins once said, *"Every day we tell ourselves stories. We create stories to give meaning to our lives, to justify what we want to experience or feel, and to give ourselves a framework upon which to build future stories."*[41] It's interesting to note that the amazing things you've been able to create and accomplish in your life have happened because there are stories you believe that have allowed you to move forward with certainty. The stories you believe have created the identity you have today. If you believe that you can lose weight, you will. If you believe that you will have success starting a business, you will. If you really believe that you will be successful, then you will.

But what about the other stories that we tell ourselves—the ones that don't serve us? Stories about why things may work for other people but not for us. Stories about why we aren't qualified or worthy to do the thing we've been called to do. Those who don't believe they will be able to stick to a diet, don't. Those who don't know if they'll be successful with their own business, aren't. It's as simple as that.

The stories you believe will form your identity and shape the direction of your life. If you change the stories you believe, you can create an identity shift and change the direction of your life.

When Craig said, "My goal in my marketing is to rewrite the story that's inside of people's heads," I realized that our only real goal in any of our marketing is to identify the false beliefs and false stories our customers are telling themselves—the ones that are keeping them from success—and to rewrite these stories inside their minds.

I always tell people that my job as head funnel nerd of the Funnel Hacker community is to get people to believe that funnels will work for them. That is my only responsibility. If I can get you to believe it will work for you, then it will. You'll put in the work and effort necessary to have success. If you don't believe it, you may start the journey, but there is no way you'll ever finish it. The same is true for the people you are leading. Your number one job is to get them to believe that the new opportunity you created for them is the key to their desired result.

The way we do that is to figure out the false beliefs that people have regarding what we are trying to offer them and what stories they are telling themselves about it, and then we have to rewrite their story. If they already had the correct story in their mind, they would have already achieved their desired result. Our job as a marketer and a storyteller is to rewrite that story.

HOW WE REWRITE THEIR STORY

The first thing you have to understand is how people write their stories and create their beliefs. It all starts with an experience that happened in their life. It could be positive or negative, but immediately after they have that experience, their mind quickly creates a story about what that experience meant. Their brain then takes the story they've created and it becomes a belief.

Now, depending on the experience and the story, that belief may serve and protect them, or it may create a false belief that keeps them from what they really want. These belief systems form the foundations for our lives. We create these beliefs to keep us safe and to safeguard our status. And while they've been developed to protect us, oftentimes they're also the things that keep us from progressing in our lives.

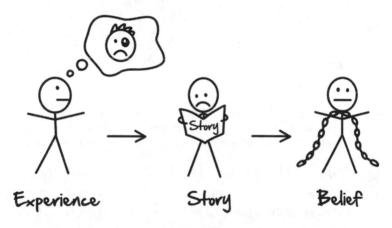

Figure 10.1:

When people have a bad experience, they create a story that they tell themselves; this story holds them back with "chains" of false belief.

This process has been happening every day of your life and has created you and the belief systems you hold on to today. Isn't it interesting that two people can have the exact same experience, but because of the story they create in their mind, it affects their beliefs about it?

When you first present your new opportunity to someone, almost instantly their subconscious mind will start looking through all the stories they have to see if what you are saying fits into their existing belief patterns. If it does, they will believe you. If not, they will be skeptical, and you will have to rewrite the story for them by telling them a better story—one that gives them the epiphany that will rewrite their story.

Let me show you how to identify the stories that we will need to rewrite with ours.

Figure 10.2:

To break someone's false beliefs, we have to identify the experience they went through that made them create the story they tell themselves. Then we have to share a story that breaks through their false beliefs and helps them form a new belief.

- **Chains of false belief:** The first step is to identify the false belief someone currently has that would keep them from believing in your new opportunity. If you struggle to figure out what your dream customer's false belief might be, think about what false beliefs you had before you went on this journey.

- **Experience:** After you've identified the false belief, determine the experience they likely had that made them believe the way they do.

- **Story:** Based on the experience they had, what is the story that they tell themselves now?

- **New Epiphany Bridge:** What story can you share that will rewrite the story that is causing the false belief holding them back, give them a new epiphany, and create a new belief?

To demonstrate how this works, I've included examples for two niches: weight loss and network marketing, or multilevel marketing (MLM). You can follow the same pattern for any niche.

Chains of false belief: What chains of false belief might your potential customer have about your new opportunity? If you're not able to think of false beliefs that your potential prospects might have, think about the false beliefs that you had before your big epiphany.

[Weight loss]

If I try to lose weight, I'm going to be miserable.

[Network marketing]

If I join a network marketing/MLM program, I could lose my friends.

Experience: Now that you have the false belief, the next step is to figure out the most likely experience your prospect had in their life that caused the false belief.

[Weight loss]

I tried to lose weight last year and had to cut out carbs; I was miserable.

[Network marketing]

One time I joined an MLM and tried to sign up my family members; they got mad.

Story: What is the false story they are telling themselves now that's creating doubt about your new opportunity?

[Weight loss]

I have to give up things that make me happy if I want to lose weight.

[Network marketing]

People have to bug their friends and family to have success in network marketing.

New Epiphany Bridge: Now it's your job to find an Epiphany Bridge story (usually from your own life, but it can also work if you share someone else's story) that shows how you once had a similar belief but because of this new story, you now have a new belief pattern and realize why the old story you were telling yourself was wrong.

[Weight loss]

I also thought I'd have to give up things that make me happy to lose weight. But then I learned about ketosis and how I can lose weight by drinking ketones instead of cutting carbs.

[Network marketing]

I also thought I might offend my friends if I joined an MLM, but then I learned that I can generate leads online. The internet is full of people who want to join my program! So I can grow my team without involving my friends or family.

Do you see how this works? When I first started to understand this concept, I realized that stories are the keys to belief. If I can identify people's false beliefs and tell stories that show them the truth, I don't need to "sell" them anything. The stories lead people to the right belief, and they sell themselves.

If you've ever heard me speak, you know I share a lot of stories. In fact, during a recent presentation, one of my friends counted the number of stories I told within the first 60 minutes. I had guessed the number might be 10 or so, but the total ended up being more than 50—almost one per minute! Some longer stories may take anywhere from 5 to 10 minutes, while others are often less than a minute. Each story I tell has a purpose, which is to break a false belief that I know my listeners have.

WHAT STORIES DO I TELL? (THE FOUR CORE STORIES)

It's important to understand that I don't just tell random stories for fun. Each story I share with my audience has a very specific purpose. It's to break a false belief that they may have and rewrite it with a new empowering belief that will give me the ability to serve them.

Inside the selling framework that you will learn in the next section of this book, I use four core stories to break the false beliefs of the people I am presenting to. The four stories are:

1) Your origin story with the new opportunity: This is the Epiphany Bridge story that tells how you discovered your new opportunity. Of all the stories you share, this is the one that will follow the Epiphany Bridge script the most closely. It is usually the first story I tell, so I spend more time going into my backstory, the journey, the guide that gave me the epiphany in this new market, the frameworks I developed, and my success as well as others' success following the frameworks, and then I end with my story of achievement and transformation.

The goal of this first story is to break the false beliefs people have about the other opportunities they may be currently using to try to get their desired result. It shows that there is a new opportunity you've discovered that you will now be sharing.

> Example: When someone hears my origin story, they should believe that funnels are the best way to achieve the result they want.

2) Vehicle framework story (how you learned or earned it): The second story I tell is specifically about the new vehicle framework. Now that my audience knows about the new opportunity, I want to tell them about the framework. The story I share is about how I learned or earned this framework, and then I share the strategy (the what) of the framework.

> Example: I would share how I created my funnel hacking framework to figure out what funnels work the best and now model those for my new funnels. My stories would show how I learned or earned these frameworks.

3) Internal beliefs story: After someone learns about the strategy behind the framework, their next false belief will be about their ability to execute on the plan. Here I tell my Epiphany Bridge story about how I discovered that I could actually do it and share examples of how others just like them have as well.

> Example: They may believe that funnels are great, but they may not believe they have the technical abilities to create them. I need to show them through stories that they can.

4) External beliefs story: After someone believes in the vehicle and their ability to execute on it, the last false belief they have will be about the external forces they believe can stop them from being successful. Here I tell an Epiphany Bridge story that will break their false beliefs that some external force will keep them from being successful.

> Example: Even if they believe they can build a funnel, because they don't know how to drive traffic to that funnel they need a story to get them to believe that it's possible for them to actually drive traffic into their funnels.

In the next section you will see inside our sales scripts where we plug these stories in. I just wanted to bring them up now because our next exercise is about creating a story inventory. I want you to categorize each of your stories based on one of these four categories so that we have them at hand in the next section of the book.

BUILDING A STORY INVENTORY

Now that you understand the power of stories and have been thinking about the stories that you could tell your audience, the last step in this section is to start building up your inventory of stories. The reason that I am able to get onstage and talk for hours without notes at a moment's notice is because I have built up an inventory of stories.

The goal with this next exercise is to start building out your own stories. I don't want you to just pick random stories, though. Each one should be specifically designed to break a false belief that someone has and rewrite the story inside their mind.

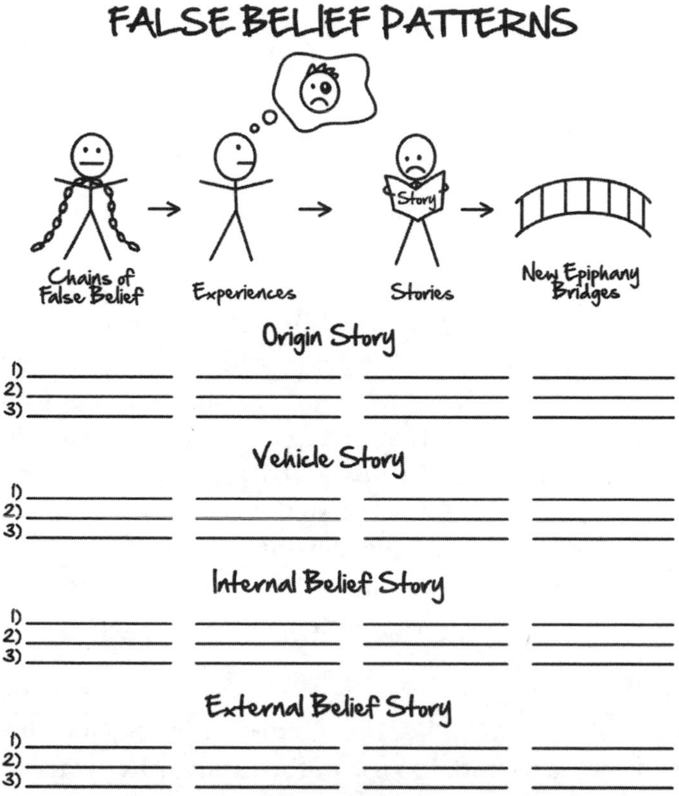

Figure 10.3:

Later you'll choose the best Epiphany Bridge story for each category, but for now you should create lots of Epiphany Bridge stories to break lots of different false beliefs.

Step #1—Chains of false belief: In the left column, list all the false beliefs your customers might have related to your new opportunity, followed by the vehicle frameworks, their internal false beliefs, and their external false beliefs. I have three lines for each category, but I'd suggest writing down dozens of false beliefs about each one.

If you struggle trying to figure them out, think about the false beliefs *you* had before you got started on this path. It's likely your audience holds those same beliefs.

Step #2—Experiences: Next to each false belief that you listed, write out what type of experience they may have gone through that gave them that false belief.

Step #3—Stories: Next to each experience, write down the story that the experience created in their mind. It's important to know exactly what story they are telling themselves so you can rewrite it with a new Epiphany Bridge story.

Step #4—New Epiphany Bridges: Think about your own Epiphany Bridge story for each of these false beliefs. What happened to change that belief for you? As you build out these steps for your customers, you'll notice that you had mostly the same beliefs, experiences, and stories. So just go back in time and remember what gave you the big aha that shattered those beliefs for you. Make sure you have a story for each false belief. If you don't have a personal story, it's okay to use stories from other people. Each of your stories will break your dream customer's false beliefs and rebuild new beliefs.

You might not use all of them, but you should start building up an inventory of stories to use in the future. After you complete all four steps, go back and practice telling your stories using the Epiphany Bridge script from Secret #9. The better you get at telling the stories, the more effective you'll become at persuading others and knowing exactly what to say when customers bring up objections.

SECTION THREE

"10X SECRETS": ONE-TO-MANY SELLING

On April 16, 2017, I received a life-changing phone call from Grant Cardone. He told me he was hosting his new "10X Event" in Las Vegas at Mandalay Bay, where 9,000 business owners and salespeople would be attending, and wanted to know if I'd be one of his keynote speakers.

Nine thousand people?! I didn't even know it was possible to get that many to attend an event like that. But I told him, "Sure, if you can pull off getting 9,000 people there, I'll come and speak."

"How much would you charge for that?" he asked.

I told him, "I want to make at *least* one million dollars if I'm going to leave my family for a weekend and come speak."

There were about five seconds of silence, and then I could hear him audibly laughing into the phone at me. "Russell, there is *no way* we're gonna pay you even a fraction of that!"

I smiled. "Okay, how about this, instead of *you* paying me one million dollars, what if I do your keynote for *free*?! But," I added, "I want to offer one of my products for sale at the end of the speech, and I'll even split the earnings with you fifty-fifty."

Grant laughed at me a second time, thinking he had easily gotten the better of me, but then he agreed. (If only he knew then how much that *one* speech would generate . . . ha ha!)

The deal was made, and after I hung up the phone, I told my team that we had a new goal. I wanted to *net* $1,000,000 in an hour. To do that, I'd have to sell $3 million in 90 minutes. Yikes, but I knew that with 9,000 people in the room, it would be possible.

We spent the next few months choreographing and strategizing how we were going to make this goal happen, and then, on February 23, 2018, at 10:30 A.M., I was scheduled to step out onto the stage. In that moment, it was kind of like Babe Ruth stepping up to the plate, calling his shot, and pointing out into the stands.

I had presented many, *many* keynotes before, but let me tell you, *nothing* can prepare you for looking out at a sea of 9,000 faces staring back at you, all of them hoping you'll have some nugget of wisdom that will change their life!

I was equal parts excited and a nervous wreck. I knew that what I was about to tell them would without a doubt change their business forever.

"Five minutes, and then you're on . . ."

The nerves turned into full-on butterflies in my stomach, and my heart started racing. My legs started fidgeting, and I began shifting my body side to side, side to side. (Anything to take my mind off the fact that I was about to talk to more than 9,000 people!)

Calm down, I commanded myself. In a fuzzy blur, I heard fragments of the blaring voice come over the loudspeaker, announcing the intro that had been written for me:

"Russell Brunson is an American Storyteller . . .

Sold hundreds of thousands of books . . .

Popularized the concept of sales funnels . . .

The internet's favorite entrepreneur . . .

Founder of ClickFunnels . . .

Internet genius . . .

PLEASE HELP ME WELCOME

MR. RUSSELL BRUNSON!"

I stepped out onto the stage, and something incredible happened—my butterflies finally went away and the excitement started pouring in. And then, slide by slide, I delivered my presentation. Just as we had agreed, at the end of the presentation I made a special offer to the audience. As soon as I made the offer, people jumped out of their chairs. They stampeded their way up the stairs and around the corner to our product tables.

The next six hours were a whirlwind. I stood in line taking pictures with each person who bought my product! After that, I went back to the hotel room to rest with my wife, Collette.

As soon as Collette and I laid down in the bed, we instantly passed out. I woke up two hours later and had to get an update. I ran up to the room where my team was processing orders and asked for the grand total.

Drum roll, please . . .

3.2 *Million* Dollars!

We did it!

$3.2 million with just one 90-minute keynote presentation, which means that my net take-home as a speaker was more than $1 million *per hour*, officially making me (at least for that one hour) the number one highest-paid speaker in the world!

ONE-TO-MANY SELLING

As I walked around the hallways over the next few days of the event, dozens of salespeople stopped me and told me that I was the greatest salesperson they had ever seen. I always smiled and said thank-you, but inside I knew I had a secret that they didn't.

I'm not the *best* at one-to-one selling, but I've mastered a different skill. I've mastered the lost art of One-to-*Many* Selling. Almost anyone could probably close a higher percentage than I could selling one-on-one, but because I'm able to speak to 100 people, or 1,000 people, or 9,000 people all at once, with *one* speech, and because I know how to craft and structure my presentation, I'm able to make *more* money in a fraction of the time!

When you are selling face-to-face, you have the unique ability to ask specific questions, get personal feedback, and resolve objections on the spot. When you're in an event, or selling inside a funnel, you can't really ask questions and get answers from *thousands* of people, so you need to create your presentation in a way that resolves all the objections that will come up for as many people as possible.

Now I know that some reading this are already thinking, *But Russell, I'm never going to speak onstage.* For those who are thinking that, I want to remind you that your platform and your funnels are your virtual stage. You will use them for your ads, the landing pages for your funnel, your live or automated webinars, your Facebook or Instagram lives, your YouTube videos, your podcasts, and more. The way you structure your selling presentations on these platforms are the same as how you structure a sales presentation from stage.

PLUGGING IN YOUR OFFER AND STORIES

In this section I will be showing you the framework I use for one-to-many selling. When you learn how to create a presentation like this and plug it into your funnels, it will give you true freedom.

While it's true that I made $3.2 million in 90 minutes doing my sales presentation from the stage, there is no leverage in that. I would have to go to another event and do that presentation again. Many people think I'm crazy that I don't travel the world speaking full time, but instead I retired from speaking publicly, because I have five amazing kids and I didn't want to miss their lives. I took those same presentations, recorded them, and plugged them into my funnels, and I do more revenue each week now on autopilot than I did from my 90 minutes onstage.

During this section you will take the Stack Slide you created with your offer in Section One (Secret #5) and the story inventory you built in Section Two (Secret #10), and you will plug them into my proven one-to-many sales framework.

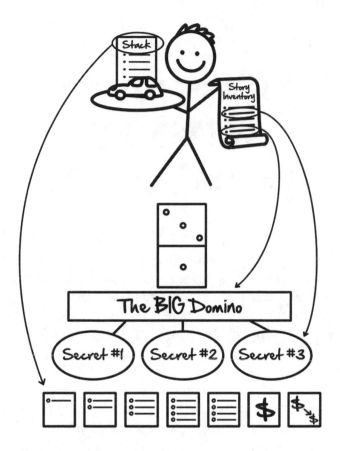

Figure 11.1:

You'll plug in your Stack Slide and Epiphany Bridge
stories into the Perfect Webinar framework.

I've perfected this script over the past decade, and it is now battle-tested in hundreds of different markets. It is the most powerful way for your dream customers to build a relationship with you as the expert, allowing you to break the false beliefs that are holding them back, rewrite the stories in their minds, and get them to take action on your offers. Of everything I've created and given to entrepreneurs in my career, this is the one that I am most proud of.

THE PERFECT WEBINAR FRAMEWORK

The first time I saw someone sell from stage, it changed my life forever. The speaker gave a 90-minute presentation and at the end made an offer. I watched in amazement as dozens of people ran to the back of the room to give this person thousands of dollars. I counted the people in the back of the room, did some simple math, and realized that he had made more than $60K in less than two hours!

I then saw the next presenter get onstage and follow a similar process, and within 90 minutes he had a table rush that made him more than $100K. I knew right then that I had to learn and master this skill at any cost.

A few months later I got invited to speak at my first event and I remember thinking that I was going to out-teach every other speaker up there. I would teach more stuff and better stuff and blow the minds of the audience, which I assumed would make people want to buy. I prepared for weeks, and when I finally got onstage I delivered the most content-packed presentation anyone had ever heard. After blowing their minds with what I shared with them, I made them a special offer to buy the new course I had just created. But what happened next shocked me.

Nothing. Nobody moved. I awkwardly walked off the stage and shook hands with some of the people in the room, and then snuck out the back door and ran to my hotel room. I was so embarrassed that I spent the rest of the event hiding in my room watching movies and eating Häagen-Dazs ice cream and coconut shrimp. It was one of the worst feelings I had ever felt to bomb like that in front of everyone.

I swore that I'd never speak or sell from stage ever again. I was going to sit behind my computer and just sell things online. But I discovered that the skills I needed to sell online were the same skills I was lacking when I spoke from the stage. So I decided to humble myself and learn. I didn't want to learn from people who were good speakers, but rather from people who could actually *sell* from their respective platforms (such as stage, teleseminars, webinars, sales videos, etc.). There's a *huge* difference.

What I discovered from the best people in the business was that teaching the best content hurts sales. But learning how to identify, break, and rebuild false belief patterns gets people to take the action they need in order to change. I learned how to tell stories, how to structure offers, and so much more. Then, for three years, I stood on stages all around the world, in front of thousands of people, and tested the presentations over and over and over again. I watched closely to see which topics (in what order) would make people run to the back of the room with their credit cards in hand. I also paid attention to what slowed my sales.

Then one day I decided I was tired of traveling and leaving my family behind. So I quit speaking from the stage, despite the fact that I was making $250,000 or more from a single 90-minute presentation. Instead I transferred these selling skills to the online environment. I tested my script on teleseminars and webinars. I used it for video sales letters, Facebook Live presentations, and more.

Each time I presented using this script, I'd watch the response and make tweaks. I did it over and over again, for years. Every so often I'll go and do an event like 10X that has a big enough crowd to make it fun, but outside of that I have retired from speaking from stages and I focus 100 percent on using this script inside my sales funnels.

A few years ago, I started teaching this script and process to my Inner Circle members. Dozens of them have implemented the script in almost any market you can dream of. It's battle-tested, it works, it's perfect. That's why it's been nicknamed "The Perfect Webinar." But in reality it's more than that. It's the perfect sales presentation, and it's worth mastering if you really want to get your message to your market.

THE FRAMEWORK

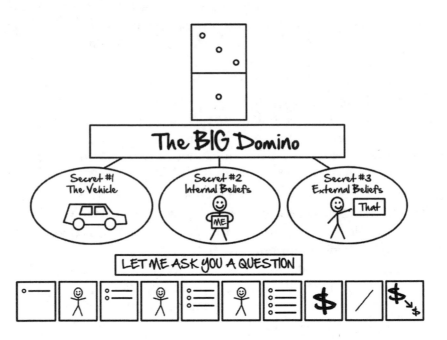

Figure 11.2:

The Perfect Webinar framework has three main parts: the Big Domino, the Three Secrets, and the Stack and Closes.

The framework revolves around three core phases.

1. The Big Domino
2. The Three Secrets
3. The Stack and Closes

I will introduce you to each of these sections as they fit into the overall framework here, and then over the next three chapters I will dive deep into each one and give you examples of how and why they work.

When I give this presentation at a live event or in a webinar, it usually fits into a 90-minute time slot. When I have 90 minutes, the time line looks like this:

- First 15 minutes: Intro, Big Domino, and Origin Story
- Next 15 minutes: Secret #1—Vehicle Framework Story
- Next 15 minutes: Secret #2—Internal Beliefs Story
- Next 15 minutes: Secret #3—External Beliefs Story
- Last 30 minutes: Stack and Closes

If I have only 30 minutes, I break it down like this:

- First 5 minutes: Intro, Big Domino, and Origin Story
- Next 5 minutes: Secret #1—Vehicle Framework Story
- Next 5 minutes: Secret #2—Internal Beliefs Story
- Next 5 minutes: Secret #3—External Beliefs Story
- Last 10 minutes: Stack and Closes

The ratios stay the same, you just expound longer on your stories and tell more short Epiphany Bridge stories to break more false beliefs if time permits.

THE BIG DOMINO

One of the biggest things to understand, and we'll go deeper into it in the next chapter, is that the presentation is not about getting your audience to believe a lot of things. The entire presentation is designed to get them to believe just *one* thing: that your new opportunity is the key to them getting the result they desire the most. That's it. If you try to get someone to believe in more than one thing, your sales will suffer.

Jason Fladlien once explained:

> *The idea is to have a **single point of belief** that your message is built around and is emphasized over and over and over again from a variety of different angles.*

The whole presentation is created to knock down that one domino, and that's it. The three secrets you're about to learn are not *new* things you're trying to get them to believe. They are the tools you use to attack the domino from a variety of different angles. That is the key to the Perfect Webinar.

Your first attempt to knock down the Big Domino is by telling your origin story about how you discovered the new opportunity. This story will kick off the presentation, build rapport between you and your audience, and introduce them to the new vehicle that you will be presenting.

THE THREE SECRETS

This is the content section of your presentation. I mentioned earlier that if you teach too much it will hurt, if not kill, your sales. This is where most people get tripped up, and the better teacher you are, the more you will struggle making sales because of this.

During the three secrets you will be teaching your frameworks, in a similar way to what you learned in Secret #2 of this book, with one exception. When you are teaching a course, you tell your story, explain the strategy, teach the tactics, and provide social proof. When you are selling, you do *not* teach the tactics. You teach the *what* (strategy) but not the *how*. Your audience's desire for the how is the reason they are going to give you money at the end of your presentation.

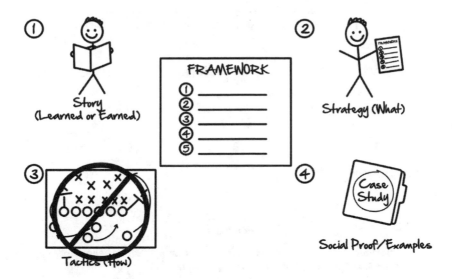

Figure 11.3:

When you're sharing your three secrets, you'll share the framework's
name, Epiphany Bridge story, strategy, and social proof/examples.

The goal of each **story, strategy, and case study** that you share
is meant to break a specific false belief pattern and rewrite the true
story in your listeners' minds. You need to identify the false beliefs
they have around the following:

1. The vehicle (new opportunity)

2. Their ability to use the vehicle (internal beliefs)

3. The number one thing they believe is keeping them
    from getting started (external beliefs)

You will teach story, strategy, and case study for each of the
three secrets.

THE THREE SECRETS

① The Vehicle   ② Internal Beliefs   ③ External Beliefs

Figure 11.4:

The three secrets are designed to break your customer's false beliefs and rebuild them into new beliefs so they're ready to take action with you.

Notice that the three secrets are not trying to get people to believe *new* things. They are simply false beliefs they already have about your Big Domino. If you knock down these three beliefs through the content section of the presentation, the Big Domino will fall and they will join your new opportunity.

STACK AND THE CLOSES

Here is where you move from the teaching to the sales portion of the presentation. You'll then present your offer in a very precise format we call the Stack, and you'll weave in some very specific closes that have been proven to persuade people to take the action they need in order to get results. And yes, you will be using your Stack Slide during this portion of the presentation.

Figure 11.5:

The Stack and the closes will help persuade people to act on your offer.

That is the bird's-eye view of the Perfect Webinar framework. After you master it, you'll be able to give a presentation like this on the fly. But it's important to really understand the objectives for each section. The next three chapters will break down each part of the Perfect Webinar slide by slide.

THE BIG DOMINO

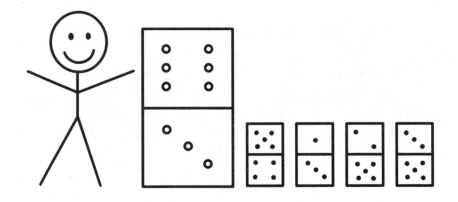

Figure 12.1:

If you can get your prospect to believe the One Thing (the Big Domino)
that will crush their other objections, then they will buy.

I was sitting in a room with about 120 other successful entrepreneurs, all of whom made at least a million dollars a year, a requirement to be in that room.[42] One of the featured keynote speakers was Tim Ferriss, the author of *The 4-Hour Workweek*. After his presentation, he opened the floor for questions. A woman stood up and asked, "Hey, Tim, you seem to get so much done. What is it that you do all day?"

He paused for a moment, then gave an awkward half-smile and said, "If you watched my daily routine, you'd be bored out of your mind.

"Most people wake up every morning with a task list of a thousand things to do," he continued. "They go through the day trying to knock down all these things. I do things differently. I wake up every morning and I meditate. I drink tea or coffee. I go for a walk, and maybe I read a book." He said he might spend three or four weeks doing that and nothing else. "My whole goal is to slow down and look around. Instead of looking for all the tasks that I could do, I try to identify the one Big Domino—the One Thing that, if I could knock *that* down, all the other dominos would either fall down or become irrelevant."

When he said that, I had an aha moment. I haven't yet figured out how to implement this in my personal life. But when it comes to how I sell things, I realize he was 100 percent right. The first step to creating belief is figuring out the *One Thing* you have to get someone to believe that will knock down all their other objections and make those objections irrelevant, or disappear altogether.

A little while later, I was talking to a friend and mentor, Perry Belcher. He told me how he had gone back and analyzed all the different offers that his companies had created and sold over the past 10 years.

He discovered that the more things they asked someone to believe in their sales pitch, the worse the offer converted. In fact, he figured out that if they tried to make more than *one* point or ask someone to focus on more than *one* thing in a sales message, conversion rates dropped by half! He said, "Look at how many things a prospect has to believe in order to buy what you're selling. If it's more than one, you need to rework your sales presentation."

After hearing that, I knew my team and I had to go back and look at everything we were selling. We asked ourselves, "What's the One Thing? What is the one Big Domino of belief that we need to knock down?" Every product has one Big Domino, One Thing that will knock down all the smaller objections and resistance. If we can get people to believe in that One Thing, then they will have to buy it.

I took a logic class in college that showed different ways to create valid arguments. One of the many valid argument forms is called "modus ponens."[43] It looks like this:

If A, then B.

A.

Therefore, B.

If I were to put this argument into a sentence, I'd say something like:

If Dallin doesn't finish his homework, then he will not get to play with his friends.

Dallin did not finish his homework.

Therefore, Dallin does not get to play with his friends.

If you think about it, you'll start to see patterns of this argument everywhere. Religion is an easy example. In Christianity, everything hinges upon the truth of the Bible. If someone believes the Bible is true, then they have no other option than to believe that Jesus Christ is the Savior. If he is truly the Savior, then all the other concerns you have about Christianity disappear.

If the Bible is true, then Jesus is the Savior.

The Bible is true.

Therefore, Jesus is the Savior.

As a Christian, if I can get someone to believe the Bible— their one Big Domino—then it knocks down every other domino and makes any other argument irrelevant to the person who has that belief.

But it's not just in religion. We see this happening everywhere around us, from politics to sports to the people we spend time with. That's why it's hard to have an argument with someone about something they truly believe in. When that seed of belief is there, it doesn't matter how much you try to convince them otherwise, it has already knocked down all the other smaller dominos that you're trying to stack back up.

THE ONE THING (THE BIG DOMINO STATEMENT)

When we launched ClickFunnels, I tried to figure out the one key belief that I needed my audience to understand and believe. I came up with this basic statement:

> **If I can make people believe that (my new opportunity/category) is/are the key to (the result they desire most) and is/are only attainable through (my specific vehicle/frameworks), then all other objections and concerns become irrelevant and they have to give me money.**

If I can get someone to *truly* believe that the new opportunity or category is the key to what they desire the most, and they can get it *only* through my vehicle or frameworks, then they have no other options but to buy. This is the key to launching your movement. Belief.

Here is what I used for ClickFunnels:

> **If I can make people believe that *funnels* are the key to *online business success* and are attainable only through *ClickFunnels*, then all other objections and concerns become irrelevant and they have to give me money.**

When someone believes they have to have a funnel (and they do), and that I present the only way they can get one, then they have to buy ClickFunnels. There is no other option.

I've helped my Inner Circle members create these statements for their businesses. We discovered that if we're struggling to make a valid argument that works, it's typically because we didn't create a new opportunity but instead have an improvement offer. If we haven't created a blue ocean, then the argument won't be valid.

For example, I've seen statements that say something like:

> **If I can make people believe that *cutting calories and exercising* is the key to *losing weight* and is attainable only through *my new weight-loss course*, then all other objections and concerns become irrelevant and they have to give me money.**

That statement is *not* true.

If the belief you are trying to give them is that they need to cut calories and exercise, there are a few problems.

- You are *not* in the Prolific Zone—you are in the mainstream.

- This is *not* a new opportunity. There are thousands of identical programs crowding the niche of "cutting calories and exercising."

- This is *not* a blue ocean. Customers could literally buy one of a hundred different products to satisfy the belief you created.

The niche and opportunity would need to change to something like this:

> If I can make them believe that *ketosis* is key to *losing weight* and is attainable only through *my proprietary framework that gets your body into ketosis within 10 minutes*, then all other objections and concerns become irrelevant and they have to give me money.

HOW TO KNOCK DOWN THE BIG DOMINO

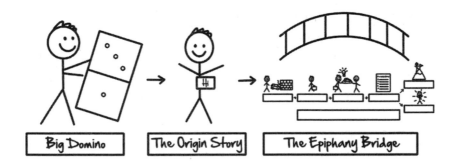

Figure 12.2:

In order to knock down the Big Domino, you can share your Epiphany Bridge story about how you discovered the new opportunity.

Now that you've identified the exact thing you need your audience to believe if they are going to take action at the end of your presentation, it's time to design everything around rewriting the stories in their minds with new, empowering stories that will better serve them.

Typically, I do this either in PowerPoint (for PCs), Keynote (for Macs), or my favorite, Google Slides, which works for everyone. Because of that, I'm going to teach the next few sessions slide by slide with an image to show the concept behind each one. If you're doing a webinar, this graphic will give you ideas on what you can put on your slides. If you're using this script as an email sequence or some other selling system, use the slides as a reminder of what you need to cover at each phase.

The first 15 minutes (or one-sixth) of your presentation is trying to knock down the Big Domino through your origin story. We break this time down into two phases: the introduction and the origin story.

THE BIG DOMINO SLIDES

Before I start creating my presentation, I want to be thinking about who it's for and what is the hook to get someone to come and watch the presentation?

Who/what statement: As a first step, I like to make a who/what statement that quickly addresses which submarket my message is for and what new opportunity they will be switching to. It reads like this:

> *I am going to teach* _____
> *(insert submarket)*
> *how to* _____
> *(insert result)*
> *through* _____
> *(insert your niche).*

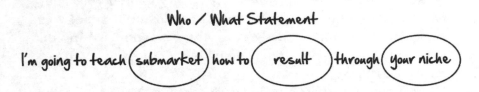

Figure 12.3:

Your who/what statement helps you quickly identify who you're serving,
what result you can deliver, and what new opportunity you've created.

Here are two examples of what that statement could look like.

I am going to teach real estate investors how to make money through flipping houses on eBay.

I am going to teach people who are sick of dieting how to lose weight by drinking ketones for energy and weight loss.

1: TITLE SLIDE

Figure 12.4:

This slide explains what your webinar is about.

The opportunity switch headline: Now that you know the *who* and *what*, you need to give the class a sexy title that will attract your dream customers. I try to create a title that focuses on the result this presentation will deliver. I do that by filling in this phrase:

> **How to (*result they desire most*) without (*thing they fear most*).**

So for my ClickFunnels masterclass, I could create something like this:

> **How to Create a Seven-Figure Funnel in Less Than 30 Minutes without Having to Hire, or Be Held Hostage by, a Tech Guy.**

Or for a Funnel Scripts presentation, our headline is:

> **How to Get *All* Your Sales Letters, Scripts, Webinar Slides, Emails, and Ads Written (in as Little as 10 Minutes) *without* Hiring an Expensive Copywriter!**

Here are some other examples for different niches:

> [Flipping houses on eBay]

> How to Make a Quick $10K This Weekend by Flipping Your First House on eBay without Getting a Loan from a Bank

> [Helping kids with ADHD]

> How to Destroy Your Kid's ADHD Naturally and Help Them Get Better Grades without Giving up Their Favorite After-School Snacks

> [Relationship coach]

> How to Reconnect with Your Wife and Find the Passion in Your Marriage without Having to Go through Painful Counseling or Wasting Time Talking

> [Weight loss through ketosis]

How to Stop Exercising and Still Lose Weight through a Little-Known Trick That Almost Instantly Puts Your Body into Ketosis, without Giving up Your Favorite Carbs

You can plug most any opportunity switch presentation into that framework and create quick titles that people will be interested in. There are many other headline frameworks you can use to title your presentation as well. We have a full chapter on headline scripts in *DotCom Secrets* you could use, or the easier route is using the funnel scripts software at FunnelScripts.com to generate headlines for your presentations.

Hey everybody! Welcome to the webinar. This is _____ and today I'm going to show you how to _____ without _____.

2: INTRO/RAPPORT SLIDES

Figure 12.5:

These slides build rapport with your attendees.

Earlier you learned about Blair Warren's one-sentence persuasion strategy. Remember he said, "People will do anything for those who encourage their dreams, justify their failures, allay their fears, confirm their suspicions, and help them throw rocks at their enemies." I like to cover this at the very beginning of my presentations as a way to build instant rapport with my audience. Here's how to do it.

Justify their failures: *Now I'm guessing for a lot of you this is probably not your first webinar. The first thing I want to mention is that if you've failed at _____ in the past, it's not your fault. There's a lot of information out there, and it can be confusing. Many times that information overload keeps you from success. It's okay.*

Allay their fears: *If you've been concerned in the past that you just can't succeed with _____, I want to put those fears to rest. You can do this. You just need the right person to explain it to you.*

Throw rocks at their enemies: *The big corporations want you to think that you need a lot of venture capital or some fancy college degree to be successful. I'm here to tell you they're wrong. They have their own reasons for wanting you to think that, but it's not true.*

Confirm suspicions: *If you've ever thought that the government and the banks want you to fail, you're probably right. They don't benefit from you succeeding. They want to keep you in debt and in need. The difference with us is that we actually care about your success and truly want to see you living the life of your dreams.*

Encourage their dreams: *So that's what we're here for. I know you have a dream to change the world and make an impact, and I want to show you how to make that happen during this webinar.*

3: THE RULER SLIDE

Figure 12.6:

This slide explains who your new opportunity is for.

The next slide is what I call the "ruler." It's the measuring stick people will use to judge your webinar. If you don't tell them what your goals are, even if you do everything perfectly they may be up-set because their goal is different than yours. So I like to tell people right away what my goals are, what I want them to get from the presentation. If they aren't looking for a similar goal, they have the opportunity to leave at that point.

The goal is always to help them to see that this new oppor-tunity will give them their greatest desires, increase their status, and help them achieve their goals. I also take this opportunity to be inclusive of any people who aren't sure whether they are in the right spot. I don't want people wondering during the whole presentation *Is this for me?* I want them to know up front that this is exactly what they need.

> *My goal for this presentation is to help two types of people. For those who are beginners, you'll get (what the presentation/ new opportunity will do for them, or how it will fulfill their desires). For more experienced people, you'll get (alternative).*

Sometimes my inclusion is for beginners versus advanced, but other times it's based on different parts of the market who may be watching. For example:

If you own a retail store, you'll get _____ from my presentation, but if you own an online store, you'll get _____ from the presentation.

4: THE BIG DOMINO SLIDE

Figure 12.7:

This slide shares your Big Domino statement.

This next slide is typically an extension of my goal, and it's where I reveal the Big Domino. Remember, they need to believe that your specific vehicle is the *only* way to get what they desire most. Remember the Big Domino sentence you created earlier? It looked like this:

If I can make them believe that (new opportunity) is key to (what they desire most), and/but it is attainable only through (specific vehicle), then all other objections and concerns become obsolete.

Here I say that my goal is to get them to believe that the new opportunity I am presenting is the secret to the result they desire the most.

> *In the next 90 minutes, my goal is to get you to believe that (new opportunity) is the key to unlock (what you desire the most), and I'm going to show you my proprietary frameworks that will make it simple for you to achieve that result.*

5: QUALIFY YOURSELF SLIDE

Figure 12.8:

This slide shares your backstory and qualifications.

You have to be careful here, because one of the fastest ways to break rapport with your listeners is to talk about how great you are, but it's also essential for them to know that you are qualified to lead them. I talk briefly about one or two things from my highlight reel, and then I quickly move into my backstory to show that I started in a place just like them.

In the past __ years I've had an amazing chance to (cool thing you've done because of your new opportunity) and I've also been able to help other people to (awesome thing you did for others), but it wasn't always that way. In fact, just a few short years ago I was just like you . . . (transition into backstory).

6. EPIPHANY BRIDGE ORIGIN STORY SLIDES

Figure 12.9:

These slides tell your Epiphany Bridge origin story.

This is where you transition into your backstory for your first Epiphany Bridge story. You will have a chance to tell the origin story that helped you discover this new opportunity.

Because we spent a whole chapter on this script, I am not going to break it down slide by slide, but I usually have at least one slide for each of the 14 steps in this script.

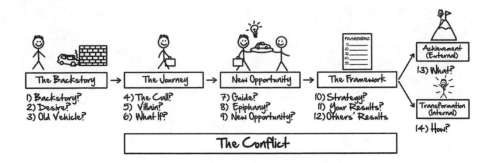

Figure 12.10:

To tell your Epiphany Bridge story, simply write down bullet
points for each of the 14 steps, then start telling your story.

This will be your first attempt to knock down the Big Domino. Some people after hearing this story will have the same epiphany that you had, and will be ready to take action when you are finished with this one story. Everything else you say from this point forward will strengthen their initial aha.

At this point you should be about 15 minutes (or one-sixth of the way) into the presentation. You've made your first attempt at getting your listeners to believe in your new opportunity, and now it's time to move on to the next phase of the script where you will be teaching the vehicle and internal and external frameworks that will help knock down the Big Domino.

THE THREE SECRETS

Figure 13.1:

If the Big Domino doesn't fall, you'll need to break
other false beliefs your audience has.

In a perfect world, you would present someone with your new opportunity, you'd know what the Big Domino was, you'd tell an Epiphany Bridge story to give them a new belief, the Big Domino would fall, and you'd have a customer or follower for life. Sometimes that does happen. One good epiphany story and they're all in. Many times, though, once you change that big belief for them, they immediately start coming up with other concerns. This is especially true with more expensive opportunities and big life changes.

STEP #1: IDENTIFY THEIR THREE CORE FALSE BELIEFS

I've found that there are three core false beliefs that come to the surface and keep someone from buying, even if they believe the new opportunity is right for them.

Figure 13.2:

Your prospects will have false beliefs about the vehicle, their own ability to use it, and external influences that will stop them from having success.

- **The vehicle:** other false beliefs they may have about the vehicle framework or new opportunity you're presenting
- **Internal beliefs:** beliefs about their own abilities to execute on the new opportunity
- **External beliefs:** false beliefs they have about outside forces that could keep them from success; things beyond the individual's control, such as time or the economy

In Secret #10, you started to build your story inventory with the false beliefs that you felt your dream customers had in each of these areas. You will be using these stories throughout the content section of the presentation, to rewrite the stories that are holding them back from success.

NEW OPPORTUNITY: NETWORK MARKETING

Chains of False Belief	Experiences	Stories	New Epiphany Bridges
VEHICLE: Network marketing doesn't work.	I tried to sign up my mom. She was mad.	If I try MLM, I'll lose my family.	You can generate leads online!
INTERNAL: I'm scared to talk to people.	I had an awkward call with a "prospect."	It's painful to do sales.	You can sell through email!
EXTERNAL: My friends won't sign up.	They made fun of me in the past.	It's impossible to close friends.	You can get interested leads online!

Figure 13.3:

This example shows the three core false beliefs that a prospect might
have when being introduced to network marketing and how a new
Epiphany Bridge can be created to break their false beliefs.

Look at the false beliefs that you listed in Secret #10, and decide which of those beliefs is the core one for each section that would keep the Big Domino from falling down. You will create Epiphany Bridge stories for each of those core false beliefs, and you'll also create Epiphany Bridge stories for the other false beliefs to use as supporting stories.

Let me show you how this works. If I were going to get someone to believe that funnels are the only way to 10X the growth of their company, and I told them my Epiphany Bridge story about why I think funnels are the greatest thing since sliced bread, here are the potential false beliefs that may come up for each section.

False Belief #1: The Vehicle

Funnels sound cool, but I don't understand how they would work for me.

False Belief #2: Internal Beliefs

I'm sold on funnels, but I'm not technically inclined, so I don't think I could build one.

False Belief #3: External Beliefs

I think I could build a funnel, but even if I did, I don't know how to drive traffic into it.

STEP #2: WRITE THREE EPIPHANY BRIDGE STORIES

Now that I have the three core false beliefs, I have to find the Epiphany Bridge stories that will break their core chains of false belief and create a new story for them.

False Belief #1: I don't understand how it would work for me.

For this, I share the Epiphany Bridge story about how I learned about the vehicle.

I tell them my Tony Robbins and Porter Stansberry stories showing them about modeling success, as well as my funnel hacking story about how we modeled the Marine-D3 funnel to build our Neuracel funnel and how they can do that with any successful funnel in their market.

I then teach them my framework to show them what the strategy is without the tactics.

False Belief #2: I'm not technical.

For this, I share the Epiphany Bridge story about how I overcame my own internal false beliefs of not being technical.

I tell the story about how I used to have a big tech team building funnels that cost thousands of dollars, and how we were able to change that after we built ClickFunnels.

I then give them my framework (strategy) for building funnels and show them a product demo so they see how easy it is, even if they are not technical.

False Belief #3: I don't know how to drive traffic.

For this, I share the Epiphany Bridge story about how I overcame external false beliefs of not knowing how to drive traffic.

I tell them my story about how I reverse engineer from where my competitors get traffic, so I can easily get traffic from the same places.

I then give them my framework to show them the strategy on how they can get traffic into their funnels.

STEP #3: WRITE THREE SECRETS

Finally, I rewrite each of the false beliefs with their accompanying Epiphany Bridge stories into a "secret" using a "how to" statement that hints at my framework being the key to their desired result. Curiosity is the key; I make sure the secrets cause curiosity so people will want to listen.

Here is how I rewrote my three core false beliefs into my three secrets.

Secret #1—Funnel Hacking: How to Ethically Steal More Than $1,000,000 Worth of Funnel Hacks from Your Competitors for Less Than $100

Secret #2—Funnel Cloning: How to Clone a *Proven* Funnel (Inside of ClickFunnels) in Less Than 10 Minutes

Secret #3—My #1 Traffic Hack: How to Get the Exact *Same* Customers Who Are Currently Going to Your Competitors to Start Coming to Your Funnel Instead!

Now that you have all these elements, you have the foundation you need to start creating the content section of your presentation. You've identified the one Big Domino that will get people to believe in your message, as well as the three core false beliefs that are holding that domino up. You'll then use stories to systematically knock down each of the beliefs holding up the Big Domino.

When all three of the core false beliefs have been knocked down, the Big Domino tumbles. When that happens, you have introduced the belief necessary for someone to take action. It's all about breaking the false belief patterns holding your prospects back and rebuilding true beliefs.

BREAKING AND REBUILDING BELIEF PATTERNS

Everything you have done to this point has been designed to encourage curiosity, build rapport, and introduce the new opportunity. Now we're transitioning to the content section of the presentation. You'll be tempted to switch into teacher mode at this point. And if you're not careful, it will destroy your sales.

This is not a teaching presentation; this is a presentation to inspire people to take action and change their lives. You can teach the strategy (what they need to do) but do not teach the tactics (how they need to do it).

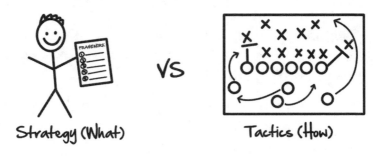

Figure 13.4:

In your Perfect Webinar, you'll teach your framework's strategy (the *what*) not the tactics (the *how*).

Teaching the tactics is what you do *after* they have purchased. If you do teach the tactics, it's the surest way to kill sales. Remember, you are providing a framework strategy, then focusing on identifying the false belief patterns behind the strategy, breaking them, and rebuilding them with the truth. If you don't break your listeners' false beliefs about the strategy, no matter how many tactics you give them, they'll never have success. They have to believe first, or everything else is pointless.

I'm sure that for some of you this concept doesn't make sense or you got a little upset about it. When I first tried to sell something I had created that I knew would change people's lives, I did it in teacher mode. I taught my best stuff, knowing that as soon as my audience heard it, they'd want more. Right? Wrong.

Instead, people told me my content was amazing, but because I didn't rewrite their stories in their minds, they went back to their same old patterns. That was a tragedy, to be that close to changing someone's life but not accomplishing it because I gave them the tactics before they were truly converted. While I was trying my best to help them, it actually hurt them because they didn't shift their beliefs, didn't buy anything, and never changed their lives. I was a failed expert and coach.

In New Testament times, Paul told the Corinthians (1 Corinthians 3:2), "I have fed you with milk, and not with meat: for hitherto ye were not able to bear it." If he would have given them the meat first, they couldn't have handled it yet, and the same is true for your dream customers. You must change their beliefs about your strategy first, then you can change their lives. But if you don't change their beliefs first, you'll never have a chance to change their lives.

I honestly believe that the greatest service you can provide for someone is getting them to buy something. The act of buying creates a commitment that causes someone to take action.

Dozens of my friends have come to my events as free guests, where someone sitting next to them had paid $50,000 to be in the same room. The strange thing is that so far none of these friends have ever launched successful businesses from the info they got at the event. None. Yet for those who paid to be in the room, our success rate is almost 100 percent.

One of my early mentors, Bill Glazer, explained that I was keeping people from success because I was teaching them. I was *so* confused, and it took a few years before I understood what he meant and how to change my method so that it would work.

Over the years, I slowly learned how to structure my content in such a way that it teaches and inspires, but also (and most important) causes people to take action. For some of you, this will feel strange at first because you aren't teaching all the cool tactics you want to share. But you need to understand that the type of teaching you are doing here is the foundation for change.

I remember being frustrated the first time I did a presentation this way, but when I was done, two very distinct things happened.

First, instead of making just a few sales like I normally did, I made hundreds of sales. And second, 10 times more people than usual told me that the content changed their lives.

It's kind of funny. Even though I wasn't teaching the tactics yet, I was breaking beliefs that had held them back for years and giving them new, empowering beliefs. This is actually teaching in its most pure form, it's just different than what you're used to. The time for teaching the tactics will come. But your customers need to come in with the right belief systems first.

THE THREE SECRETS SLIDES

For many people, the initial story will get them excited, but objections and false beliefs will also start to pop up as soon as you introduce the new opportunity. This is where you transition to the content section of the webinar, where you will start breaking and rebuilding their false belief patterns.

7: TRANSITION TO THE THREE SECRETS SLIDE

Figure 13.5:

This slide lists the three secrets.

Introduce what you're going to teach during the webinar. You already created the titles of these three secrets, so you can plug them in here and introduce them to everyone.

Here's what we're going to cover during the next 45 minutes or so:

Secret #1—Funnel Hacking: How to Ethically Steal More Than $1,000,000 Worth of Funnel Hacks from Your Competitors for Less Than $100

Secret #2—Funnel Cloning: How to Clone Their Proven Funnel (inside ClickFunnels) in Less Than 10 Minutes

Secret #3—My #1 Traffic Hack: How to Get the Exact Same Customers Who Are Currently Going to Your Competitors' Funnels . . . to Start Coming to Your Funnel Instead!

8: STATE SECRET #1 SLIDE

Figure 13.6:

This slide states the first secret to break false beliefs about the vehicle.

Here you quickly state the first secret.

*Secret #1: How to Ethically Steal More Than $1,000,000
Worth of Funnel Hacks from Your Competitors for Less Than $100*

INTRODUCE YOUR FIRST FRAMEWORK (THE VEHICLE)

During the next set of slides you will be presenting the first framework you alluded to during your origin story.

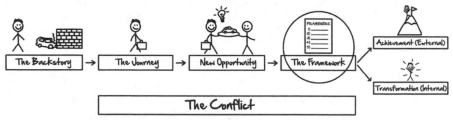

Figure 13.7:

**When you share your framework for the vehicle, it's the same framework
you discussed in your Epiphany Bridge origin story where you explained how
you discovered a proprietary framework to succeed with your new opportunity.**

They've heard you talk about it, they've seen your results with it as well as the results of others, *and* they've already seen how it's transformed you as a person. That information will become the first framework you introduce to them.

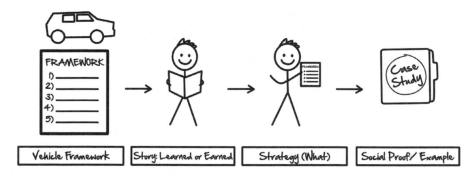

Figure 13.8:

**You'll introduce the vehicle framework's name, share the Epiphany Bridge story that you
learned or earned, teach the strategy (the *what*), and share social proof and examples.**

In this process we introduce the framework, share the story about how we learned or earned it, teach the strategy (what it is), and show case studies of others who have applied the framework.

9: INTRODUCE THE FRAMEWORK SLIDE (THE VEHICLE)

Figure 13.9:

This slide introduces the framework's name.

This slide introduces the framework your audience will be learning. They've already heard about it in your initial Epiphany Bridge story, so here you're going to remind them what it is and tell them what it's called. This is where they will start taking notes and open their minds to learn.

> *Remember earlier I told you about the framework we developed that helped me to (desired result)? Take out your pen and paper to take notes because I'm going to walk you through this framework. I call it (proprietary name for your framework).*

You're not teaching them the strategy behind the framework yet, you're just telling them what it's called and reminding them of what it did for you.

10: SHARE LEARNED OR EARNED STORY SLIDE (THE VEHICLE)

Figure 13.10:

This slide shares the Epiphany Bridge story that you learned or earned.

Now that they are ready to learn the strategy, you need to step back and tell them the story about how you learned or earned this framework. Without this preframe, your audience won't value the gold that you are about to give them.

Epiphany Bridge origin story vs. Epiphany Bridge vehicle story: Many people get confused here because they are not sure how this story is different from the origin story you told during the introduction. That story is your origin story about how you discovered the new opportunity and turned it into a framework. This story is about how you actually developed the framework.

Epiphany Bridge origin story: In my webinar that built ClickFunnels initially, the origin story I told was my potato gun story. The quick version is this:

> **Backstory:** I wanted to make money to support my wife.

Journey: I started selling potato gun DVDs, but got shut down by Google.

New opportunity: Mike Filsaime told me about an upsell; I discovered funnels.

Framework: I built funnel frameworks to grow my companies.

Achievement: I made a ton of money and my wife retired so she could have kids and be a stay-at-home mom.

Epiphany Bridge vehicle story: This second Epiphany Bridge story I am telling here is all about the vehicle framework. How did I discover it? For those who have seen that presentation, here are the highlights inside the Epiphany Bridge framework:

Backstory: Tony Robbins said to model people who were successful.

Journey: I launched a supplement company; it struggled.

New opportunity: I funnel hacked a competitor and saw their funnel; my team and I modeled it and sales 10Xed overnight.

Framework: How to funnel hack

- Step #1: Find a funnel to model.
- Step #2: Funnel hack it (buy the product and see the funnel structure).
- Step #3: Create a blueprint for the funnel you need to build.
- Step #4: Build that funnel in ClickFunnels.

Achievement: My success story and lots of stories from other Funnel Hackers!

You'll notice that here I was able to tell the story about the framework and then show the step-by-step strategy of the framework.

11: TEACH THE STRATEGY SLIDES (THE VEHICLE)

Figure 13.11:

These slides teach the strategy (the *what*) of the framework.

This is when you teach the strategy of each step of the framework. Often, if time permits, I tell a mini Epiphany Bridge story for some of the steps in the framework. For example:

Step #1: Find a funnel to model.

Step #2: Funnel hack it (buy the product and see the funnel structure).

Backstory: I found another supplement to funnel hack.

Journey: Their funnel wasn't great; I modeled it and it did okay.

New opportunity: I found a supplement funnel that was really good.

Framework: I modeled the look, feel, layout, and price points.

Achievement: The funnel 10Xed almost overnight.

Step #3: Create a blueprint for the funnel you need to build.

Step #4: Build that funnel in ClickFunnels.

You'll notice that I showed may audience *what* to do (find a funnel, buy the product, create a blueprint, and build the funnel in ClickFunnels) but I didn't show them the tactical *how*. The how would be me showing them where to find a funnel, the criteria of a good funnel to model, things I look for in a funnel, such as structure, design, etc. That stuff—the how—is reserved for the training they are buying. If you spend time in the weeds teaching the tactics here, you will lose them. Once again, your only goal is to get them to believe the strategy will work for them. After they believe, then you can teach them the tactics inside your training.

12: CASE STUDY SLIDES (THE VEHICLE)

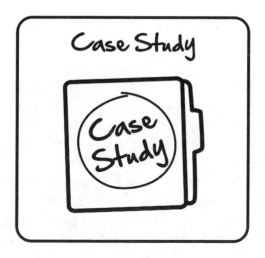

Figure 13.12:

These slides share case studies of people who've had success using your framework.

Here you will show case studies of others you have shared your framework with and the results they achieved by following them.

13: SHARE OTHER SUPPORTING EPIPHANY BRIDGE STORIES SLIDES

Figure 13.13:

These slides break other related false beliefs.

You just shared your Epiphany Bridge story about how you discovered your framework and then taught the strategy behind your framework. If time permits, you can also share shorter versions of additional stories that can help knock down other false beliefs your audience may have about the vehicle framework. These are the supporting stories that you identified in your story inventory list. It's time to revisit that list and use those stories to break any other core beliefs customers might have related to the vehicle.

I learned a cool way to do this from Jason Fladlien. We were doing a webinar and he kept track of every objection he could think of during the whole thing. At the end, he spent about 90 minutes busting every objection on the list. He'd say, "You're probably thinking (*insert false belief*), right? Well, (*tell quick Epiphany Bridge story*)."

You're probably thinking you need a lot of money to drive traffic, right?

Well, actually, you only need 100 clicks a day.

You're probably thinking you need to know how to code, right?

Well, actually, you can just model other people's funnels right inside ClickFunnels.

He went on and on like that for about 50 false beliefs that I hadn't even mentioned in the main webinar. I was starting to sweat because we'd been on for three hours and he was still talking. What were people going to think? But what happened was amazing.

At the end of the webinar, we sold three times more during his 90 minutes of "You're probably thinking X, right?" than we sold in the first 90 minutes of the webinar. We were live for three hours and had a record-breaking day. He just kept breaking false beliefs until there were no more objections anyone could possibly think of. There was absolutely no resistance left.

I told my Inner Circle about what happened, and almost immediately Brandon and Kaelin Poulin plugged in these supporting epiphany bridge stories after they were done teaching each secret. They reported back that this one technique more than doubled their sales from their webinars!

So go back to the list of false beliefs you created in your story inventory, find the ones associated with this secret, and quickly break the beliefs that may be holding your followers back. These stories are usually told in 30–60 seconds. Just mention the false belief and give a quick story in a few sentences about why that belief is wrong and what the truth is.

14: INTRODUCE YOUR SECOND SET OF FRAMEWORK (INTERNAL BELIEFS) SLIDES

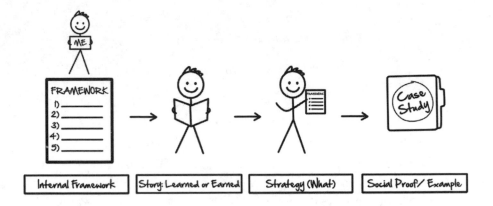

Figure 13.14:

After you've finished Secret #1, you'll follow a similar flow for Secret #2.

As we transition from Secret #1 to Secret #2 (breaking internal false beliefs), almost everything will be the same, so I'll just list the steps to follow below:

- State the secret
- Introduce the framework's name
- Share the Epiphany Bridge story that you learned or earned
- Teach the strategy of the framework
- Show case studies
- Share other supporting Epiphany Bridge stories

The only difference is that you will be sharing your Epiphany Bridge story about your internal frameworks. Let me give you an example of how this will look so you can model it for your presentation.

In my Funnel Hacks presentation, after telling my origin story and teaching the strategy behind my funnel-hacking framework, my audience is sold on the fact that they need funnels if they are going to grow their company online. So the internal false belief that starts to creep up is usually along the lines of: *I'm not technically inclined, so I don't think I could build one.* That's when I need to introduce a framework that will show it is possible for them to do it.

Backstory: I used to have to hire expensive programmers and designers.

Journey: My business partner Todd said he could build software that would make it easy.

New opportunity: He developed ClickFunnels, which made building tunnels simple for people like me!

Framework: How to Build a Funnel in 10 Minutes

Step #1: Pick a template you love (or use our share funnels).

Step #2: Drag and drop elements to make the template match your brand.

Step #3: Type in your copy and plug in your images to each page.

Step #4: Make sure it looks awesome on mobile.

Step #5: Launch your funnel!

Achievement: In less than 10 minutes, with no tech skills, I have a funnel live!

15: INTRODUCE YOUR THIRD SET OF FRAMEWORK (EXTERNAL BELIEFS) SLIDES

Figure 13.15:

After you finish Secret #2, you'll follow a similar flow for Secret #3.

Again, moving on to Secret #3 (breaking external false beliefs), you'll follow the same format with your slides as you did for Secrets #1 and #2:

- State the secret.

- Introduce the framework's name.

- Share your Epiphany Bridge story that you learned or earned.

- Teach the strategy of the framework.

- Show case studies.

- Share other supporting Epiphany Bridge stories.

This third secret is all about your customers' external false beliefs. They believe that the funnel is the right vehicle, and they also believe that they could actually build one now, but their fear is that there is some external force that will hold them back from success. The false belief my customers have sounds something like this: *"I think I could build a funnel, but even if I did, I don't know how to drive traffic into it."* Secret #3 is where I introduce my framework for helping them get traffic.

Backstory: I created a funnel, but it was hard to get traffic.

Journey: I tried Google, Facebook, and other ads, with little success.

New opportunity: I found software that would show me where my competitors were buying ads, and I could just buy them in the same places they were!

Framework: How to Get the Same Customers Who Are Going to Your Competitors' Funnels to Come to Yours Instead

Step #1: Find a competitor who already has your dream customers.

Step #2: Figure out what sites they are buying ads on.

Step #3: Look at what their banner ads look like and model them.

Step #4: Buy ads on the same websites as your competitors.

Achievement: Without learning keywords, interest targeting, or any of the technical things, I got a stream of dream customers coming to my funnels every day!

That is how you teach the content section of the webinar. If you've done it right, you've gotten your audience to believe that your vehicle is the key to them getting their desired result. They should believe that they can actually do it, and that there is no external force that could hold them back from success. If those things are true, then they have to give you money to unlock the tactics they need to be able to implement the strategies you just taught them.

The last step in this script is making the offer. You are about one hour into the presentation (or four-sixths of the way done), and now you have 30 minutes (or two-sixths) left to do the Stack and the close. You've taken them to the finish line, and now it's time to position your offer in a way that they have to say *yes*!

THE STACK AND CLOSES

I was sitting in the back of a stuffy conference room in Chicago, about to watch one of my first mentors step onstage. I had heard that he was one of the best stage closers in the world, and I wanted to see him in action. In the room were about a thousand people, all with their notepads out ready to take notes.

His name is Armand Morin, and I watched in amazement as he closed almost 50 percent of that room on his $1,000 course. There was a huge table rush to the back of the room, and I watched for more than 30 minutes as the order forms were collected and everyone was dismissed for the night.

I stood in the corner of the room waiting for everyone to clear out so I could go and talk to Armand. As I approached him, he held up a stack of order forms that was so thick he could barely hold it in his hands.

"You know what each of these are?" he asked me.

"An order form?" I responded, a little confused by his question.

"No, each of these is a thousand dollar bill," he said with a laugh.

I was blown away. I had been trying to speak on various stages for almost a year at that point, and my biggest day was about $15K in sales. He must have had close to half a million dollars in his hands. And then he started into the real reason why we were meeting.

"When you speak at BigSeminar in two weeks, I think you can make over $100K, but you have to change something about how you sell." As one of the most coachable humans on this planet, I was *so* excited to find out what he wanted to share with me. "Did you notice what I did the last 30 minutes of my presentation?" he asked.

My mind raced trying to figure out what he was talking about. "Um, I'm not sure . . . I might have missed it," I confessed.

"I did something I call the Stack." He then explained to me how it works, and ended by saying, "If you use the Stack at my event, you'll have your first real table rush."

I took notes and tried to model it as closely as possible in my presentation. Two weeks later I was onstage at Armand's BigSeminar. Speaking at this event was a huge deal for me because just three years earlier it was the first seminar I had ever attended. When I was sitting in the room at that first event, I dreamed of being on that stage someday, and now it was actually happening!

I did my presentation the way I normally do, and then at about the hour mark, I transitioned to the Stack. I felt silly doing it, but before I even finished, I watched in amazement as people jumped up and ran to the back of the room to sign up! The deeper I got into the Stack, the more people were in the back of the room, and by the time I finished, it was hard to hear anything above the noise of people signing up. That day I had my first table rush, and it was the first six-figure day I had ever experienced. Since that day I have never sold anything without using the Stack.

STACK PSYCHOLOGY

What Armand taught me when he showed me the Stack was that the only thing prospects remember when you sell is the last thing you show them. He explained that most sales presentations focus on the core offer, then the presenter will offer a bunch of different bonuses, and then give a call to action.

The problem is that if people can only remember the last thing you showed them, they only remember the last bonus, and then they associate the value of the offer with the last bonus instead of the full offer.

The Stack solves this problem by changing how you structure the way you introduce and show your offer and its bonuses. It all starts with the Stack Slide you created in Secret #5.

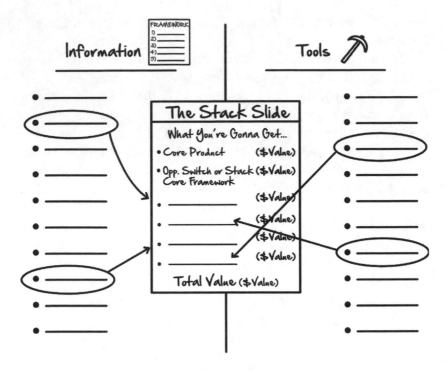

Figure 14.1:

By adding your offer elements one at a time on the same slide, you allow
your prospects to see the value build in front of their eyes.

When you transition to the close, you are going to walk people through your offer. You do this by introducing the first part of your offer, telling the story behind how you created (learned or earned) it, and listing that one thing on a slide with the total value.

You then move to the second element of your offer, tell the story about how you created (learned or earned) it, and come back to the Stack Slide and show elements #1 and #2 with the new total.

Figure 14.2:

By keeping all offer elements on one slide, you allow your prospects to associate the price of your offer with all the elements combined, instead of just the last thing you said.

Do this for each element in the offer—talk about it, then add it to the Stack Slide—so the audience sees the value adding up. The *last* thing you show them before you reveal the price is the full Stack Slide with the entire offer. When you present it this way, the audience associates the price with the *full offer*, not just the last thing you mentioned.

This small shift in how you present your offer will do more to increase your sales than almost anything else you could possibly do. Let's walk through the slides for this section of the script.

THE STACK AND CLOSES SLIDES

Figure 14.3:

After you share the Big Domino and three secrets, you'll transition to the Stack and closes.

16: THE TRANSITION TO SELLING SLIDE

Figure 14.4:

This slide recaps everything your audience has learned.

As I start to move from the content section to the Stack and closes, I use a few techniques to cement the new concepts into their minds and make a simple, non-stressful transition to the selling section of the presentation.

The first thing is to show how they could get the results they desire most, if they follow what I showed them. I'll go back through my three secrets and say something like:

> *So let me ask you a question. If you followed what I showed you in Secret #1 and found a funnel that is already working, then you did what I showed you in Secret #2 and used ClickFunnels to build out a similar funnel in just 10 minutes, and then you used Secret #3 to get traffic from the SAME place your competitors are getting it from, do you think you could be successful?*

When you break it down like that so they can connect the dots, they have to say yes. If they've said yes to that question, that means all the internal beliefs have been knocked down, and the Big Domino has fallen.

When I'm speaking onstage and can actually see the audience, those who are nodding their heads to that question are the ones who end up running to the back of the room to buy. If someone isn't nodding, something in my presentation didn't convince them the Big Domino was true.

When you sell in person, you have the ability to ask follow-up questions and figure out their specific false beliefs. Then you can address those concerns and close them. You don't have that luxury in one-to-many sales like webinars or inside your funnels. So you have to include as many objections and false beliefs in the presentation as possible.

That first transition question will help you gauge whether they are sold. And it will help them convince themselves that they are sold as well.

17: THE QUESTION SLIDE

Figure 14.5:

This slide asks for permission to share something with your audience that will help them.

Now it's time to start the actual sales section of the webinar. You've taught the three secrets. You've broken false beliefs. It's time to reveal what you have to offer. For most people, the hardest part of selling on a webinar is transitioning into the close. They get nervous and shaky—the hesitation and lack of confidence shows in their voice and body language. I used to get nervous too, until I learned a magic question from Armand. He taught me that the best way to make that transition is to simply say:

Let me ask you a question . . .

That's the secret. It takes off all the pressure and lets you make a seamless transition. I like to follow up with a couple of questions.

How many of you are excited about what we just talked about?!

How many of you are feeling a little overwhelmed because we've covered so much?

Then I try to get them to laugh by showing them a picture of someone with a fire hose in their mouth. That usually gets a laugh, and it allows me to explain how it's impossible to show them everything they need to get results in a 60-minute presentation, but that I tried to cover as much as possible. I tell them that I created a special package for those who are ready to move forward and want to implement this new opportunity.

Then I *ask permission* to share it with them.

Is it okay with you if I spend 10 minutes going over a very special offer I created to help you implement _____?

If I'm in front of them live, then I wait until they say yes or I see heads nodding. If it's in a video or virtual, I still pause for a moment to get them to agree. I want them to say yes first. Once you get permission, all the awkward feelings about selling disappear.

In the rare times when no one speaks or there is an awkward silence, I say something like:

If you don't want to learn this, that's totally okay. I already know all this. I can leave right now.

Then I wait and say:

Who here wants me to spend 10 minutes going over this?

And the second time, everybody always says yes.

If you've followed the script up to this point, they're going to say yes and you can introduce your offer. This transition helps you recap everything you've said in the webinar up to that point, and once again sets those new belief patterns in place. Once you transition into your sales pitch, you're going to use one of my favorite techniques—the Stack.

18: WHAT YOU'RE GONNA GET SLIDE (THE CORE PRODUCT)

Figure 14.6:

This slide shows the core product/service you're selling.

This is a good time to show a digital image representing the core product you're selling. It could be an information product, a service you sell, or a physical product. Tell the story about how and why you created this core product for them.

19: YOU'LL BE ABLE TO . . ./YOU'LL BE ABLE TO GET RID OF . . . SLIDES

Figure 14.7:

This slide explains how the product/service will move your customers away from pain and toward pleasure.

You want your audience to realize that investing in this thing shouldn't cost them any money, it should only save them money. Remind them not only what they are now able to do, but also what they will be able to get rid of. Hopefully the money they save will be more than what they are actually paying. That way, it's a truly irresistible offer.

When you have this product, you'll be able to _____.

When you have this product, you'll be able to get rid of _____.

20: THE PROBLEM THIS PRODUCT SOLVED FOR YOU SLIDE

Figure 14.8:

This slide shows the roadblocks you ran into when you tried
to get the same desires your customers want.

*When I was first figuring this stuff out, I ran into a big
roadblock. I didn't know how to _____. So I had to create
_____ for myself.*

21: HOW MUCH TIME/MONEY
THIS PRODUCT WILL SAVE THEM SLIDE

Figure 14.9:

This slide tells them they will save time and money by using your product/service.

Talk about all the time and money you had to spend to overcome that big roadblock the product saved you from. Maybe you had to spend a year developing email templates, or you had to hire expensive lawyers to draft just the right contracts. Then explain that they won't have to because you're going include the tool for them.

> *Way back then, I had to spend _____ and _____ to figure out an efficient way to handle this problem. But I don't want you to have to re-create the wheel. I've already got proven _____. And I'm just going to give it/them to you with this package. Sound cool?*

or

> *When you use this product, not only will you save the time and money I spent to develop it, but you'll also save what could be months or years of wasted time and money because you'll be doing it right the first time. There's no trial and error period.*

22: BREAK RELATED BELIEFS ABOUT THE PRODUCT SLIDES

Figure 14.10:

These slides break other false beliefs they may have.

As we've done in other sections, here I mention any false beliefs they may have about the product or their ability to use it, and I quickly break and rebuild those belief patterns.

23: STACK SLIDE #1

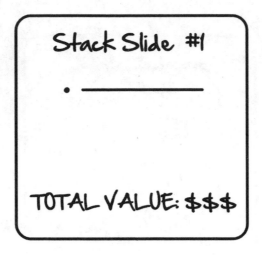

Figure 14.11:

This slide lists the value of your core product/service.

Reveal the first Stack Slide with the product on it. Be sure to include the total value of the item on the slide.

When you sign up, you're going to get instant access to my product, a total value of $_____.

24: INTRODUCE ELEMENT #2 (THE FRAMEWORKS) SLIDES

Figure 14.12:

These slides explain the frameworks they'll also receive.

It's time to introduce people to your opportunity switch or stack frameworks. Often this will be a digital course or live workshop or event to help them implement the frameworks. For some of you, your core product is your frameworks, and that is okay too. Here you will tell the story behind why and how you created these frameworks.

25: QUICK HIGH-LEVEL RECAP
OF DELIVERABLES SLIDE

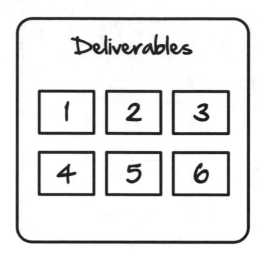

Figure 14.13:

This slide goes through a quick outline of what they'll receive with the frameworks.

A big mistake people make is going deep into each module explaining what will be covered each week. Don't do that. It overwhelms and confuses your audience. Just give them a high-level look at each module. Go through this really quickly. It should take only about 30 seconds.

Here's what we're going to cover. Week 1, we're going to talk about _____. Week 2, we'll go over _____. Week 3, we dive into _____. Then by Week 4, you'll be ready for _____. Week 5, we look at _____. And finally, in Week 6, we wrap it all up with _____.

Now let me show you some people who've had a chance to go through this process already.

26: CASE-STUDIES SLIDES

Figure 14.14:

These slides share case studies of people who've found success with your frameworks.

Here you will highlight the success stories from people who have used your frameworks. Over time, you'll add in other success stories as they happen.

Let me introduce you to . . . (share case study #1.)

Then there's . . . (share case study #2.)

And probably my favorite story is . . . (share case study #3.)

27: WHO THIS WORKS FOR (ALL-INCLUSIVE) SLIDE

Figure 14.15:

This slide reminds them who your offer is for.

After you present the case studies, people often think: *That's great, but it won't work for me.* They think: *That person lives in Australia,* or *That person is in a different industry.* They think their business or personal circumstances are different from the case study details, so it won't work for them. This is where you make a blanket statement about all the different people it works for. Be as inclusive as possible here. I've also included a few niche examples.

So I want to go back and make sure you realize who this is for.

It's for people who . . .

[Business]

It's for people just starting out or those who are already successful and want to scale.

[Weight loss]

It's for people who have 100 pounds to lose or those who have only 5 more to go. It even helps people who don't need to lose weight but want to build healthy muscle.

28: DESTROY THE #1 REASON
PEOPLE DON'T GET STARTED SLIDE

Figure 14.16:

This slide breaks any objection to starting right away.

Usually there's a common reason people don't get started right away. It's the elephant in the room. Address it head-on so they don't keep thinking about it through the rest of your presentation. The biggest excuse I hear from people about ClickFunnels is that they don't have a product to sell yet. So I tell them they don't need to have a product. They can use affiliate products. And I teach them how to make a product, if that's what they want to do. Destroy your audience's number one objection to the training right here.

You might be thinking you can't get started with this because . . . Here's why that's a mistake that will hold you back from success.

29: STACK SLIDE #2

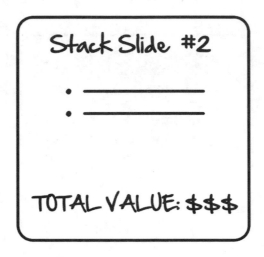

Figure 14.17:

This slide adds the value of your frameworks to your offer.

This is where the magic starts happening. Show the Stack Slide again with the core product/service on top and the frameworks on the second line. Then update the total value price at the bottom to show what the offer is now worth.

30: REPEAT THIS PROCESS FOR ALL OTHER ELEMENTS OF YOUR OFFER

You will continue to introduce new elements to your offer, tell the story behind how you created it so they can see the pain and cost you put in to learn or earn it, and then show them the ease and speed with which they will experience it because you are just giving it to them!

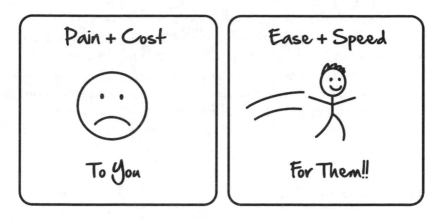

Figure 14.18:

Introduce additional elements of your offer by sharing the pain and cost it took
you to learn or earn them and the ease and speed they'll get by using them.

Between each new element, make sure you restack the slide so
they can see what the total value of your offer has grown to.

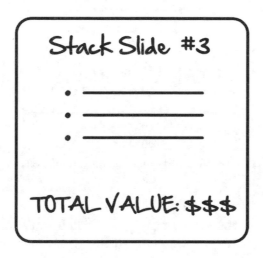

Figure 14.19:

This slide goes after each element you introduce
so they can see the total offer value rise.

As you do this, remember that each new element you create should be helping to knock down false beliefs they have about why they may not be successful. If I know that people aren't going to buy my product because they are afraid they won't be able to get traffic into their funnels, then I will create a bonus that shows them how to get traffic. Yes, each part of your offer should be created in a way that removes all false beliefs they may still have at this point.

31: THE BIG STACK SLIDE

Figure 14.20:

This slide shows the entire offer with the total value.

I call this the Big Stack Slide because it has all the elements of the offer, including the value of each part. You'll want to total everything up and have the value be 10 times as much as the actual price will be. (If the value doesn't reach that level, consider adding something more valuable to your offer.)

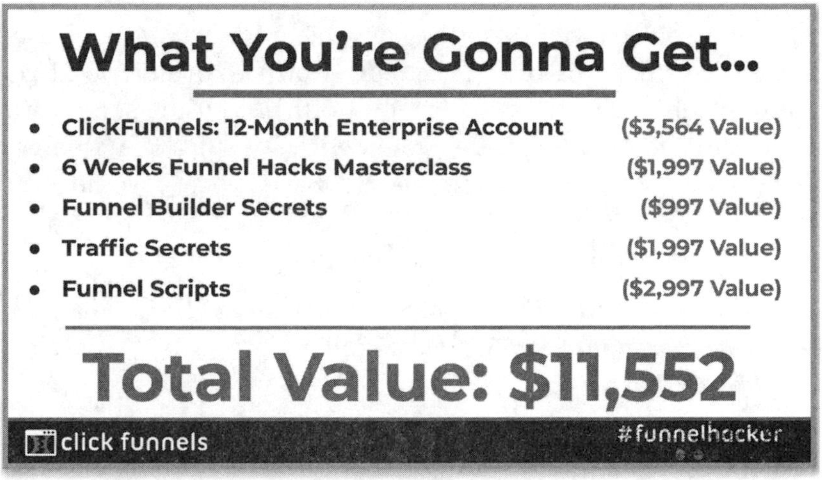

Figure 14.21:

Your Big Stack Slide shows all the offer elements, their
individual value, and the total value of the offer.

32: IF ALL STATEMENTS SLIDES

Figure 14.22:

These slides compare the price to the value of the
result they will receive when they buy.

Now that you've given them the big value price, you need to convince them that this offer is actually worth that much and get them to admit it to themselves. You do that by using something Dave VanHoose calls "If all" statements. An "If all" statement reads like this: "If all this package did was _____, would it be worth $_____?"[44]

I usually transition by saying something like:

> *Now obviously, I'm not going to charge you $11,552. But if I DID charge you $11,552, and all it did was _____, would it be worth it to you?*

Then do three "If all" statements based on your three secrets.

> **Vehicle (Secret #1):** *If all this system did/got you was _____ (related to Secret #1), would it be worth $_____?*

Stop and wait for them to say yes in their mind.

> **Internal Beliefs (Secret #2):** *And if all it did was _____ (related to Secret #2), would it be worth $_____?*

Stop and wait for them to say yes in their mind.

> **External Beliefs (Secret #3):** *And what if all it did was _____ (related to Secret #3), then would it be worth it?*

Stop and wait for them to say yes in their mind.

They've now said yes three times when you asked them if what you are selling is worth the total value, usually a 10-time markup. Now when you discount the price to what you're actually selling it for, they are getting a 90 percent discount from what they believe (and have said) it's worth.

33: I HAD TWO CHOICES SLIDE

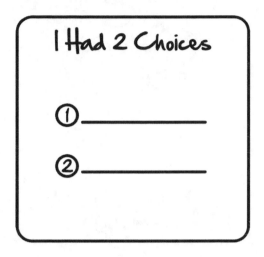

Figure 14.23:

This slide explains you could price it low or require a higher investment.

I like to use the "I had two choices" close at this point because it gets people to agree that I should charge them more in order to make the program better.

> *I had two choices with this. I could go as cheap as possible and try to sell as many as possible. But the problem with that is I couldn't really stack on the value for you. So I decided to go with a second option, which obviously requires a slightly higher investment on your side. But in exchange for that, my team can dedicate more time, energy, and resources to help guarantee your success.*

34: WHAT WOULD THE END RESULT BE WORTH SLIDE

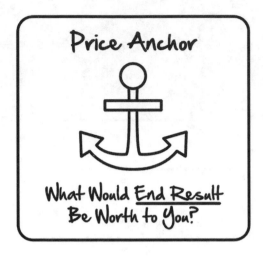

Figure 14.24:

This slide asks how much the end result is worth.

Before you reveal the actual price, ask what the end result would be worth to them.

> *So if you had a successful funnel today that was making you money, what would it be worth to you?*

Then *stop* and wait for them to answer the question in their minds.

> *How much would you pay to have that one successful funnel?*

Then *stop* and wait for them to think about it for a few seconds.

> *You can probably see why people pay $_____ for a similar result from me, because it's not a cost—it's an INVESTMENT.*

35: PRICE DROP SLIDE

Figure 14.25:

This slide drops the price from the "value" amount to the "retail" amount.

Now I come back to the full price I showed them right before the "If all" statements.

You've already seen how it's worth $_____.

And even at $_____, which I charge the public, it's a great deal.

But because of _____, I'm going to give you a very special offer . . .

36: PRICE REVEAL SLIDE

Figure 14.26:

This slide reveals the price for attendees.

Here is the first time you reveal the price of your offer. Tell them the real price and give your first call to action (asking them to click on a button, go to a certain website, or call a phone number). Every slide after this will have a call-to-action link so that when they are ready, they can sign up.

37: PRICE JUSTIFICATION SLIDE

Figure 14.27:

**This slide justifies the price compared to the
retail price or the cost to get similar results.**

For years, I ended my sales presentations with the price on the last slide. As I gained experience, I realized the elements that come *after* the initial price reveal are vitally important to closing the sale. So I give the initial price, and some people will still have sticker shock. I need to let that price marinate for a while as I justify why it's actually not that expensive.

My first price justification is usually related to either showing what the full price would be outside the current presentation or comparing it to the price of other options for getting a similar result (apples vs. oranges).

[Full price]

Now let me put this into perspective for you. If you went to my regular website right now, you could buy this same product for $_____. But because you've invested this time with me, and you've proven that you really want to get this result, I'm making a special offer just for this webinar.

[Apples vs. oranges]

If you were to hire a professional to do this for you, it might cost $_____. But because you're learning how to do it yourself AND I'm giving you all the tools and resources to make it happen fast, you pay only $_____.

38: YOU'VE GOT TWO CHOICES SLIDE

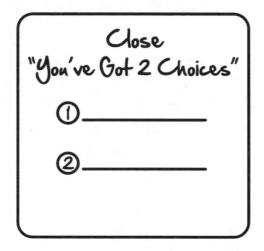

Figure 14.28:

This slide explains that they can do nothing or they can test it out.

Now I like to mention the choices they can make.

At this point you have two choices. You can choose to do nothing. If you do nothing with the information you've learned over the last hour, what will you get? Nothing.

Or you can choose to take a leap of faith. Just test it out to see if it will work for you.

39: GUARANTEE SLIDE

Figure 14.29:

This slide reverses the risk and explains your guarantee.

Then I reveal that it's okay if it doesn't work for them, because they're covered with a 30-day money-back guarantee. They can test-drive it now and see if it will work for them. They have nothing to lose.

40: THE REAL QUESTION IS THIS . . .

Figure 14.30:

This slide explains that even if it does only *half* of what you've claimed, it will pay for itself soon.

Now that they know they have nothing to lose, I like to make their choice as simple as possible. Help them see that this really is a no-brainer.

> *The real question is this: Is it worth gambling a few minutes of your time to check this out? Even if it does only HALF of what I've claimed today, it will pay for itself as soon as _____.*

41: LAST STACK SLIDE

Figure 14.31:

This slide recaps each element to show the entire offer.

Next I show them the Big Stack Slide one last time, with everything they're going to get and the total value. I go through each element line by line one last time to cement the offer in their minds before my final pitch.

42: URGENCY/SCARCITY BONUS SLIDE

Figure 14.32:

**This slide shows a time-sensitive or number-specific
(or both) bonus to push them to act.**

The two most valuable tools in marketing are urgency and scarcity. Here you're going to add a bonus upgrade that's only available right then. You can create urgency and scarcity by offering something special to a certain number of people, or for a certain amount of time (or both).

Do not skip this part! It is the key to getting people to buy immediately. If they leave the webinar, the chances of them coming back and buying later are almost zero. In fact, I usually give a bonus only for those who are actually on live that I don't offer to those who watch only the replays later. That encourages people to show up live, but it also gives them a reason to sign up before the presentation is over. The deadline is the key.

43: CLOSING CALL TO ACTION/Q&A SLIDE

Figure 14.33:

This slide stays up during your Q&A session.

This is the slide I end my presentation with, and it stays up during the entire question-and-answer session. There are a few key components to this slide.

- Recap of the offer
- Countdown clock for 30 minutes
- Price
- Call to action

Then it's time to answer questions. Sometimes I'll take questions live from the audience, and other times I'll write many of the questions in advance that I know people typically have. I then go through those questions and give another call to action after each one. That gives me lots of opportunities to repeat the link for people to buy.

I also try to think about any other false beliefs they may still have, returning to the sentence:

You're probably thinking _____, right?

And that is the Stack. That single concept has made me more money than anything else I've ever done in this business. Study it. Master it. There is no greater gift I could give you than this.

TRIAL CLOSES

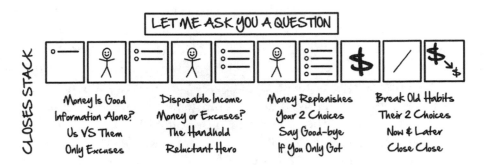

Figure 15.1:

Trial closes and mini closes will help persuade attendees to buy your offer.

Years ago, I had heard rumors about a guy nicknamed "The Pied Piper of Selling." People call him this because he's so good at selling from the stage that he would have hundreds of people line up behind him, waving their credit cards in the air, and walking with him to the back of the room to buy his programs. One day I had the chance to witness this in person, and it was one of the coolest things I had ever seen.

His real name is Ted Thomas, and the first time we met was when I was speaking at an event and noticed that Ted was in the audience. One of the best closers in the world was about to watch me try to close this room. I did my best to ignore the butterflies in my stomach and delivered a pretty good presentation. While I did get a lot of signups, I didn't get the huge table rush I was hoping for.

After my presentation, Ted introduced himself and invited me to lunch. As we ate, he started asking me casual questions. After a few minutes, he grinned. I asked him why he was smiling. He laughed and said, "What's your head doing right now?" I realized I was nodding my head up and down—and had been since the moment we started talking.

He said, "What I've been doing is a little technique I call trial closes. I've been asking you dozens of little yes-or-no questions where the only answer is yes. You instantly started nodding, and you didn't stop until I pointed it out just now."

He went on to explain that the reason I didn't get a table rush was because the first time I asked the audience to say yes was when I was asking for their money. "When you watch me speak, you'll notice that all the heads in the audience are nodding the entire time. If you are standing in the back of the room and you are looking at the heads of the audience members, it looks like the waves in the ocean going up and down. I am constantly asking simple questions to get people to say yes over and over again, so when I ask them to give me money at the end, they've already told me yes hundreds of times before that."

I thought that was pretty cool. But to be completely honest, I thought he was oversimplifying his skills. I didn't think his trial closes could possibly have that big of an impact on sales. But I decided to test it out.

At the time, I had an automated webinar that had been running profitably for five or six months. I rewatched the video and found a few dozen places where I could add in trial closes. I then recorded just the trial closes and inserted them into the video file. I didn't expect much, but what happened was amazing! That webinar went from making $9.45 per registrant to $16.50 per registrant—just by me adding in the trial closes.

From that day forward, I was sold. I wrote out simple trial closes on note cards and put them around my desk. As I worked through my various presentations, every time I'd see a card I'd use that trial close. Here are some examples of trial closes that I've used dozens of times in each of my presentations.

- Are you ready to get started?

- Are you all getting this?

- Is this making sense?

- Can you imagine if that happened to you?

- Who here wants a free copy of _____?

- Would you like to be our next case study?

- You've heard them talk about this before, right?

- Isn't that cool?

- Isn't that exciting?

- Am I right?

- Can you see yourself doing _____?

- I'm sure you've noticed this too, right?

I could go on and on. It's become ingrained in how I write and speak. You've seen me using trial closes throughout this book, haven't you? (See what I did there?) (Whoa! I did it again, didn't I?) Get used to using lots of little statements that get your audience to think or say yes over and over again. The more you can get them to say yes, the more likely they will be to accept the epiphanies you've shared with them and the offer presented. Trial closes are a huge part of telling effective stories.

The most powerful times to use trial closes are right after you've shared a case study or success story from one of your students. Many times people will share their story and then quickly move on. If you notice when I share any story, I'll always pause, and then drop a half dozen trial closes before I move on. *"Did you hear that? Isn't that amazing? Can you imagine what your life would be like if that happened to you? Are you getting this?!"* These are all examples of the types of trial closes I would use right after sharing a success story.

16 MINI CLOSES

When you get to the end of the presentation and start the Stack, there are lots of really good closes you can use, but I have 16 favorites that I use repeatedly. Several listed here I've learned from Jason Fladlien's Webinar Pitch Secrets 2.0; Jason has kindly let me share them with you here.[45] I don't use all of them in all presentations, but I pick a handful of those that help strengthen my argument.

I already built some of my favorites for you into the Stack I've shared with you. I want to show you all of them, though, so you can pick and choose which ones to plug into your presentations. Some will work better than others for different types of presentations. Choose the ones that flow naturally and make the most sense.

For each close below, I will briefly explain the concept, then show you how I would use that close in my own presentations.

Money is good: The goal is to get people to disassociate from their fear about spending money with you. Money is a tool for exchange. You spend money to get something greater in return.

I want you to think about something for a minute. What is money? A lot of people have fear about money, and even bigger fears about spending money. But you need to understand that money is good. It's just a tool that was created for exchange.

Other than that, there is no real value in money. You can't use it to stay warm, you can't eat it, you can only trade it for something else that you want. Just think, everyone who exchanges money for something does it because they believe that what they are getting in exchange is greater than keeping the money or using it for something else. At least that's what I expect when I buy something. I don't actually know for sure until I do buy it, try it out, and can see the results.

But my question for you is this. Would you exchange that money for those results? If the answer is yes, then you need to get started right now. And if you have any fear that it might not be what you expected, or that you might not be able to get those results, just let us know, and we'll give you your money back.

Disposable income: The goal is to help them realize that they are spending their disposable income on things that aren't serving them well, and by spending that money on things that will help them grow, they will have long-term fulfillment. When you use the disposable income close, people get that they *do* have the money to invest.

Most people in this world live paycheck to paycheck. Every couple of weeks you get paid and then you pay your fixed costs like rent and food. Then there's usually some money left over. We call that disposable income.

Most people are going to blow that every single month. If they have $1,000 in disposable income, they're going to spend it until it's gone. They might spend it on movies or ice cream or travel—all short-term pleasures that are gone in an instant.

But the cool thing is that money replenishes. Every two weeks—boom! There's another $1,000 in disposable income you can spend. Most people spend that cash on things that don't really add value to their lives in a meaningful way. You should be investing that money into products, programs, and services that will actually help you.

That's the power of disposable income—it comes back. Every two weeks—boom! There's more money.

Money replenishes: The goal for this close is to help people realize that while each month money comes back, time does not, and if they're not careful, they will run out of time.

Do you think it's okay to dip into your savings or leverage your credit and spend money you might not have to get started today? This is a serious question. Do you think it's okay or not? Some people say yes and some say no. Let's talk about this for a minute.

Every month, money replenishes, right? But this is the key—time does NOT replenish. It disappears. So you could go out and spend months or years of your valuable time to figure something out—but you will never get that time back. Instead, you could save that time and effort, because I've already spent it for you, and work directly with me instead. It will cost you money to get started, but that money will come back, whereas the time away from your family in trial and error is wasted effort and is gone forever.

Break old habits: The goal for this close is to help them realize that if they leave today without investing, nothing in their life will change.

Habits are really hard to change. I could leave the webinar right now and go enjoy the rest of the afternoon. I'm already successful with _____. This is already working for me. But this is not about me. This is about you. If YOU leave now, you might think you learned a lot of cool stuff, but my guess is that by morning tomorrow you'll have already slipped back into your normal routines. Right? You'd just do what you've always done. That's what most people do.

But because I'm your coach, your friend, your mentor, I'm not going to let you go back to your old habits. I'm going to make sure you're successful by breaking them. If you want real, lasting change, you need repeated exposure to the full system. That's what you'll get when you invest today.

Information alone: My goal for this close is to help them understand that, while they have gotten some awesome information, they can't rely on information alone. They need coaching and accountability too.

Now I've told you how the whole system works. I've shown you how you can _____. I've shown you that you only need _____ to make this all work. But you know what? To be successful with this, you're going to need more than information alone.

I know you can be successful with this system, but you're going to need coaching. You will have questions that need answering. And you might need help in the accountability department too. Let me tell you, I take my job as a coach very seriously. I won't let you quit on yourself. We will get through everything together. I can't do that with just a few videos and some PDFs. Information alone won't cut it.

My success rate when people go at this by themselves is almost 0 percent. But my success rate for those who work with me is closer to _____ percent. If information were enough, then you could have just turned to Google. You need a guide who has been there before, who can take you there right now.

Money or excuses: The goal of this close is to get them to quit making excuses about why they can't buy.

I've been in this business a long time. And I've found there are only two kinds of people: those who are good at (making money, losing weight, etc.) and those who are good at making excuses. You can't be both. If you're the one making excuses, I hate to say it, but I think you're going to have a really hard time _____.

The good news is that you get to choose. In this moment, you can choose which type of person you're going to be. Don't be someone who makes excuses, be someone who actually_____.

Your two choices: The goal of this close is for them to understand why you are charging so much money, and to make sure they are okay with that.

When we were deciding how to price this, we had two choices. The first was to go as cheap as possible and sell as many as we could. Now the problem with that is we would have no real incentive to pile on the value. It would cost us more for those bonuses than the whole course would be worth. Our second choice was to raise the price a little, and give you absolutely everything you need to succeed.

Their two choices: The goal for this close is to help them realize they are crazy if they don't invest with you today.

The way I see it, you've got two choices. Your first option is to do nothing and not take this leap of faith (which is 100 percent risk-free).

Your second option is to pony up this tiny investment today (compared to all the value you'll get in return) and give it a shot. See if it'll work for you. If it doesn't—for whatever reason—you get your money back. There's no risk. You have nothing to lose but the stress and headaches.

Us vs. them: The goal for this close is to call people out as either doers or dabblers.

I'm guessing there are two kinds of people listening to me right now. You're either a doer or a dabbler. The dabblers love to sit and listen and learn, but they rarely ever do anything and often look for any excuse not to move forward.

Some of you are doers. You're not sure how this is going to work for you, but you see how it's worked for me and for other people, so you have faith that it will work for you as well. And what I've found is that it's the doers who get ahead in life, while the dabblers don't ever really seem to progress.

The handhold: This close is where you walk them through the sign-up process.

When you are ready to change your life, this is what you need to start doing. First, open up a browser window—I don't care if it's Google Chrome, Firefox, or Safari. I'm going to open Chrome right now and show you how this works.

Type in www._____.com. On this page, you're going to see _____. Then you're going to click here and fill out this form. After that, you'll be taken to this page, where you can create your account. If you have any issues, this link will connect you to my support desk, where _____ can answer any of your questions.

Say good-bye: In this close I want to show them all the pain that will instantly disappear after they invest.

> *Once you've been through this training and have everything set up, you can say good-bye to the stress of _____. You'll never have to worry about _____ again. Can you imagine what life will be like when those things have instantly disappeared from your life? What will you do with all the extra (time, energy, money, etc.)?*

Now and later: In this close, I want to paint a picture of their life now compared to what it could become if they invest.

> *I want to paint a picture of where I was before I started with (the new opportunity). I struggled with _____. I wasn't able to _____. Things were hard because _____. Does that sound familiar?*

> *But now I want you to get a vision of what life could be like. Ever since (new opportunity), I've been able to _____. Now I'm able to _____, and things are amazing. Can you imagine what that would be like?*

Only excuses: The goal of this close is to call out any excuses that might be keeping them back and diffuse them.

> *If you didn't sign up immediately, you're probably thinking one of two things. First, you might be thinking _____. Don't worry. We spend the whole first module showing you _____. I'm also going to show you how we figured out _____. I'm going to give you templates to help you figure it out. I promise you, by the end of Week 1, you'll know exactly how to _____.*

> *Second, you're probably a little nervous about setting it all up. I get that. But I promise you, it's not hard. On Week 2, we're going to walk step-by-step through the whole setup process. I know _____ can be scary, but we'll be there for you.*

> *The third reason might be that you think it's too expensive. If that's your reason, I don't know how I can help you. This is*

an investment and a decision you need to make for yourself. When I invested in learning this process, I paid $_____, but I got back_____ within _____.

Reluctant hero: The goal of this close is to help them believe they can actually do it.

I want you to know something about me. I'm no one special. I don't have any supernatural gifts or anything. I actually really struggle with _____. And that's what I love about this system—I don't have to worry about that anymore!

If you only got: The goal of this close is to show them what they already got for free, and what they can possibly achieve when they invest with you.

Okay, so I could stop right here. If I stopped right here and you only got _____, it would still be worth the investment, right? But you're also getting _____ and _____. But you're also going to get _____ and _____ and _____. I want to make sure that nothing is standing in the way of your success.

Close close: This close is the final push to get them over the edge. I typically do this one several times during the question-and-answer section at the end of the webinar.

If you're still on the fence, now is the time to open a new browser window, go to www._____.com, and get started. Remember there is no risk, and we have a 100 percent money-back guarantee. But the only way for you to know if this is right for you is to get started right now. You can get your account at _____.com.

There you go—16 closes you can use throughout the Stack to help sell your offer. I like to use a close right before I introduce a new element in the Stack. Sometimes I'll even use two or three closes in between elements. They just flow naturally one into the other.

CREATING YOUR OWN CLOSES

The closes above are powerful, but it's even more powerful to start developing your own closes. A good close in its more pure form is just an Epiphany Bridge story to break a false belief about why they shouldn't buy. For your own closes, you can use any of the stories from your Story Inventory that you haven't used for your presentation.

One of the closes that I use often when I speak I call "Investing vs. Buying," and it goes a little something like this:

Backstory: *I had just moved into the dorms and gone to my first wrestling practice, where I had an awesome time meeting my teammates and coaches.*

Journey: *That night, there was a knock on my door. When I opened it, there stood my wrestling coach, Mark Schultz. He was an Olympic gold medalist in freestyle wrestling as well as the winner of UFC 9, when he stepped into the Octagon with less than 24 hours notice and no formal training and destroyed his opponent.*

New opportunity: *As he walked in my dorm room, he handed me a videotape titled "Total Violence"; the footage held the highlights of his wrestling career.*

As I took the tape, he asked me to give him my wallet. A little surprised, but too afraid to say anything to the strongest man I had ever personally met, I pulled my wallet out of my pocket and gave it to him. He opened it, took all my money out, and handed me back an empty wallet. I was kind of confused, but too nervous to say anything.

Framework: *He then told me, "Russell, if I gave you that tape for free, you'd never watch it. But because you've paid for it, I know you're going to watch it and learn from it." And with that he walked out the door. That night my coach taught me the power of investment, and he was right.*

Achievement: *Because I had made that investment, I did watch the tape over and over again, and I became a better wrestler because of it.*

I share that close almost anytime I'm going to ask somebody to make an investment with me. They may have a false belief that they don't have money to buy something that will cost them money, but they do have money to invest in something that will make them money.

Creating your own closes from your Epiphany Bridge stories is the most powerful type of close you can use.

In this section you have been given the framework for the Perfect Webinar as well as the strategies and tactics you need to master it. As you start creating your slides, use this book as a reference manual to make sure you cover all the pieces of the script in the correct order. In the next section of the book I am going to show you some different selling situations where you can use this framework inside your value ladder.

BECOMING YOUR DREAM CUSTOMER'S GUIDE

The focus of this book so far has been to help you become an expert. We've talked about how to find your voice and build your tribe. We've discussed how to build frameworks and make offers that are truly new opportunities. We've spent time mastering story structure and organizing those stories in a way that gets people to move. But the focus has been on you, telling your stories about the experts and guides who gave you the epiphanies that caused you to transform into who you are today.

For this next section, I want you to take a step back and realize that now you are becoming the guide in your dream customer's story. Right now they are stuck in a red ocean somewhere, trying to get a result they desire, but every opportunity they've tried so far hasn't worked for them.

Figure 16.1:

Your dream customers are likely at the same point where you started: stuck.

YOUR DREAM CUSTOMER'S TWO JOURNEYS

Your dream customers are stuck there just like the hero in any story is stuck in their "ordinary world." They are frustrated, they are waiting for their mentor, their expert, their guide to take them on their hero's journey.

In *Building a StoryBrand*, Donald Miller explains that your *brand* is not the hero. He says your *customer* is the hero, and your brand's role is to successfully guide the hero through the challenges they will face.[46] Therefore, he explains that your brand should be like Yoda to Luke Skywalker.

When you look at your business through that lens, you will see that all you are really doing is looking for congregations of people (heroes who have challenges), throwing out hooks to grab their attention, and becoming the guide to lead them through their challenges so they can achieve the results they desire.

Figure 16.2:

**Your job as the expert is to guide your dream customers
on their own Hero's Two Journeys.**

Backstory: It starts by understanding that your dream customers are in their backstory now. Your job as their future guide is to go to where they are, find the red oceans they are frustrated and stuck in, and start throwing out hooks to grab their attention. My *Traffic Secrets* book goes deep into the strategies and frameworks showing how to do this, but understand that is the first step.

As you try to remember when you were in your backstory, and what you felt, what you were searching for, and what other opportunities you were trying before you found your new opportunity, it will help you to identify where you can find your future customers. Your job then is to throw out hooks to try to grab their attention and get them to start on their journey.

Journey: After you grab someone's attention, you are giving them a literal calling to leave their ordinary world (Facebook, Google, email—wherever they are seeing your ad) and start a journey with you. Just like our hero in any story physically leaves their home, your dream customers are leaving where they are comfortable and coming to your funnel.

On this page is where you are giving them their calling. It's the first real offer where they have to decide whether they want to go on this journey with you. If they give you their email, you'll give them some lead magnet. It could be an e-book, a video, a webinar. The deliverable matters less than the commitment they make in deciding to start this journey with you.

New opportunity: Now that they have joined your list and started on this journey with you, you have the ability to make them a presentation. During this presentation you will do the following things:

1.   Introduce yourself to them as their new guide

2.   Tell them your story to give them an epiphany

3.   Present them your new opportunity

This presentation can happen in a lot of different formats, depending on which type of funnel you use. Inside *DotCom Secrets*, I showed you many different types of funnel structures based on what you are selling, and at which price points, but regardless of what funnel type you use, you are still going to make a presentation with those three elements.

When they've finished watching the presentation, they have the chance to choose whether they accept this new opportunity or not. If they do, they become customers and you are then able to give them your frameworks and work to ascend them up your value ladder, helping them achieve what they desire the most and transform into the person they want to become.

In this last section of the book I will be sharing with you how to weave your presentations into the different funnel types you learned about in *DotCom Secrets*. The presentation is about telling your story (as a guide), but the funnels are about creating their journey, where they are the hero.

TESTING YOUR PRESENTATION LIVE

A few weeks after we officially launched ClickFunnels, I got invited to speak at a friend's event. He asked if I would give a presentation about funnels and then create and sell a $1,000 offer that included access to ClickFunnels at the end of my presentation. I was a little deflated because my team and I had been trying for weeks to figure out the best way to get people to buy the software. We tried free trials, we tried special promotions, but nothing seemed to be working very well, and now he wanted me to sell a $1,000 version? If people weren't taking a free trial, why would they take me up on this offer?

I tried to back out of the presentation, but he told me that my face was already on the website as a keynote speaker and people were expecting me to be there. The event was happening Thursday, Friday, and Saturday, so I booked a flight to get me there early Saturday morning, a few hours before I was supposed to speak. The event was also being streamed live, so on Thursday and Friday, I had it playing on my computer while I was working on my presentation.

The first thing I did was create my Stack Slide. I knew they were going to get ClickFunnels, but what else could I add to the offer to make it sexy enough that people would pay $1,000? I added in a course I hadn't made yet called Funnel Builder Secrets. I added in software and training that would help them get the copy written on their pages and traffic into their funnels. I bundled in a few months of ClickFunnels for free, and soon I had an offer that I felt was worth $10,000, so I could easily sell it for $1,000.

The next step was creating the presentation to sell this new offer. I took out my Perfect Webinar framework and went through the same process I did with you in Section Three. I figured out my Big Domino and what origin story I would tell to try to knock it down. I wrote out three secrets, created a framework for each, and plugged in the story behind how I learned or earned them. Then I created my Stack Slides and finished just in time to jump on a plane to San Diego.

When I got there, I walked into the same small room that I had been watching on my computer the prior two days. There were about 100 people in the room, and the energy was really low. I walked over to the guys who were running the audio and video for the event and handed them my USB drive with my presentation. I had no idea whether it was going to work, and I had no time to practice.

A few minutes later the emcee was announcing my name and I was giving the first version of my Funnel Hacks presentation. I told my potato gun story, I showed them my funnel-hacking framework, I showed them a demo of the software, and finished by showing them my traffic framework. As I nervously transitioned to the close, I asked them, "Are you okay if I spend about 10 minutes going over a special offer I created for you, where I can help you get a funnel created for your business?" The audience who had been almost asleep before I got onstage were all now very attentive and everyone said *"Yes!"*

I went through my Stack and closes, and before it was over I saw people running to the back of the room to sign up! It had worked! The next few hours were crazy, collecting order forms and answering questions, but when the dust settled, I learned that over a third of the room had signed up for ClickFunnels!

That night I went to dinner with my two co-founders, Todd Dickerson and Dylan Jones, along with a few of our other future partners, and I told them something that I had never said before. "We're going to be rich. I saw it in their eyes, I've spoken on stages for 10 years, and I've never seen something like this before."

FOCUS ON ONE FUNNEL UNTIL IT HITS THE TWO COMMA CLUB

I've had successful presentations in the past, but I knew that if we really wanted to grow ClickFunnels, I couldn't do what I normally do. As you can probably tell I'm obsessed with building funnels, so what I (and many of the successful entrepreneurs I coach) do is create a funnel, launch it, make some money, and then move on to the next one—each time getting paid well, but never really building anything sustainable. As we sat at dinner that night, we talked about how to make sure this wasn't just a flash-in-the-pan payday, and instead a launchpad for ClickFunnels.

I told them a story about a conversation I had a few months earlier with my friend MaryEllen Tribby. MaryEllen has a unique ability to take companies that are doing well and quickly scale them to much higher profitability. One of her successes was with the company Weiss Research. She took the company from $11 million in sales to $67 million in just 12 months. She had similar results with several other companies. I asked her to share her secret. How could she possibly grow a company that fast?

She said, "Internet marketers like you are so smart and so dumb at the same time."

I was a little shocked, but she had my interest. "What do you mean?"

She went on to say that what we do each month is the equivalent of creating a Broadway show. "You hire the best playwrights in the world. You hire the best actors. You practice for months, then you open the show in downtown Boise, Idaho. (Because that's where you happen to live and you spend a month promoting it.) You open the show to a sold-out crowd and they give you a standing ovation. That night after the show is done, you pull everything down and start writing your next play to open next month in the same auditorium in Boise."

I kinda laughed nervously. "Okay, then what should I be doing? What would you do differently?"

"I take companies like yours that have an awesome show in Boise—I take them on the road. I take that show to Chicago, to New York, to L.A., and I keep running it until it stops making money."

I realized then and there what I was doing wrong. I needed to learn how to take my show on the road. In other words, to drive more traffic to the same webinar every week. I made a commitment to my partners that I would focus on doing this presentation live every week for the next 12 months.

As a side note, we now have a rule inside my Inner Circle that no one is allowed to work on their second funnel until their first one has made it into the Two Comma Club. I would give you that same recommendation: Do your presentation live for a year, or until it hits the Two Comma Club, whichever comes sooner.

PERFECTING THE PRESENTATION

The next morning, as I was leaving the event, one of the attendees who heard the presentation told me she loved it, but since she was a coach and didn't have a supplement to sell, she couldn't use ClickFunnels.

I gave her a puzzled look.

She pointed out that all the examples I had shown were people selling supplements, but she didn't have one. I told her that I use ClickFunnels for my coaching business and showed her a few of my funnels. She got so excited; she ran back into the event and grabbed two of her friends. They all filled out order forms and handed them to me before I left the hotel. I closed three people who hadn't signed up before!

This interaction revealed that my presentation wasn't perfect. So on my flight home, I tweaked it by adding a few more slides showing different funnels and giving examples of how other industries can use ClickFunnels. On that same flight I started sending emails to everyone I knew (my Dream 100) telling them I had a presentation that was converting, and asking them if they would like to do a webinar with me. By the time I landed, I had more than a dozen presentations lined up.

The first one was just a few days later. The partner was able to get about 600 people to show up live on the webinar. I did my presentation (with the updates I had made on the plane) and when it was over, we had sold about $30K, which wasn't too bad, but I knew it could have been more. I was supposed to give the same presentation to another group of entrepreneurs a few hours later, so I decided to look at all the questions that people had asked during the earlier presentation. I downloaded their questions and comments and read through them. Quickly I was able to see four or five places in the presentation when I could tell people were really confused by what I was saying, or the offer wasn't clear, so I went back to my slides and added in new things to make sure people's questions were answered before they asked them.

A few hours later, I delivered this revised presentation to a smaller group of about 500 entrepreneurs, and this time we sold $120K live! I repeated this same process 60-plus times over the next 12 months—doing a live webinar, exporting questions, and adjusting the presentation.

It's probably why Joe Lavery, one of my friends and conversion experts, said this after watching my presentation:

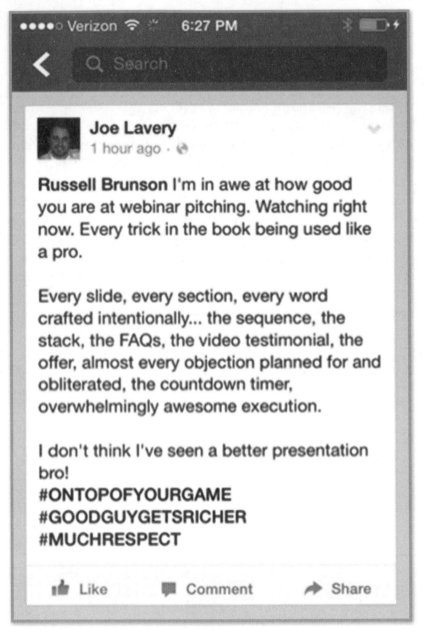

Figure 16.3:

After reading the comments from my previous webinar, I learned there
were sticking points where I hadn't overcome my audience's objections.
I fixed the slides and made four times the profit on my next webinar.

People ask me all the time, "If you were to start ClickFunnels over today, or launch a new start-up, how would you do it?" The answer is simple: I would create a presentation, and then I would deliver that presentation live every week for a year, until I had it perfected.

I now have this presentation memorized. I could recite it in my sleep. I can tell you with almost 100 percent accuracy how much money I'll make on a webinar based on how many people show up. The close rate stays the same, because it's the same presentation. This is the reason I knew that I could do more than $3 million at the 10X event. I knew how many people were in the room, I know my conversion rates, and so there were no doubts.

The problem most people have is they create what they think is a good presentation, record it once, and then put it into their funnels. You can do that, but the problem is that if you haven't perfected it, you have no idea what people's real objections are. Even if you do it live a half dozen times, at least you'll know where the sticking points are and you can get those ironed out. It's a little hinge that swings a huge door. The difference between 10 percent conversion and 15 percent conversion is the difference between a 7 figure-a-year webinar vs. an 8 figure webinar.

THE LIVE PRESENTATION MODEL

After I committed to "taking the show on the road" and doing a live presentation at least once per week, I sketched out a model and told my team I was going to stick to this model for at least the next 12 months.

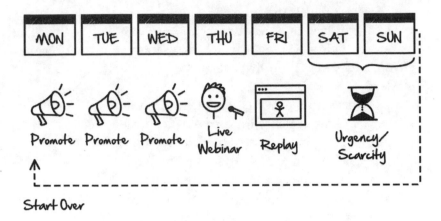

Figure 16.4:

I recommend doing your Perfect Webinar live every week for a year,
or until you hit the Two Comma Club, whichever comes sooner.

My favorite day to do webinars is Thursday, because then I
have adequate time to promote it during the week. I start my pro-
motions on Monday and keep pushing hard until Thursday before
the webinar goes live. I send emails. I drive Facebook ads. I work
with joint venture partners, and I engage in a whole bunch of
other activities that drive traffic to my sign-up page. Whatever I
can do to get people onto this live event, I do. When the webinar
starts, I stop all promotion because the rest of the week is about
converting prospects into buyers.

Every market is different, but I like to spend only $3–$5 per
webinar registrant. If the costs are getting above that, then my
landing page isn't right, my message isn't interesting, I'm targeting
the wrong people, or something else is off. In the "funnel audi-
bles" chapter in *DotCom Secrets*, I show you how to diagnose and
increase conversions on these types of pages. Use that as a resource
if your numbers aren't where you need them to be.

As your costs climb higher into the $7–$8 range, it becomes
challenging to stay profitable on the front end. Here are my personal goals for this funnel each week. Your goals may be different,
but this will give you an idea of what to shoot for.

Weekly Live Webinar Stats

- 1,000 people register ($3,000 ad spend at $3 per registration)

- 250 attend webinar (25 percent show-up rate)

- 25 buy course (10 percent close rate; $25,000 in sales at $997 each)

- 25 buy in follow-up replays ($25,000 in sales at $997 each)

- $47,000 net profit ($50,000 sales – $3,000 ads)

With that formula, I'm putting $3,000 a week into ads and making back $50,000 a week in sales, while adding 1,000 new people to my list! These are the goals each week. Some weeks, we don't get the full 1,000 registered; other times we'll get 2,500 people or more. But setting that as the goal and doing a webinar every week (yes, the *same* webinar over and over again) is the recipe for new consistent leads and cash flow into your company.

So each week I do a *live* webinar selling people on my new opportunity. I spend Monday through Thursday morning promoting that webinar to get as many people as possible to show up on Thursday night. I present the webinar live on Thursday night and make my special offer. Then I show replays on Friday, Saturday, and Sunday. At midnight Sunday, I take down the offer for those who had registered. Then I start again on Monday filling my event for the upcoming Thursday. That's it. That's the whole model.

When you are first starting out, don't try to get 1,000 people right away. Test with a smaller group. I like to have at least 100 people live to test my presentation, so that usually means I need at least 300 to register. Start with a lower ad budget at first. Run your webinar a few times to get the kinks out and know what conversion rates to expect. Then you can spend more money on ads because you'll know what kind of return you're likely to get.

In the beginning, all kinds of things could happen. Facebook could mess up your ads. Your webinar software could fail to record or function properly. You could lose power in the middle of your broadcast. Things happen. Sometimes no one even shows up at all!

It's important not to get discouraged. Stick to the plan, and work it week in and week out. The beginning can be rough for some people. Don't quit! It won't be long before you start hitting consistent numbers.

THE LIVE PRESENTATION (WEBINAR) FUNNEL

Now that you know the model, let's take a look at the funnel you'll be using to move people from registration through the purchase.

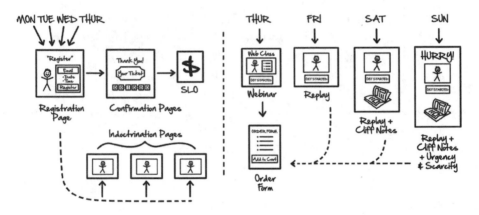

Figure 16.5:

Monday–Thursday, you'll promote your webinar and warm up your registrants with your follow-up funnel. Thursday you'll hold your webinar, and Friday–Sunday you'll promote the replay. On Monday, start the process over.

Step 1: Send Traffic to the Webinar Registration Page

The key to a high-converting webinar registration page is . . . *curiosity*. That's it. If your registration page isn't converting well, it's because you're showing people too much and they assume they know the answer. If they think they know what you're going to talk about, then they won't register or show up. If they can't figure out what it is without registering, then you'll get them to register *and* show up.

The headline I showed you earlier, "How to _____ without _____," is typically the key to getting people to register. Here is an example of the type of headline I used on my Funnel Scripts webinar:

> How To Get *ALL* Of Your Sales Letters, Scripts, and Webinar Slides Written (In Under 10 Minutes) *WITHOUT* Hiring An Expensive Copywriter!

Figure 16.6:

Your webinar registration page should have a curiosity-based headline.

Sometimes I tweak my headline to increase the curiosity factor. This is the main registration page we used the first year for the Funnel Hacks webinar.

Figure 16.7:

If you're not getting a high enough registration rate, you should split-test your headline, adding more curiosity.

I want you to notice a few things about this page.

The picture makes *no* sense: When you look at it, you have no idea what it is or why I'm doing it. It arouses curiosity. Find a picture of you that's kinda related to the topic but kinda strange to help increase your conversions dramatically. I do *not* recommend putting video on a webinar registration page. Rarely (if ever) will it beat a strange image. But if you do a video, be sure to test the page without a video as well.

The headline builds a *ton* of curiosity:

My Weird Niche Funnel That's Currently Making Me $17,947 Per Day . . . And How To Ethically Knock It Off In Less Than 10 Minutes!

This headline gives you a hint about the presentation, but it leaves *so* many unanswered questions like:

- What niche is it?
- Is it really possible to make $17,947 per day?

- Can you really knock it off *ethically*? How?
- In just 10 minutes?

The page uses urgency and scarcity: Nothing gets people to act (register, show up, and buy) more effectively than urgency and scarcity. These are your secret weapons—use them.

Step 2: Send Registrants to a Thank-You Page with a Self-Liquidating Offer

After people register, we take them to a thank-you page where we give them the basic information for the webinar. On this page, I *do* like to include a video, with me talking about why I'm so excited for the webinar. They *need* to feel my passion for the subject or they won't show up. Remember, the registration page is about curiosity. The thank-you page is about your passion and excitement for what they are about to experience on the webinar.

Figure 16.8:

On the thank-you page, you should offer a "self-liquidating offer" to recoup your ad costs.

One of the biggest secrets about the thank-you page is that you can (and should) use it to sell people something! We call this a "self-liquidating offer," or SLO. There are a few reasons you want to include this offer here.

- It's called a self-liquidating offer because it's meant to liquidate your ad costs. That's right—often you can completely cover your ad costs from the product you offer on your thank-you page. That means everything you sell on the webinar is pure profit!

- If they buy something that complements what the webinar is about, they are more likely to show up live.

- Buyers in motion tend to stay in motion, unless you do something to offend them. That means if they buy from you *before* the webinar, they are a lot more likely to buy from you *on* the webinar.

I like my SLO offers to be lower ticket, usually $37–$47 or a free (or $1) trial to a membership site. When we launched the Funnel Hacks webinar, we decided to give away a free trial to ClickFunnels on the thank-you page. Looking at the stats from the first year of following this model, more than 15,000 people had created ClickFunnels trials from that link, and more than 4,500 are still active. If you do the math, we have more than $450K per *month* in recurring cash coming in just from our thank-you page!

Step 3: Send a Series of Indoctrination Emails

Between the time someone registers for the webinar to the time you deliver it live, there are about 10 million distractions that could keep them from showing up. If you're not careful, the people you paid for with advertising won't remember who you are by Thursday.

During the in-between time, I send registrants videos to help introduce them to my philosophy, get them excited about the webinar, and presell them. For me, each of the videos is preselling the framework that I will teach during each of my three secrets. Remember, each of the three secrets is tied to a false belief pattern. So I make a video talking about that belief pattern, and explain that on the webinar I will give them the framework that will help them overcome their problem and get to their desired result. Don't answer the questions, just increase the curiosity for what they're going to learn on the webinar.

The main concern people share with this sequence is "But what if they register on Wednesday and they only get one or two of the indoctrination emails before the webinar?"

Here's the thing—the indoctrination sequence is *not* essential to the sale. It's an amplifier. If they only see one video and then they attend the webinar, that's okay. Videos two and three may come after the webinar, and that's fine. Don't stress about it. Oftentimes one of the indoctrination emails is the thing that gets them to watch a replay or to purchase after the webinar is over.

Step 4: Send Reminders

The reminders start on Wednesday. Just send quick emails and/ or text messages that say something like: "Hey, don't forget we're talking about _____ *live* tomorrow at _____." People don't always read every email, so I like to send one the day before we go live, one the morning of the webinar, one an hour or so before we start, another about 15 minutes before, then a final one that says, "We're live—join us!"

Step 5: Present the Webinar Live

I like to present my webinars on Thursdays. Others might prefer Tuesdays or Wednesdays, but that matters less than following the pre-webinar indoctrination series, the Perfect Webinar framework, and the follow-up sequences.

ClickFunnels doesn't have its own webinar platform. It will build all the pages for registration, indoctrination, order forms, etc., but the webinar must be delivered live on a webinar platform.

The two we use are GoToWebinar.com and Zoom.us. Both are great and both integrate easily with your ClickFunnels account.

The best time of day for your webinar depends a lot on your market. I schedule my webinars during the day because most people in my market are entrepreneurs who usually have more freedom over their schedules during the day. Other markets where people have 9-to-5 jobs usually require nighttime webinars. So *when* you present the webinar will depend on your particular audience.

Typically, about 25 percent of registrants show up on the webinar. If fewer than 25 percent attend, focus more on the indoctrination sequence, sending text message reminders before the webinar, emails one hour before the webinar, and again 15 minutes before. You've paid a lot of money to get them registered, and you're going to have to push hard to get them to show up.

When I transition from the content to the pitch, I check how many people are still on the webinar, and I base my closing stats on that number. So if I have 250 people who are still on the webinar when I start the pitch at the 60-minute mark, and I know that I typically close 15 percent, I'll probably make about $37,500.

What will your close rate be? At first, it will probably be pretty low. That's why you need to do your presentation live so many times. When you have a 5 percent close rate, you have a good webinar and are likely going to be profitable on the front end. When you get it to 10 percent, then (I believe) you have a million-dollar-a-year webinar. When you get above 10 percent . . . well, I'll tell you that at 15 percent, we did just shy of $10 million the first year. So it pays to keep refining your conversion rates by tweaking and regularly presenting your new opportunity live.

Step 6: Send Follow-Ups and Create Last-Minute Urgency

As soon as a webinar is over, I shift focus to the replay campaign. Some people get *really* intense with their replay campaigns, but the basics are urgency and scarcity. That's what gets people to take action. I usually *double* my sales between the time I end the webinar and when we close down the offer Sunday at midnight.

Friday, Saturday, and Sunday I deliver follow-up emails that include the webinar replay link. The first day, I talk about what a great response we had on the live call and offer them a chance to watch the replay . . . if they access it quickly. When the cart closes, the replay link disappears as well.

Sometimes in my follow-up sequence I'll send a PDF cheat sheet (similar to CliffsNotes) that briefly summarizes what we covered in the webinar or even a PDF version of my slides so they can see what we covered in the webinar. Some people would rather read text than watch a video. People are busy and they may not have time to go watch your 90-minute presentation—but they *will* scan over your PDF. In this email, I also remind them that the offer is live only until Sunday. These few days are about amping up the urgency and scarcity. If people think they have all the time in the world to buy, they won't.

On the last day, I send a couple of emails reminding them that the cart closes at midnight. I recap the main reasons they should buy and leave it at that. It's amazing how many people will hit the Buy button one minute before midnight!

Step 7: Close the Cart

Sunday at midnight, it's time to close the cart. The offer is done, and the Buy buttons are deactivated. That's it. You've completed your Perfect Webinar funnel.

Step 8: Repeat

Monday morning, you start all over again with Step 1: driving traffic. Each time you go through this process, you will improve. You'll figure out different ways of presenting that get more people to buy. You'll answer more questions. You'll fine-tune your ad targeting. The point is to never stop after one try—*especially* if you had disappointing results.

No one showed up for Liz Benny's first live webinar. She had a few hundred people registered, yet for some reason no one showed up. She had spent months preparing, and not a single soul attended. But she didn't give up. She kept refining her process. And she wound up making it into the Two Comma Club in her first year. Would that be okay with you? If you knew you could make six or seven figures in a year, would you keep going in the face of disappointment? Yeah . . . me too.

What happens if you get great results from your first live webinar? Should you automate it and move on to something else? No! This is a huge mistake people make—automating too soon. I ran the Funnel Hacks webinar 60-plus times before we finally decided to automate it. One full year of the same webinar, week in and week out. Some weeks I did it five or six times. In fact, to this day I still do it live a few times a month.

By the time we finally automated it, that presentation was as tight as it could be. We had every objection covered. We knew exactly how to get traffic. We had just the right follow-up sequences. And now it's all down to the numbers. Because we spent so much time perfecting the webinar, we get predictable results from the automated version.

So the last step is to repeat your webinar. Again and again. Run it every week for a full year, and watch what happens to your bank account and your expert status.

THE PERFECT WEBINAR SHORTCUT

As you can see, it takes time to create a Perfect Webinar presentation. Most people spend a week or two creating their first one. And even though I've been using the format for years, I'll often spend a couple of days creating one presentation. While that's really not a long time to create the foundation of millions of dollars in a business, sometimes you want to test out a new offer quickly.

For example, a few years ago I was helping a close friend launch a new company that sold automated webinar software. His sales process looked very traditional, and the company was getting average sales driving traffic into his funnel. Then he decided to launch an affiliate contest where the winner would receive $50K.

I thought it would be fun to compete, but I knew the only way I could win was to change how he was selling his product. I had planned on creating a Perfect Webinar presentation, but as the deadline to win the $50K got closer, I ran out of time. I was competing against 100 other affiliates who had been promoting for several weeks, and I was way behind. There were only a few days left before the contest ended.

I was about to give up and just blow it off, but then I had an idea. What if I could quickly create a Perfect Webinar and launch it—in 10–15 minutes? Ha! (I had to laugh at myself for a minute. Then I got serious.) I knew I could never pull it off with traditional PowerPoint or Keynote slides. But what if I just wrote out the key components on a whiteboard?

I had no idea if it would work, but it was my only shot. So I started asking myself a lot of the questions I've covered throughout this book. I'm going to run through them quickly for you right now—because that's all I was able to do in the 15 minutes before I went live with this presentation. (NOTE: All these elements could have been much stronger if I'd had more time, but I had only 15 minutes before I went live, so I had to think *really* fast.)

I want you to see what you can pull together when you use the concepts in this book as guidelines.

Question #1: What's the *new opportunity* I'm offering? For this product, we were selling automated webinar software, which was nothing new. So I offered a *new* opportunity to sell more through webinars using my weekly webinar framework. This was a new opportunity that most people (at the time) had never heard of:

Increasing webinar sales using my weekly webinar model

Question #2: What *special offer* can I create for those who purchase? I spent five minutes writing out my Stack on a whiteboard, including everything I would give people who purchased through my affiliate link. My friend's software helped people conduct webinars, so I brainstormed things I already had that would complement what he was selling. Here is what my Stack looked like:

What You're Gonna Get . . .

- *The Perfect Webinar Script* *$497*
- *The Perfect Webinar Training* *$9,997*
- *Video of My Closing Live* *$2,997*
- *Perfect Webinar Funnel* *$997*
- *My Webinar Funnel . . .* *Priceless*

Total Value: *$14,988*

Question #3: What is the one Big Domino for this offer? If I can get them to believe that doing webinars through my model is the only way they can get to 7 figures in the next 12 months, then they have to give me money. So I wrote out this title:

How to Make (at Least) Seven Figures
Next Year with This Webinar Model

Question #4: What is my Epiphany Bridge origin story to attempt to knock down the Big Domino? I told the story about how I bombed at my first event and Armand Morin taught me how to do the Stack. From there I designed the Perfect Webinar framework.

The Perfect Webinar framework is
the framework I will teach in Secret #1.

Question #5: What is the framework I'm teaching and the false belief I'm trying to break? (Vehicle)

- **Framework:** The Perfect Webinar framework

- **False Belief:** Perfect Webinars don't work for me

- **Truth:** You just need the right script

- **Story:** The story about how I developed the Perfect Webinar framework

Secret #1 Title: It's All about the Script

Question #6: What is the framework I'm teaching and the false belief I'm trying to break? (Internal Beliefs)

- **Framework:** The weekly webinar framework

- **False Belief:** I did a webinar once and it bombed

- **Truth:** You have to do it consistently every week for a year

- **Story:** The story about how ClickFunnels grew when I did it weekly

Secret #2 Title: Understanding the Model

Question #7: What is the framework I'm teaching and the false belief I'm trying to break? (External Beliefs)

- **Framework:** Transitioning to autowebinar framework
- **False Belief:** I have to do live webinars for the rest of my life
- **Truth:** After you've perfected the pitch you can automate it
- **Story:** The story about how we turned my Funnel Hacks to autowebinar after 60 live webinars

Secret #3 Title: You Have to Do This Live Until . . .

Now these probably weren't the best titles in the world, and I'm sure with a few days of massaging them, I could have made them amazing. But I only had about 15 minutes for the whole process.

Then I had to figure out how to promote this message to the most people in the least amount of time. I didn't have time to set up a webinar funnel and get people into a sequence. I needed to start getting sales *immediately.* So I opened up two of my phones, turned on Facebook Live and Periscope, and clicked "Go Live" on both platforms. Because I already have strong followings in both places, I was live in front of hundreds of people within seconds!

Figure 17.1:

If you're short on time, you can prepare a Perfect Webinar in as little as 15 minutes.

I did the presentation by just talking off the top of my head, sharing my Epiphany Bridge stories, then going into my Stack and close.

Within 26 minutes and 32 seconds, my presentation was done. I had no idea whether it was good or bad—it was all so quick. But as I looked at my stats, I saw the sales flooding in.

Afterward, I was able to promote these presentations on Facebook and other places for the next three days until the contest was over. During that time, more than 100,000 people saw my presentation. We ended up doing more than $250,000 in sales and I won the $50,000 cash prize! Not bad for only 15 minutes of preparation!

And while I thought that was pretty cool, even more exciting was the fact that Kaelin and Brandon Poulin saw what I did and decided to model it. Later that day, they launched a Facebook Live session and did almost the same thing. They had their Stack written down on a whiteboard, and Kaelin wrote her three secrets on paper, which she showed as she was teaching and telling her stories.

Figure 17.2:

Kaelin and Brandon Poulin saw my Facebook Live and modeled it for LadyBoss.

Their first try at this process made them more than $100,000, and they've gone on to do it monthly. In fact, recently they brought in more than $650,000 from *one* Facebook Live presentation, using the Perfect Webinar script without any PowerPoint slides—just a whiteboard and a few sheets of paper.

Pros: The biggest benefits of doing the Perfect Webinar shortcut is that 100 percent of the people who see your presentation actually see your presentation. With a traditional webinar, you lose people at each step. From the people who hit your landing page, maybe 40 percent register, and from there maybe only 20 percent show up. When you do it live, everyone who sees the presentation (either live or afterward) can be hooked into watching it immediately.

The other big pro is that when your presentation is done, if it's good you can turn it into an ad and drive people to it all the time. I won the affiliate contest and Kaelin generated more than $650,000 from one presentation by continually promoting these videos through ads for as long as they continued to convert.

Cons: I would not recommend going the Perfect Webinar shortcut route until you've practiced presenting in a live webinar environment first. Going live on Facebook or Instagram can be intimidating when you are trying to remember a script, and people in comments can be brutal. I think practicing in a more private setting first to master your presentation skills is a smart approach. After you get very comfortable with the script, then you could test going live on Facebook or Instagram and see how it feels.

As you master the Perfect Webinar script and you get better at telling stories and delivering your offer, you can use it to sell almost any product with just a few minutes' notice. The Perfect Webinar is perfect. The only time it doesn't work is when people mess it up by not following what I've laid out in this book. In fact, if you try it and it doesn't work, I can tell you from experience it's probably for one of these reasons:

- You picked a bad market and no one wants to hear what you have to say.

- You built an improvement offer and no one wants to buy it.

- You slipped into teaching the tactics before you sold your audience on the strategies.

If you pick a good market, make a new opportunity that is truly irresistible, and use your presentation to break and rebuild your audience's belief patterns around that new opportunity, it works. I promise!

As you follow what I do online, you'll see me using this script and story process in all sorts of situations, including video sales letters, teleseminars, product launch videos, Google Hangouts, Facebook Live videos, and even in my email sequences.

PERFECT WEBINAR CHEAT SHEET

You can use this cheat sheet to structure your Perfect Webinars quickly.

1. What *new opportunity* am I offering?

2. What *special offer* can I create for those who purchase?

3. What is the one *Big Domino* for this offer?

4. What is my Epiphany Bridge *origin story* to attempt to knock down the Big Domino?

5. What is the framework I'm teaching and the false belief I'm trying to break? (Vehicle)

6. What is the framework I'm teaching and the false belief I'm trying to break? (Internal Beliefs)

7. What is the framework I'm teaching and the false belief I'm trying to break? (External Beliefs)

8. How can I structure the Stack and close to increase my sales conversions?

THE 5-MINUTE PERFECT WEBINAR

"Did you know that the most powerful ingredient for your skin does not come from plants? I know it sounds crazy because we're so used to hearing about herbal oils and essential oils, and herbal extracts . . . but the truth is there is something even more powerful for your skin, and today I'm going to share with you three secrets that are going to revolutionize the way you care for your skin and the condition of your skin! Hi, I'm Jaime Cross and I'm a master herbalist . . ."

Wait, what? Did she just say "three secrets"?!

Earlier that day I had met Jaime Cross at her first Inner Circle meeting. I didn't know her story or the journey she had gone on to be in that room, but when she got on our little stage I found out that what she was doing was unique.

Jaime owned a skin care company that she and her husband had started a few years earlier. They sold their handcrafted lotions and soaps at farmers' markets. During that time she found one of my videos on YouTube that pulled her into a funnel, and a few months later she was at Funnel Hacking LIVE, learning about the Perfect Webinar script.

The reason why I said that what Jaime was doing was unique is because most people in my community who sell physical products didn't understand how the Perfect Webinar could work for their type of business. Countless ecommerce sellers told me that this framework was only good for authors, speakers, coaches, and consultants. While I had tried to convince them that the principles were universal, almost all of them told me that their business was different. All except for Jaime.

When she learned about the Perfect Webinar, she asked, "How can I make this work for my business? How can I make it work for soap?" She tried to create a 90-minute webinar selling a $200 package of her soaps and lotions, but had no success. So she decided to take the framework and modify it to sell a $39 product. After months of tweaking, she launched a new five-minute version of the Perfect Webinar and it took off! Within six weeks she had passed $130K in sales and made almost $2 million in her first year!

Figure 18.1:

Jaime created the 5-Minute Perfect Webinar to sell her lower-priced lotion bars.

As I sat there that night watching her five-minute version of my framework, I knew that we finally had a powerful way for *any* business to use the Perfect Webinar. This mini version of the Perfect Webinar works great for ads, landing pages, video sales letters, and more. In the next chapter I'll show you which funnels and where you can plug it in, but I want you to understand from Jaime's story that the Perfect Webinar framework will work for any business, you just need to apply your art to the proven framework.

THE 5-MINUTE PERFECT WEBINAR SCRIPT

After Jaime's success, I wanted her to show other e-commerce sellers, as well as anyone who is running any type of ad or who needs a shorter version of the Perfect Webinar, how they can take what they've already learned in this book and modify it to make a shorter version. She worked with Jim Edwards (my business partner at FunnelScripts.com) to make a simple script that anyone can use to create their own 5-Minute Perfect Webinar quickly. Here is the script that they developed.

Script Structure

Hey, did you know that (**big misconception**)?

I know it sounds crazy because we're so used to hearing about (**usual thing**), and while that is important, I'm going to share three secrets with you today that are going to revolutionize the way you (**area of their life you'll revolutionize**).

I'm (**your name**) and I am (**your role**) who has helped (**accomplishment**).

So what is (**the big idea or thing you'll reveal**)?

It's (**the thing**).

It's (**more details about the thing**).

So, I'm going to share with you three secrets about (**the thing**) and how you can (**big payoff**).

And I know what you're probably thinking: (**objection**).

But again, I'm going to show you a great way you can (**action they can take**) and get amazing results.

So the first secret is (**first secret**).

The big idea here is (**first secret big idea**).

This is important because (**why first secret is important**)!

The second secret is (**second secret**).

The main thing to understand here is that (**second secret big idea**).

This means (**why second secret is important**).

The third secret is (**third secret**).

The main thing to understand here is that (**third secret big idea**).

This is key because (**why third secret is important**).

Now, I know what you're thinking.

It's (**next objection**).

Well the tricky thing is that (**real truth behind the objection they don't realize**)!

And so I've (***verb* ending in *ed***) this (**the thing you've developed/created/found**) you can (**what they can do with this amazing thing you've just revealed to them**).

(**What makes this so special.**)

And so what this is going to do is (**what this will *do* for them**)!

And I, as (**your role**) who has (**cool accomplishment/ thing about you**), what I do is (**the superpower/secret of your success**).

So what I've done is I've (**what you've created/done for them**).

If you click the link, you can (**what they can do when they click the link**).

I honestly don't know how much longer we'll keep this (**the thing you've developed/created/found**) available, and prices will probably go up because (**why you can't keep this offer up forever**).

So click the link to get it today while it's still available.

We're always here to help and I can't tell you all the amazing results we've gotten for (**target audience**) just like you who are struggling with (**problem**).

We also have (**the next thing you'll offer them in an OTO**), but today I'm talking about (**the thing you've developed/created/found**), which is amazing.

I can't wait to see you on the inside.

Have a great day.

And that is the 5-Minute Perfect Webinar script. Use it as a powerful way to do Facebook Lives that will become ads that drive people into your funnels. You can also use it as the sales page on your funnels, especially for products that are lower on your value ladder (with a price point of less than $100). The higher the price point, typically the longer your presentation will need to be, but now that you've seen the 90-minute version as well as the five-minute version, hopefully you'll be able to take the framework and modify it for your needs.

PLUGGING "EXPERT SECRETS" INTO YOUR VALUE LADDER

We've seen it in every movie: The hero (your dream customer) finds a guide (you) who leads them to their destination. I hope that you're now seeing that this role as an expert or guide is one of the greatest callings we can have in this life.

Throughout this section I want to show you how and where you will be weaving your personality, stories, and frameworks into the value ladder that you learned about in *DotCom Secrets* so you can guide your dream customers to the results they desire the most. You now have all the selling tools you need; you just need to understand where in these frameworks you'll be plugging in each "epiphany" element.

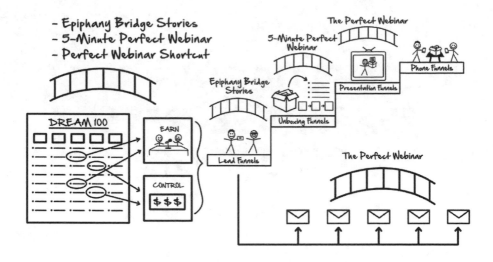

Figure 19.1:

You can use Epiphany Bridge stories in your lead funnels, 5-Minute Perfect Webinars in your unboxing funnels, and Perfect Webinars in your presentation funnels.

EPIPHANY ADS

In *Traffic Secrets* you will go deep into how to fill your funnels with your dream customers. As you dive into that book, you'll notice that most of the hooks we use to grab our dream customers' attention are based on all the things you have learned in this book.

When I'm trying to develop hooks to grab my dream customers, this is the list that I pull ideas from:

- Your Epiphany Bridge stories
- Your frameworks
- The red ocean that you are throwing rocks into
- Your new opportunity
- Elements of your future-based cause (your platform, identity shifts, manifesto, milestone awards)

- Your offers

- Your presentations

All the things that you've been developing for your tribe are the things that will get your people to stand up and follow you. Every message you post and every ad you create will have your personality and stories weaved into it.

While we are always testing lots of different hooks in our ads, these are my three favorite and most profitable types of ads.

Epiphany bridge stories: Most of my ads are simply a story about how I created the lead magnet, webinar, book, or whatever the call to action is on the ad. I follow the five simple phases of an Epiphany Bridge story.

- **Backstory**

- **Journey**

- **New Opportunity**

- **Framework** (what I'm offering in the ad)

- **Achievement**

Then I give people a call to action to click and get access to the framework. Sometimes they are taken to a page where they give me their email address for the framework; other times they have to get on a webinar, or buy a book, or watch a video. But the CTA is always pushing back to the framework I shared in the story.

5-Minute Perfect Webinars: Ever since Jaime showed me her 5-Minute Perfect Webinar (which, by the way, she uses as both her ad and the video on her landing page), I've become kinda obsessed with them. I've built out 5-Minute Perfect Webinar ads for every product I have.

Perfect Webinar Shortcuts: I love to use these when I'm launching a new product or service. I will typically create a Perfect Webinar short-cut that I use to launch the new product with a bang. If it converts well, I continue to buy ads to it for as long as it remains profitable.

EMAIL EPIPHANY FOLLOW-UP FUNNELS

One of my biggest breakthroughs happened when I realized that I could use this Perfect Webinar process in *all* areas of my marketing, including email. In *DotCom Secrets*, I talked about a concept I learned from André Chaperon called Soap Opera Sequences (SOS), which are the emails you send to someone when they first join your list.[47] He called them Soap Opera Sequences because each email ends with a hook that draws you to the next episode, just like a soap opera does.

For years, I had been using SOS emails with different story structures. But when I started seeing people use the Perfect Webinar in different situations like Facebook Live and video sales letters, I had a thought . . . *I wonder if this would also work as an email sequence?* In fact, I wonder if I could do *all* the selling by email, and not even direct people into attending a presentation. It seemed so crazy, I figured it just might work. So I took the Perfect Webinar and broke down the four core stories and the Stack, added each into an email, and tested it out. The results were amazing! So much so that we are now going back and adding them into every funnel we have.

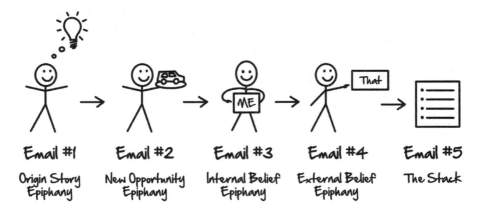

Email #1	Email #2	Email #3	Email #4	Email #5
Origin Story Epiphany	New Opportunity Epiphany	Internal Belief Epiphany	External Belief Epiphany	The Stack

Figure 19.2:

You can use the Perfect Webinar framework in your follow-up sequences.

There are a few different ways we've successfully used this so far. The first was writing out each story for the emails. The second was making videos telling each story and linking to the video inside the emails. Honestly, the way you transmit the story matters less than following the actual story structure.

One of the keys to a soap opera sequence like this is that every email needs to pull people into the story in the next email. Think about how good soap operas, reality shows, and most TV shows are able to pull you through the commercial breaks and week to week by getting you excited by what is about to happen, then cutting it off. We do the same thing in these emails, teasing about the next email that's coming so they are anxiously waiting for it.

Some people have asked how this fits in with the frameworks I taught in both *DotCom Secrets* and *Traffic Secrets* about moving from emotion to logic to fear in your email sequences.

Figure 19.3:

In your follow-up sequences, you should focus your first five emails on emotion, the next two on logic, and the last two on fear.

Although the Perfect Webinar framework does have emotion, logic, and fear weaved inside of it, in the email sequence, the first five emails fit into the emotional category. On email five, I introduce the Stack, which is the last of the emotional emails. After that my follow-up emails shift to logic and then fear to close out the campaign. This means you are delivering your presentation over the first five emails, and then your next two to four emails are focused on logic and fear.

EPIPHANY LEAD MAGNETS

Most of my lead funnels are simple. The majority of the time I tell the story for the lead funnel inside of the ad. Often I summarize or retell the Epiphany Bridge story quickly to show people the value of the framework they are going to trade for their email address. This can be done through video or through the copy on the page.

Figure 19.4:

You can share your Epiphany Bridge stories in your lead magnets.

Here is the simple framework I use on these pages:

- **Backstory**
- **Journey**
- **New opportunity**
- **Framework** (what I'm offering for them to become a lead)
- **Achievement**

EPIPHANY UNBOXING FUNNELS

As we move up the value ladder, we now find ourselves with the unboxing funnels. These funnels typically have lower-priced products that are being sold on the front end. You don't normally need a full 90 minutes to get someone to pay for shipping on a free book or a $39 lotion bar.

This is where the 5-Minute Perfect Webinar comes in handy. Yes, we use it as an ad, but we can also use it as the sales video on our sales pages.

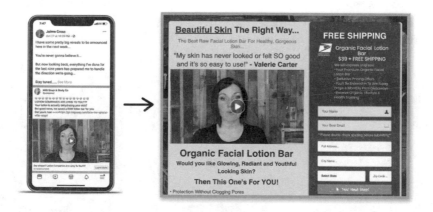

Figure 19.5:

Jaime Cross showed how to use her 5-Minute Perfect
Webinar framework in her ads and her unboxing funnel.

You'll notice I do the same thing inside all my unboxing funnels.

Figure 19.6:

I use the same 5-Minute Perfect Webinar framework in my unboxing funnels.

EPIPHANY VIDEO SALES LETTER (VSL) FUNNELS

Your video sales letter funnels are simply a Perfect Webinar presentation that has been recorded and put onto a sales page. Sometimes I use my full 90-minute webinar recording, and that becomes my presentation; other times I use the Perfect Webinar shortcut to make a 30-minute version, and I've had success with both.

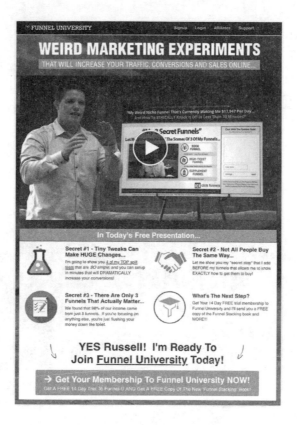

Figure 19.7:

You can use the Perfect Webinar framework for your video sales letters (VSL).

EPIPHANY AUTOMATED WEBINAR FUNNELS

In both your webinar (live) funnels and your automated webinar funnels, you are using the full Perfect Webinar presentation. We already talked in detail about how live webinars work. With an automated webinar the funnel structure is similar, but instead of using GoToWebinar.com or Zoom.us to host a live webinar, you take the recording of your Perfect Webinar presentation and plug it into a ClickFunnels page.

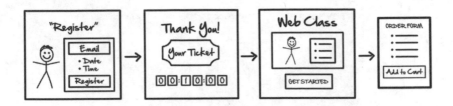

Figure 19.8:

You can also use the Perfect Webinar framework in your automated webinar funnels.

Figure 19.9:

We followed the Perfect Webinar framework for Funnel Scripts.

When you go to the top of the value ladder and look at phone funnels, the people who are having the most success right now in our community are doing a basic webinar funnel, following the Perfect Webinar framework, and then the call to action directs them to an application form instead of an order form. In *DotCom*

Secrets you get access to both of the sales scripts that we use after someone fills out an application form.

EPIPHANY PRODUCT LAUNCH FUNNELS

Another type of presentation funnel is called the product launch funnel, which was made popular by Jeff Walker.

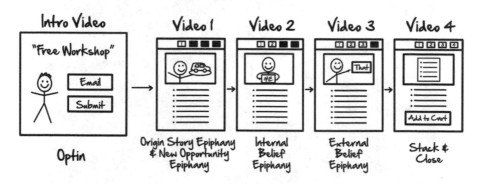

Figure 19.10:

You can use the Perfect Webinar framework in your product launch funnels.

In the first video, your audience gets your epiphany origin story as well as the frameworks you teach in Secret #1. In the second video, they get the frameworks of Secret #2, and in the third video they get the frameworks of Secret #3. The last video in the series is simply your Stack and your close. Jeff Walker calls this funnel a sideways sales letter, but I might call it a sideways Perfect Webinar.

Figure 19.11:

I used the Perfect Webinar framework in my Funnel Hacks webinar.

Are you able to see how your voice as the guide is weaved into the framework of your dream customers' journey? You are the one who hooks them in the ads, you give them the call for their new journey, you are the one who presents them with the new opportunity, and you help guide them to the achievement and transformation they want the most.

CONCLUSION

I ran my Inner Circle for almost a decade before I decided that I needed to take a break. I resolved to put my highest-level coaching program on pause for a few years while my kids were in high school so I could spend more time with them. The group decided to gather for our last meeting, and members from around the world flew to Boise for one last time to mastermind together.

On the last day, after we had finished with all the fun, I stood on our little stage and thanked everyone for allowing me to serve them over the past few years. It had been a huge honor that had blessed my life so much. I got a little teary-eyed and choked up, so I had to stop for a second. One of our members raised her hand and asked if she could have the mic for a minute.

Her name is Liz Benny, and as she started to talk, a memory of how we first met popped into my head. It was about a year before my team and I had launched ClickFunnels. In fact it was a secret project that only a few people knew we were working on when Liz joined my Inner Circle. Because she lived on the other side of the planet from me in New Zealand, we had to do the call at a strange hour so we could all be online at the same time. I could tell that she was excited, and within a few minutes of our conversation I knew that she was going to change the world; she just needed a little direction.

"I remember five years ago, I used to see Russell's ads in my newsfeed every day. At first I was annoyed, thinking, *Who is this 12-year-old kid who keeps telling me to click on his ad?* Eventually I clicked and went to his funnel and bought the book he kept trying to sell me," she said into the mic.

"I kept getting emails from him, and I watched some videos, and eventually I got an invitation to join this group. I watched a presentation he made that showed me why I needed to be in this room. A few days later I was wiring him $25,000 that I didn't have to spend." She started to get a little choked up.

"At the time I was scared. I knew I had a bigger mission in life, but I wasn't sure how to accomplish it. By following Russell's advice over the past five years, I've found my own voice, built a great brand, and have had the chance to change the lives of countless people around the world. I am so grateful that five years ago, I decided to click on his goofy ad. It changed my life."

The tears were now streaming down my face, so much so that I couldn't even say a word, but as I sat there waiting to regain composure, I felt such gratitude that I got to be a little piece of her journey to transform not only herself, but the countless other people she's impacted.

If you haven't yet, you'll soon find out that the feeling you get as the expert or the guide in someone else's journey—when someone you've helped has accomplished their goal and enjoyed success—is a thousand times better than the feeling you get from your own success. It becomes addictive, and soon all you want to do is help more people with your message.

I've been so grateful that you've trusted me on this journey so far. Your message matters, and if what you learned in this book helps you reach one more person with your God-given gifts, then it will have been a success.

Remember, this is a playbook. Don't just read it once and go on with business as usual. Keep it handy, and refer to it often. This book is also just one part of a three-part series.

DotCom Secrets is the framework. It was written to help you master the science of funnel building. (Get a free copy at DotComSecrets.com.)

Expert Secrets is the fire. It was written to help you master the art of the sales and persuasion tactics you will need to change the lives of the customers you've been called to serve.

Traffic Secrets is the fuel. It will show you how to fill your websites and funnels with your dream customers. (Get a free copy at TrafficSecrets.com.)

I hope that you can use these secrets to find more of your dream customers and serve them at your highest level. They are waiting for you to find them so that you can change their lives. If you focus on that, your business will be a catalyst of change for them in their lives, and that's the real purpose behind business.

Thank you for allowing me to serve you through these pages and this series. It's truly been an honor, and I can't wait to see what you do with the frameworks you've been given. Come hit me up on any of the social media platforms, say hi, and please share with me how these "secrets" have changed your life.

Thanks,
Russell Brunson

P.S. Don't forget, you're just one funnel away . . .

ENDNOTES

Introduction

1. Churchill, Winston S. "Quote by Sir Winston Churchill." *Goodreads*. Accessed December 16, 2019. https://www.goodreads.com/ quotes/67420-to-each-there-comes-in-their-lifetime-a-special-moment.

SECTION ONE

Secret #1

2. Abraham, Jay. "Jay Abraham - People are silently begging to be led." *Facebook*. Last modified July 27, 2012. https://www.facebook.com/ JayAbrahamMarketing/posts/264556476981874.

3. Bilyeu, Tom. "Tom Bilyeu on Instagram: There it is. Those are the steps." *Instagram*. Accessed December 16, 2019. https://www.instagram.com/p/ Bs1wFllFveP/?igshid=1tzi9m1felum7.

4. James, Vince. "The 12-Month Millionaire." *The 12-Month Internet Millionaire*. Accessed November 22, 2019. https://www.12monthinternetmillionaire.com.

5. Lee, Bruce. September 12, 2017. "Research Your Own Experience." Podcast audio. *Bruce Lee Podcast*. https://brucelee.com/ podcast-blog/2017/9/12/63-research-your-own-experience.

6. Indie Film Hustle. "Screenwriting: The Hero's Journey with Chris Vogler - IFH Film School - Indie Film Hustle." *YouTube*. October 18, 2017. http:// www.youtube.com/watch?v=7ZzeTuFen9E.

7. Guo, Jerry. "The World's Best Guinea Pig." *Newsweek International*. Accessed February 4, 2020. https://www.questia.com/magazine/1G1-246190621/ the-world-s-best-guinea-pig.

8. Barry, Nathan. "Endure Long Enough to get Noticed." *Nathan Barry* (blog). February 18, 2019. https://nathanbarry.com/endure.

9. Dwinwell, Mason. *Eat the Sun*. DVD. Directed by Peter Sorcher. San Francisco: Sorcher Films, 2011.

10. "Bulletproof Coffee: Everything You Want to Know (Plus the Recipe)." *Bulletproof*. Accessed February 4, 2020. https://www.bulletproof.com/recipes/ bulletproof-diet-recipes/bulletproof-coffee-recipe.

11. Kennedy, Dan. "Renegade Millionaire System." *Dan Kennedy's Magnetic Marketing*. Accessed February 4, 2020. https://store.nobsinnercircle.com/ renegade-millionaire-system-cd-dvd-manual-and-book.html#.XjnoD2hKjIU.

12. Abraham, Jay. "Famous Quotes from Jay Abraham." *Famous Quotes*. Accessed February 4, 2020. http://famousquotefrom.com/jay-abraham/.

13. Warren, Blair. *The One Sentence Persuasion Course*. Warren Production Services, Inc, 2013.

14. Roosevelt, Theodore. "20 Inspirational Theodore Roosevelt Quotes." *Dose of Leadership*. Accessed February 4, 2020. https://www.doseofleadership.com/20-inspirational-theodore-roosevelt-quotes.

Secret #2

15. "Strategy vs. Tactics: What's the Difference and Why Does it Matter?" *Farnam Street* (blog). Accessed February 4, 2020. https://fs.blog/2018/08/strategy-vs-tactics.

Secret #3

16. Kim, W. Chan and Renée A. Mauborgne. Blue Ocean Strategy. *Harvard Business Review Press*, 2016.

17. Ramadan, Al, Dave Peterson, Christopher Lochhead, and Kevin Maney. *Play Bigger: How Pirates, Dreamers, and Innovators Create and Dominate Markets.* HarperCollins US, 2016.

18. "David Ogilvy (businessman)." *Wikipedia*. Accessed February 4, 2020. https://en.wikipedia.org/wiki/David_Ogilvy_(businessman).

19. Maynard, Navah. "The Dove Effect: Ogilvy on Positioning." *Medium*. May 10, 2016. https://medium.com/ogilvy-on-digital-advertising/the-dove-effect-ogilvy-on-positioning-4a88f68c48bc.

20. Ferreira, Miguel. "The Man Who Invented Orange Juice." *Medium*. December 11, 2018. https://medium.com/@_miguelferreira/the-man-who-invented-orange-juice-2721147b8498.

21. Polish, Joe and Tim Paulson. *Piranha Marketing.* Nightingale Conant, 2004.

Secret #4

22. Shedden, David. "Today in Media History: Apple's Steve Jobs Introduces the iPod in 2001." *Poynter*. October 23, 2014. https://www.poynter.org/reporting-editing/2014/today-in-media-history-apples-steve-jobs-introduces-the-ipod-in-2001.

23. Hoffer, Eric. *The True Believer: Thoughts on the Nature of Mass Movements.* HarperCollins US, 2019.

24. Sullivan, Dan. *The Dan Sullivan Question.* Strategic Coach, 2010.

25. Poulin, Kaelin Tuell. "Swap 7 Bad Habits for Good Ones in 7 Days and Move on Forever!" *LadyBoss* (blog). Accessed February 4, 2020. https://ladyboss.com/blog/lifestyle/swap-7-bad-habits.

Secret #5

26.   Bilyeu, Lisa. *Instagram.* Accessed February 4, 2020. https://www.instagram.com/lisabilyeu.

27.   "Samuel Brannan." *Wikipedia.* Accessed February 4, 2020. https://en.wikipedia.org/wiki/Samuel_Brannan.

Secret #6

28.   Runyon, Joel. "Impossible Case Study: Sir Roger Bannister and the Four-Minute Mile." April 5, 2014. *Impossible.* https://impossiblehq.com/impossible-case-study-sir-roger-bannister/#Roger_Bannister_changed_his_story.

29.   "Four-Minute Mile." *Wikipedia.* Accessed February 4, 2020. https://en.wikipedia.org/wiki/Four-minute_mile.

30.   Humphrey, Jack. "John Reese: The Million Dollar Man." *Jack Humphrey* (blog). Accessed February 4, 2020. https://jackhumphrey.com/john-reese-the-million-dollar-man.

31.   "You Are Only ONE 'Swipe' Away from Becoming Rich . . ." *Warrior Forum.* Accessed February 4, 2020. https://www.warriorforum.com/copywriting/894257-you-only-one-swipe-away-becoming-rich-swipe.html.

32.   Gibson, Mel. *Braveheart.* Santa Monica: Icon Entertainment International, 1995.

33.   "Napoleon on War." *Napoleon Guide.* Accessed February 4, 2020. http://www.napoleonguide.com/maxim_war.htm.

SECTION TWO

Secret #7

34.   Spice, Byron. "Most Presidential Candidates Speak at Grade 6-8 Level." *Carnegie Mellon University.* March 16, 2016. https://www.cmu.edu/news/stories/archives/2016/march/speechifying.html.

35.   McAvoy, James. *X-Men: First Class.* DVD. Directed by Matthew Vaughn. Los Angeles: Twentieth Century Fox, 2011.

Secret #8

36.   Seastrom, Lucas. "Mythic Discovery within the Inner Reaches of Outer Space: Joseph Campbell Meets George Lucas." *Star Wars.* October 22, 2015. https://www.starwars.com/news/mythic-discovery-within-the-inner-reaches-of-outer-space-joseph-campbell-meets-george-lucas-part-i.

37.   Campbell, Joseph. *The Hero with a Thousand Faces.* New World Library, 2008.

38.   Future Artists. "Lucasfilm Fan Club - George Lucas Joseph Campbell Mythology, Religion, Creativity." *YouTube.* August 11, 2018. https://www.youtube.com/watch?v=-TpXdM3i5V0.

39. McGuire, Sara. "What Your Favorite 6 Movies Have in Common (Infographic)." *Venngage*. June 25, 2018. https://venngage.com/blog/heros-journey.

40. Hauge, Michael and Christopher Vogler. *The Hero's 2 Journeys*. Audiobook. Accessed February 4, 2020. https://www.audible.com/pd/The-Heros-2-Journeys-Audiobook/B002VA8MWA.

Secret #10

41. Robbins, Tony. "Are You Telling Yourself the Full Story?" *Tony Robbins* (blog). Accessed February 4, 2020. https://www.tonyrobbins.com/stories/date-with-destiny/are-you-telling-yourself-the-full-story.

SECTION THREE

Secret #12

42. Ferriss, Tim. Presentation at Genius Network, New York, New York.

43. "Modus Ponens." *Wikipedia*. Accessed February 4, 2020. https://en.wikipedia.org/wiki/Modus_ponens.

Secret #14

44. VanHoose, Dave. "Dave VanHoose on Automated Webinars that Sell." DishyMix. Podcast audio. http://podcasts.personallifemedia.com/podcasts/232-dishymix/episodes/157047-dave-vanhoose-automated-webinars.

Secret #15

45. Fladlien, Jason. "Webinar Pitch Secrets 2.0." Jason Fladlien (blog). Accessed February 4, 2020. https://jasonfladlien.com.

SECTION FOUR

46. Miller, Donald. *Building a StoryBrand*. HarperCollins Leadership, 2017.

Secret #19

47. Chaperon, André. "André Chaperon." Andre Chaperon (blog). Accessed February 4, 2020. http://www.andrechaperon.com.

ACKNOWLEDGMENTS

I wanted to start by giving a very special thanks to Daegan Smith. A few years back, we had a conversation about belief, and what's possible when someone truly believes in something. We then talked about how we could create that true belief in the minds of the people we were trying to serve. That one conversation took me on a journey that lasted for more than five years and has resulted in this book. You will see many things I learned that day and over the next few years from Daegan woven into these pages. Without his ideas, this book wouldn't have been possible.

I want to thank Perry Belcher for helping me understand new opportunities and status, Dan Kennedy for teaching me how to use character and communication, Michael Hauge for showing me story structure, Blair Warren for his work with persuasion, Jason Fladlien for teaching me how to break and rebuild belief patterns, and Armand Morin for creating the Stack. Those concepts created the foundation on which this book was built.

I'm so grateful for my Inner Circle members and people inside our Funnel Hacker community who are willing to take these crazy ideas and test them in literally hundreds of different markets. You've given us the ability to test things at scale in a way that has never been possible in the history of direct response marketing. We're able to see what things work in which markets, and make adjustments based on that feedback. This book is infinitely better because of your real-world, in-the-trenches testing of these concepts.

I also know that none of this would be possible if it weren't for my team here at ClickFunnels—Todd Dickerson, Dylan Jones, Ryan Montgomery, and the rest of the development team—for building ClickFunnels and continuing to make it better every day. This platform is what has given entrepreneurs like me the ability to get our messages out to the world. Thank you to John Parkes, Dave Woodward, and the rest of our marketing team for helping us get ClickFunnels and this message into the hands of every entrepreneur in the world. Brent Coppieters and his support team for creating the best possible customer experience for our entrepreneurs. And everyone else who is helping to serve our community. There are so many amazing people who are part of the movement we are creating here at ClickFunnels, it would be impossible to name them all.

I want to thank Steve J Larsen for being a constant sounding board during this book project. Without your excitement for this book, it never would have been completed. And Julie Eason, for dedicating the better part of a year to help me write this book . . . twice. If it weren't for you, this would still be just a bunch of random thoughts inside my head. And last, I want to thank Joy Anderson for making this second edition possible. I can't believe how much we got done in such a short period of time!

Thank you.

ABOUT THE AUTHOR

Russell Brunson started his first online company while he was wrestling in college. Within a year of graduation, he had sold over a million dollars of his own products and services from his basement. Over the past 15 years, he has built a following of over a million entrepreneurs, sold hundreds of thousands of copies of his books, popularized the concept of sales funnels, and co-founded the software company ClickFunnels, which has helped tens of thousands of entrepreneurs quickly get their message out to the marketplace. He lives in Idaho with his family, and you can visit him online at RussellBrunson.com.